LF339 LINUX DEVICE DRIVERS AND KERNEL INTERNALS

COURSE MANUAL

The official training manual from The Linux Foundation

Version 1.0

Contents

List of Figures

List of Tables

Chapter 1

Introduction and Preliminaries

We lay out our objectives and describe our target audience. We'll discuss our procedures. We'll describe the use of the **staging** drivers tree. Finally we'll point to some sources of documentation.

1.1 Objectives

- **Linux Device Drivers and Kernel Internals** is designed to show experienced programmers how to develop device drivers for **Linux** systems, and give them a basic understanding and familiarity with the **Linux** kernel.

- Upon mastering this material, you will be familiar with the different kinds of device drivers used under **Linux**, and know the appropriate **API**'s through which devices (both hard and soft) interface with the kernel.

- We will focus primarily on **Device Drivers** and only secondarily on the **Linux Kernel**. These are impossible to separate, since device drivers are an integral part of the kernel. However, most device drivers use only a limited set of kernel functions and one need not learn everything about the kernel to do a device driver. Yet while device drivers don't control important kernel features such as scheduling or memory management, the more you know about how **Linux** handles such things the better a device driver you can write.

- In many other operating systems, which are closed source, there is a cleaner separation between a device driver and the kernel proper. Because **Linux** is **open source**, the device driver developer has full access to all of the kernel. This is both powerful and dangerous.

- While we will discuss kernel internals and algorithms we will examine deeply only the functions which are normally used in device drivers. More details on things such as scheduling, memory management, etc., belong more properly in a higher level treatment (or lower level depending on how you define things.)

- Developing device drivers is a big subject both in depth (from deep inside the kernel to usage in user-space) and in breadth (the many types of devices.) In order to keep things manageable we are going to limit our range both vertically and horizontally.

- This means sometimes we won't look very deeply into the kernel's inner plumbing even as it relates to device drivers. And for particular types of device drivers we will stop before we get to detailed aspects of particular devices or classes of devices and hardware. It also means we are going to just ignore whole classes of devices, such as **SCSI** and **wireless**, as any treatment of these subjects would rapidly become both huge and specialized.

- Our order of presentation is not axiomatic; i.e., we will have some forward referencing and digressions. The purpose is to get you into coding as quickly as possible. Thus we'll tell you early on how to dynamically allocate memory in the simplest way, so you can actually write code, and then later cover the subject more thoroughly. Furthermore, the order of subjects is somewhat flexible.

1.2   Who you Are

- You are interested in learning how to write device drivers for the **Linux** operating system. Maybe you are just doing this for fun, but more likely you have this task as part of your job. The purpose here is to ease your path and perhaps shorten the amount of time it takes to reach a level of basic competence in this endeavor.

- How much you get out of this and how bug-free, efficient, and optimized your drivers will be depends on how good a programmer you were before you started with the present material. There is no intent or time here to teach you the elements of good programming or the **Linux** operating system design in great detail.

- You should:

    - Be proficient in the **C** programming language.
    - Be familiar with basic **Linux** (**Unix**) utilities, such as **ls**, **rm**, **grep**, **tar**, and have a familiarity with command shells and scripts.
    - Be comfortable using any of the available text editors (e.g., **vi**, **emacs**.)
    - Know the basics of compiling and linking programs, constructing Makefiles etc.; i.e., be comfortable doing application developing in a **Linux** or **Unix** environment.
    - Have a good understanding of systems programming in a **Unix** or **Linux** environment, at least from the standpoint of writing applications.
    - Experience with any major **Linux** distribution is helpful but is not strictly required.

- If you have had some experience configuring and compiling kernels, and writing kernel modules and or device drivers, you will get much more out of this material.

- If you have a good grasp of operating system fundamentals and familiarity with the insides of any other operating system, you will gain much more from this material.

- While our material will not be very advanced, it will strive to be thorough and complete. It is worth repeating that we are not aiming for an expert audience, but instead for a competent and motivated one.

1.3   Procedures

- You will need a computer installed with a current **Linux** distribution, with the important developer tools (for compiling, etc.) properly deployed.

- The emphasis will be on hands-on programming, with most sections having laboratory exercises. Where feasible labs will build upon previous lab assignments. The solution set can be retrieved from **http://training.linuxfoundation.org/course_materials/LF339** As they become available, errata and updated solutions will also be posted on that site.

- Lab **solutions** are made available so you can see at least one successful implementation, and have a possible template to begin the next lab exercise if it is a follow up. In addition, **examples** as shown during the exposition are made available as part of the SOLUTIONS package, in the EXAMPLES subdirectories. Once you have obtained the solutions you can unpack it with:

```
$ tar zxvf LF339_SOLUTIONS*.tar.gz
```

or

```
$ tar jxvf LF339_SOLUTIONS*.tar.bz2
```

substituting the actual name of the file.

- In the main solutions directory, there is a **Makefile** which will recursively compile all subdirectories. It is smart enough to differentiate between kernel code, user applications, and whether multi-threading is used.

- There are some tunable features; by default all sub-directories are recursively compiled against the source of the currently running kernel. One can narrow the choice of directories, or use a different kernel source as in the following examples, or even pick a different architecture:

```
$ make SDIRS=s_22
$ make KROOT=/lib/modules/3.0.0/build
$ make SDIRS="s_0* s_23" KROOT=/lib/mdoules/linux-3.0.0/build
$ make ARCH=i386
$ make ARCH=arm CROSS_COMPILE=arm-toolchain-linux-gnueabi-
```

where KROOT points to the kernel source files. On an **x86_64** platform, specifying ARCH=i386 will compile 32-bit modules. ARCH=arm sets the architecture to ARM and overrides autodetection. To build a kernel for ARM on an x86 host, we need a cross-compiler installed and the CROSS_COMPILE flag set. The CROSS_COMPILE flag is used to specify the compiler-prefix. The actual prefix used by your toolchain may vary e.g. arm-linux-eabi-gcc binary will have arm-linux-eabi- as compiler prefix. The **genmake** script in the main directory is very useful for automatically generating makefiles, and is worth a perusal.

- For this to work, the kernel source has to be suitably prepared; in particular it has to have a **configuration file** (.config in the main kernel source directory) and proper dependencies set up.

- One should note that we have emphasized clarity and brevity over rigor in the solutions; e.g., we haven't tried to catch every possible error or take into account every possible kernel configuration option. The code is not bullet-proof; it is meant to be of pedagogical use.

- If you have any questions or feedback on this material contact us at: *trainingquestions@linuxfoundation.org.*

locate <file name>

- The provided solutions will from time to time contain functions and features not discussed in the main text.

- This is done to illustrate methods to do more than the minimum work to solve the problem and teach extra material.

- If there is anything that **must** be used and is not covered in the material, its omission is a bug, not a feature, and should be brought to our attention.

1.4   Hardware

- Sometimes when people teach device drivers they use simple devices hanging off an external port. Rather than do this we will use the hardware already on the machine such as network cards and input devices, and piggyback our device drivers on top of the already installed ones using the kernel's ability to share interrupts.

- Questions often come up of the following variety:

  - How many I/O ports does my device use, and what addresses do they use?
  - What IRQ?
  - Do I read bytes or words, how many per interrupt, etc?
  - What standards does the device conform to?

- These questions can be answered **only** from the hardware's specifications, and sometimes by examining the hardware itself. When you are writing a device driver you **must** have such knowledge and if you don't you can't write a driver. (Of course it is possible to figure out a lot by probing a device which keeps its specifications secret, and a lot of drivers have been reverse engineered this way. But as **Linux** has matured this has become much rarer and time and energy are better spent encouraging manufacturers to cooperate if they want their devices supported, than in doing this kind of dirty work.)

- Get as much information as you can from the hardware people, but be prepared for some of it to be wrong or out of date, especially with new devices. It is not unusual for the hardware and the specifications to not be in sync or for a device to fail to completely follow specifications. Sometimes this is because device manufacturers are content with making sure the device works adequately under the market-dominant operating system and then stop asking questions at that point.

1.5   Staging Drivers

- Beginning with the 2.6.28 kernel a new area in the kernel source was added for so called **staging** drivers. It is understood that drivers included in this manner are not to be expected to possess the quality of those already included in the main kernel tree.

- These drivers may or may not work, may utilize user-space interfaces that are more than likely to change. It is more than possible that some of these drivers won't even compile under some ranges of kernel options.

- Furthermore, use of any of these drivers **taints** the kernel.

- The purpose of the **staging** drivers directory is to give a zero-height barrier to entrance to the kernel source tree, and to expose the source to a wider range of developers. This is partly intended to silence critics who complain about how hard it is to get things accepted by the main kernel developers.

- Any drivers which do not improve or garner much attention while residing in the staging tree will be removed after a period of time.

- The original notion of the staging tree has also been expanded to include drivers which are on their way out of the **Linux** kernel, either because they are no longer maintained, or have been obsoleted by newer drivers. If no developers step forward to bring these drivers back up to proper standards, eventually these drivers will be removed.

1.6 Documentation and Links

- The **best** source of documentation about the **Linux** kernel is the source itself. In many cases it is the **only** documentation. Never trust what you see in books (including this one) or articles without looking at the source.

- The **/usr/src/linux/Documentation** directory contains a many useful items. Some of the documentation is produced using the **docbook** system (see **http://www.docbook.org**.) To produce this you go to **/usr/src/linux** and type

```
$ make { htmldocs | psdocs | pdfdocs | rtfdocs }
```

the different forms giving you the documentation in either as web-browseable, postscript, portable document format, or rich text format, which will appear in the **/usr/src/linux/Documentation/DocBook** directory. Warning: producing this documentation can take longer that compiling the kernel itself! For this to work properly you may have to install additional software on your system, such as **jade** or **latex**.

Books

- ***Linux Device Drivers, Third Edition***, by Jonathan Corbet, Alessandro Rubini, and Greg Kroah-Hartman, pub. O'Reilly, 2005.

  The full, unabridged on-line version can be viewed at **http://lwn.net/Kernel/LDD3/** and downloaded from **http://lwn.net/Kernel/LDD3/ldd3_pdf.tar.bz2**. and source code for the examples in the book can be retrieved at **http://examples.oreilly.com/linuxdrive3/examples.tar.gz**.

- ***Understanding the Linux Kernel, Third Edition***, by Daniel P. Bovet and Marco Cesati, pub. O'Reilly, 2005.

- ***Understanding Linux Network Internals***, by Christian Benvenuti, pub. O'Reilly, 2006.

- ***Linux Kernel in a Nutshell***, by Greg Kroah-Hartman, pub. O'Reilly, 2006.

  The full text of the book can be viewed or downloaded at **http://www.kroah.com/lkn/**.

- ***Linux Kernel Development, Third Edition***, by Robert Love, pub. Addison-Wesley, 2010.

- ***Linux Debugging and Performance Tuning: Tips and Techniques***, by Steve Best, pub. Prentice Hall, 2005.

- ***Writing Linux Device Drivers: a guide with exercises***, by Jerry Cooperstein, pub. CreateSpace, 2009.

- ***Linux Program Development: a guide with exercises***, by Jerry Cooperstein, pub. CreateSpace, 2009.

Kernel Development and Mailing List Sites

- **http://lwn.net**
  Linux Weekly News: Latest Linux news including a Kernel section. This very important site is supported by user subscriptions, so please consider making an individual or corporate contribution!

- **http://ldn.linuxfoundation.org/book/how-participate-linux-community**
  A complete view of the kernel development process and how to join it.

- **http://lwn.net/Articles/driver-porting**
  A compendium of Jonathan Corbet's articles on porting device drivers to the 2.6 kernel.

- **http://www.linuxfoundation.org/collaborate/lwf**
  The **Linux Weather Forecast** tracks ongoing kernel developments that are likely to achieve incorporation in the near future.

- **http://lkml.org/**
  Archive of the Kernel Mailing List, updated in real time.

- **http://www.tux.org/lkml**
  The Kernel Mailing List **FAQ:** How to subscribe, post, etc. to the kernel mailing list, plus related matters such as how to submit and use patches.

- **http://linux.yyz.us/patch-format.html**
  A detailed guide for how to submit patches to the official kernel tree.

- **http://linux.yyz.us/git-howto.html**
  The **Kernel Hackers' Guide to git**, the source code management system, used by many senior kernel developers.

- **http://lxr.linux.no**
  The **lxr** kernel browser: Can be run though the Internet or installed locally.

- **http://www.kernelnewbies.org**
  kernelnewbies: An excellent source of documentation; while starting at the lowest level and going to advanced.

- **http://www.kernelnewbies.org/LinuxChanges**
  Comprehensive kernel changelog: A detailed list of changes in the kernel and its **API** from one release to another. .

Other Documentation

- **http://www.linuxsymposium.org/2007/archives.php/**
  http://ols.fedoraproject.org/OLS/
  Full proceedings of Ottawa **Linux** Symposium from 2001 on, containing many important talks and papers.

- **http://www.ibm.com/developerworks/linux**
  IBM's Linux developer page, with white papers and other documentation.

- **http://www.tldp.org**
  contains a lot of material from the **Linux Documentation Project (LDP)**, including all current **HOWTO** documents.

- **http://training.linuxfoundation.org/lp/sign-up-for-the-free-linux-training-webinar-series** has a series of free webinars on important topics from **Linux** contributors.

Chapter 2

Kernel Configuration and Compilation

We'll examine the layout of the **Linux** kernel source. We'll consider methods of browsing the source. We'll also give the procedures for configuring, compiling, and installing updated or modified kernels. Finally, we will discuss some details of the kernel and module build process.

2.1 Installation and Layout of the Kernel Source

- The source for the **Linux** kernel must be made easily available by all distributors. Both the newest and older kernel versions are generally available for download. (Remember that `finger @www.kernel.org` will give a quick enumeration of the most recent kernel versions.)

- The pristine source for all kernel versions can always be obtained from directly from the kernel maintainers at **http://www.kernel.org**, or from the distributors, most of whom make (possibly quite extensive) changes to the source. These changes must also be freely available.

- The exact location of the source is on your system is neither mandated nor important. When external modules have to be built against the source, the directory `/lib/modules/$(uname -r)/build` either contains the actual source, or is a symbolic link pointing to it.

- For convenience, we'll often pretend the kernel source resides at `/usr/src/linux`, and for the purpose of displaying code, create a symbolic link from there to the real code. This should not be construed as a recommendation to do this on normal development systems. Under `/usr/src/linux` (or the real location) we find:

Table 2.1: **Layout of the Kernel Source**

Directory	Purpose
arch	x86_64, ia64, alpha, arm, sparc, sparc64, mips, mips64, m68k, ppc, s390... Architecture specific code for boot, synchronization. memory and process management.
kernel	Generic main kernel routines.
mm	Generic memory management code. swapping, mmaping, kernel malloc, etc.
init	Generic kernel start-up code.
drivers	char, block, net, scsi, fs, cdrom, pci ... Device drivers sorted by type.
sound	**ALSA** (**A**dvanced **L**inux **S**ound **A**rchitecture), including sound card drivers.
block	Low-level infrastructure for the block device layer. Specific block device drivers are under `drivers/block`.
fs	Filesystems, with subdirectories for each type.
net	Ethernet, ip, decnet, ipx, ipv4, ipv6, appletalk and other network code.
security	Security models, including **SELinux**.
crypto	Cryptographic algorithms.
lib	Some standard library routines, mostly for strings.
ipc	System V Inter-Process Communications code.
usr	User-space interaction; so far only **intramfs** code.
scripts	Various scripts used to compile and package kernels.
Documentation	Various documentation resources; sometimes not up to date.
virt	Virtualization infrastructure.
firmware	Firmware that is packaged with kernel.
samples	Sample kernel code used for tracing, profiling and debugging purposes.
tools	User-space tools, used for performance counting.
include	System header files.

- Here is a count of lines in the source code for the most recent vanilla kernel. (For each directory all subdirectories are included.)

```
/usr/src/linux-3.0

   Directory           .S files      .h files      .c files        TOTAL

   .                     339158       2473651      10875599       13688408
   ./drivers               2057       1039058       6637523        7678638
   ./arch                334418        748410       1546271        2629099
   ./fs                       0         86547        900009         986556
   ./sound                  218         69525        614364         684107
   ./net                      0         21136        659279         680415
   ./include                  0        474883             0         474883
   ./kernel                   0          7005        171553         178558
   ./mm                       0           265         83071          83336
   ./security                 0          5529         54425          59954
   ./tools                    2          4715         49989          54706
```

./crypto	0	10359	40183	50542
./lib	0	1309	42370	43679
./scripts	0	3612	26477	30089
./block	0	668	21019	21687
./Documentation	0	0	9714	9714
./ipc	0	178	7696	7874
./virt	0	228	5725	5953
./init	0	76	3069	3145
./firmware	2425	0	280	2705
./samples	0	148	1952	2100
./usr	38	0	630	668

- Most of the lines of code are for drivers, either for peripherals or different types of filesystems. A fair comparison with other operating systems should observer that the sources for the **X**-window system and the various Desktops, etc., are not included. However, we have included all architectures.

- Here is how the total number of lines has changed with kernel versions:

```
Kernel Version  TOTAL LINES

    2.6.18       7082952
    2.6.19       7308043
    2.6.20       7400843
    2.6.21       7522286
    2.6.22       7744727
    2.6.23       7818168
    2.6.24       8082358
    2.6.25       8395801
    2.6.26       8535933
    2.6.27       8690888
    2.6.28       9128690
    2.6.29       9871260
    2.6.30      10419567
    2.6.31      10765122
    2.6.32      11403137
    2.6.33      11765938
    2.6.34      11861616
    2.6.35      12250679
    2.6.36      12539782
    2.6.37      13006967
    2.6.38      13289311
    2.6.39      13600071
    3.0         13688408
```

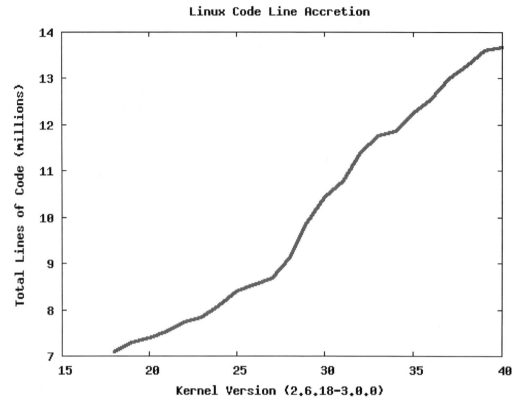

Figure 2.1: **Source Line Counts**

2.2   Kernel Browsers

- One often has to browse the kernel source in order to understand the inner workings of the kernel, compare kernel versions etc. Often the best tools for doing so are the simple text utilities such as **grep** and **find**.

- One modern tool is the **Linux Cross Reference Browser** (**lxr**) which can be accessed at **http://lxr.linux.no**. This website contains browseable source code repositories for virtually every linux kernel ever produced, as well as source code and instructions for a local installation of **lxr**.

- The master **lxr** repository uses version 0.9.4 of the browser, which while very robust is relatively slow and more difficult to install compared to older versions. A sample installation of the simpler version 0.3.1 can be found at **http://users.sosdg.org/ qiyong/lxr/source**

- Local use of **lxr** requires running a web server (typically **apache**) and several hundred MB of disk space per kernel being indexed.

- A purely text-based browser is offered by the **cscope** utility, which is a standard offering on most **Linux** systems. To use on the kernel sources one need merely run `make cscope` in the kernel source directory, creating the various index files needed, and then simply run **cscope** in the main kernel source directory. From then on the use is interactive and intuitive.

- Another approach is afforded by the use of **GNU Global**, which can be obtained from **http://www.gnu.org/software/global**. Many distributions offer this as a package. Once **global** is installed one need go only to the kernel source directory and do `gtags ; htags`, wait until the cross-indexing is done and then navigate the results using your favorite browser, simply by pointing to `/usr/src/linux/HTML/index.html`. One disadvantage of **global** is its use of over 2 GB of disk space per kernel.

- All these methods will work, and there are some others such as just doing **make tags** and using the generic tags files that can be used by **emacs** and **vi** experts. For what it's worth, we confess to having a preference for **lxr** (older versions) because of the easy comparison of different kernel versions.

2.3   Kernel Configuration Files

- Kernels provided by **Linux** distributors usually differ from those whose sources are directly obtained from the official "vanilla" kernel repository at **http://www.kernel.org**. Patches, sometimes quite extensive, have been made to the kernel source, including the addition of new features and device drivers that have not yet made it into the "official" kernel tree, as well as bug fixes and security enhancements.

- The default configuration for the vanilla sources has only a few kinds of hardware turned on (such as one network card) as well as various subsystems turned off, with the actual default choices probably reflecting the actual hardware Linus Torvalds has (or had at one point), such as his choice of sound card, network driver etc.

- When you configure the kernel you produce a configuration file, `.config`, in the main kernel source directory. If configured to do so, the contents of the `.config` file can be stored right inside the kernel. If the `CONFIG_IKCONFIG_PROC` option is turned on, information can be read out directly from `/proc/config.gz`.

- Running the `scripts/extract-ikconfig` utility on a kernel image (**compressed** or **uncompressed**) built with `CONFIG_IKCONFIG` turned on, causes a dump of the configuration file. (Beware, this utility needs to be run from the main kernel source directory, or requires some minor modifications to work.)

- If you don't have the full kernel source install, you can still find your `.config` file in the directory `/lib/modules/$(uname -r)/build/`, as well as find an additional copy in the `/boot` directory.

- In these configurations, drivers for almost all conceivable hardware are compiled as kernel modules. This is the correct thing to do because one cannot know in advance precisely what hardware the end user will have, so all possibilities must be prepared for.

- On the other hand, by configuring only the hardware actually present the kernel compilation can be sped up considerably. In addition, the configuration process goes much faster as you only have to turn on what you need.

2.4   Kernel Building and Makefiles

- The **Linux** kernel building process has become quite complex, and was completely reworked for the 2.6 kernel. Fortunately, using it is quite easy. Full documentation can be found under **/usr/src/linux/ Documentation/kbuild**.

- Important components include:
  - The top-level `Makefile`.
  - The configuration file, `.config`.
  - The top-level architecture-dependent `Makefile`.

- – Subdirectory `Makefiles`.
- – In each directory with a `Makefile`, there is a file named `Kconfig`, which interfaces with the kernel configuration utilities.

- The documentation that comes with the kernel does an excellent job of explaining the relationship of these quantities, so we won't try to repeat it.

- Here is an example of a simple Makefile:

```
obj-$(CONFIG_FOO1)      += foo1.o
obj-$(CONFIG_FOO2)      += foo2.o
obj-$(CONFIG_FOO3)      += foo3.o

foo3-objs               := foo3a.o foo3b.o foo3c.o

ccflags-$(CONFIG_FOO_DEBUG) += -DDEBUG
```

(Note we have `.o`, not `.ko`.)

- As the **make** proceeds, three environmental variables are constructed according to the `CONFIG_*` values:

  - – `obj-y`: Those source files to be compiled into the kernel itself.
  - – `obj-m`: Those source files to be compiled into modules.
  - – `obj-`: Those source files to be ignored.

- If more than one file must be compiled and linked together that is done as in the `foo3-objs` example.

- The variable `EXTRA_CFLAGS` can be used to augment compiler flags.

- To get your new facility in the configuration utilities requires modifying one more file, `Kconfig` in the same directory, which is written in a customized scripting language, but is easy to hack. This consists of a series of sections such as:

```
config FOO1
        bool "FOO1 Driver"
        default y
        help
          Here is the help item on the foo1 driver.
config FOO2
        tristate "FOO2 Driver"
        default n
        help
          Here is the help item on the foo2 driver.
```

- There are other directives in this file for indicating dependencies, etc.

- Slightly fancier **Makefiles** are required if you need to recurse through subdirectories, etc, but looking at the examples in the kernel source gives good enough guidance.

- To repeat, there are three main ingredients; the `Makefile`, the `Kconfig` file, and the source itself.

2.5 Labs

Lab 1: Building a Kernel for an ARM target

- In this exercise you will build a **Linux** kernel, tailored to specific needs of hardware/software. You won't actually modify any of the source for the **Linux** kernel; however, you will select features and decide which modules are built.

- Use whatever exact file names and version numbers are appropriate for the sources you have, rather than what is specified below.

Step 1: Obtain and install the source

- **Note:** As shortcut, we have a source tree already in /home/lftraining/training/linux-3.0-arm of the classroom VM.

- Depending on your **Linux** distribution you may already have the source installed for your currently running kernel. You should be able to do this by looking at the **/lib/modules/kernel-version/** directory and seeing if it has active links to **build** or **source** directories. If not you'll have to obtain the kernel source in the method detailed by your distribution.

- If you are using a vanilla source, then download it from **http://www.kernel.org** and then unpack it with:

  ```
  $ tar jxvf linux-3.0.1.tar.bz2
  ```

  (putting in the proper file and kernel version of course.)

Step 2: Make sure other ingredients are up to date.

- The file **/usr/src/linux/Documentation/Changes** highlights what versions of various system utilities and libraries are needed to work with the current source.

- To build the kernel, we need a cross-compiler available. Your virtual system image has a version installed in the folder **/opt/cross/bin**. Always make sure your PATH includes this folder (check with 'echo $PATH') and you set CROSS_COMPILE accordingly.

  On the training VM we've 3 different cross-compilers installed:

  ```
  lftraining@lftraining-instance:~$ ls /opt/cross/bin/
  arm-2009q3-linux-gnueabi-addr2line  arm-2009q3-linux-gnueabi-readelf
  arm-2011.03-linux-gnueabi-gprof     arm-eabi-gcc
  arm-2009q3-linux-gnueabi-ar          arm-2009q3-linux-gnueabi-size
  arm-2011.03-linux-gnueabi-ld        arm-eabi-gcc-4.5.4
  arm-2009q3-linux-gnueabi-as          arm-2009q3-linux-gnueabi-sprite
  arm-2011.03-linux-gnueabi-nm        arm-eabi-gccbug
  arm-2009q3-linux-gnueabi-c++         arm-2009q3-linux-gnueabi-strings
  arm-2011.03-linux-gnueabi-objcopy   arm-eabi-gcov
  arm-2009q3-linux-gnueabi-c++filt     arm-2009q3-linux-gnueabi-strip
  arm-2011.03-linux-gnueabi-objdump   arm-eabi-gdb
  arm-2009q3-linux-gnueabi-cpp          arm-2011.03-linux-gnueabi-addr2line
  arm-2011.03-linux-gnueabi-ranlib    arm-eabi-gdbtui
  arm-2009q3-linux-gnueabi-g++          arm-2011.03-linux-gnueabi-ar
  arm-2011.03-linux-gnueabi-readelf   arm-eabi-gprof
  arm-2009q3-linux-gnueabi-gcc          arm-2011.03-linux-gnueabi-as
  ```

```
arm-2011.03-linux-gnueabi-size       arm-eabi-ld
arm-2009q3-linux-gnueabi-gcc-4.4.1  arm-2011.03-linux-gnueabi-c++
arm-2011.03-linux-gnueabi-sprite     arm-eabi-nm
arm-2009q3-linux-gnueabi-gcov         arm-2011.03-linux-gnueabi-c++filt
arm-2011.03-linux-gnueabi-strings    arm-eabi-objcopy
arm-2009q3-linux-gnueabi-gdb          arm-2011.03-linux-gnueabi-cpp
arm-2011.03-linux-gnueabi-strip      arm-eabi-objdump
arm-2009q3-linux-gnueabi-gdbtui       arm-2011.03-linux-gnueabi-elfedit
arm-eabi-addr2line                   arm-eabi-ranlib
arm-2009q3-linux-gnueabi-gprof        arm-2011.03-linux-gnueabi-g++
arm-eabi-ar                          arm-eabi-readelf
arm-2009q3-linux-gnueabi-ld           arm-2011.03-linux-gnueabi-gcc
arm-eabi-as                          arm-eabi-run
arm-2009q3-linux-gnueabi-nm           arm-2011.03-linux-gnueabi-gcc-4.5.2
arm-eabi-c++                         arm-eabi-size
arm-2009q3-linux-gnueabi-objcopy      arm-2011.03-linux-gnueabi-gcov
arm-eabi-c++filt                     arm-eabi-strings
arm-2009q3-linux-gnueabi-objdump      arm-2011.03-linux-gnueabi-gdb
arm-eabi-cpp                         arm-eabi-strip
arm-2009q3-linux-gnueabi-ranlib       arm-2011.03-linux-gnueabi-gdbtui
arm-eabi-g++
```

This translates to:

- CROSS_COMPILE=arm-2011.03-linux-gnueabi- (our default)

- CROSS_COMPILE=arm-2009q3-linux-gnueabi- (older but known to work well)

- CROSS_COMPILE=arm-eabi- (recent android toolchain / linaro)

Step 3: Configuring the Kernel

- You can use any of the following methods:

  - **make ARCH=arm CROSS_COMPILE=arm-2011.03-linux-gnueabi- config**
    A purely text-based configuration routine.
  - **make ARCH=arm CROSS_COMPILE=arm-2011.03-linux-gnueabi- menuconfig**
    An **ncurses** semi-graphical configuration routine.
  - **make ARM=arm CROSS_COMPILE=arm-2011.03-linux-gnueabi- xconfig**
    An **X**-based fully-graphical configuration routine, based on the **qt** graphical libraries.
  - **make ARCH=arm CROSS_COMPILE=arm-2011.03-linux-gnueabi- gconfig**
    Also an **X**-based fully-graphical configuration routine, based on the **GTK** graphical libraries, which has a somewhat different look..

  You'll probably want to use **make xconfig** or **make gconfig**, as these have the nicest interfaces. At any rate, the content and abilities of all the methods are identical. They all produce a file named **.config**, which contains your choices. (It is generally advised not to edit this file directly unless you really know what you are doing!)

- If you have an old configuration, you can speed up the process by doing:

  ```
  $ make ARCH=arm CROSS_COMPILE=arm-2011.03-linux-gnueabi- oldconfig
  ```

  which takes your old configuration and asks you only about new choices. If you begin from the default choices from **kernel.org** doing:

```
$ make ARCH=arm CROSS_COMPILE=arm-2011.03-linux-gnueabi- vexpress_defconfig
```

will supply such a reference configuration.

- For convenience, we provide an alias:

```
alias armcrossmake='make ARCH=arm CROSS_COMPILE=$MYCROSSPREFIX'
```

For using the default toolchain (arm-2011.03-linux-gnueabi-gcc) we only have to type then:

```
armcrossmake menuconfig
  - or -
armcrossmake
```

- The **ketchup** utility is very useful for going from one kernel version to another. It will download patches and/or full sources as they are needed and can check source integrity.

- For instance upgrading from 2.6.38 to 2.6.39 would involve going to the source directory and just typing:

  ```
  $ ketchup -G 2.6.39
  ```

- If your distribution does not have **ketchup** in its packaging system, it can be obtained from **http://www.selenic.com/ketchup**.

  Note: To work with 3.0 you need a new version of ketchup. A version working for 3.0 is available at **https://github.com/psomas/ketchup** .

- Take your time configuring the kernel. Read the help items to learn more about the possibilities available. Several choices you should make (for this class) are:

  - Under **Processor type and features:**
    Pick the proper CPU (Choosing too advanced a processor make cause a boot failure.)
  - Under **Loadable module support:**
    Turn **on** "Enable loadable module support."
    Turn **on** "Module unloading."
  - Under **Block Devices:**
    Turn **on** "Loopback device support."
    Turn **on** "RAM disk support"
    Turn **on** "initial RAM disk (initrd) support"
  - Under **Multi-device Support (RAID and LVM):**
    Turn **on** "Device Mapper Support"
  - Under **Instrumentation Support**:
    Turn **on** "Profiling Support" and "Oprofile"
    Turn **on** "Kprobes"
  - Under **Kernel Hacking:**
    Turn **on** "Magic SysRq key".
    Turn **on** "Debug Filesystem".

- Make sure you turn on drivers for your actual hardware; i.e., support for the proper network card and if you have a **SCSI** system the proper disk controller, and your particular sound card.

- You can short circuit this whole procedure by obtaining a `.config` file that should work for most common hardware from **http://training.linuxfoundation.org/course_materials/LF339** with a name like `config-3.0.1_arm_vexpress`. In this template we turn on the most common network cards etc and pick the options that will provide kernels that can handle the exercises we provide.

- For detailed guidance on configuring kernels an invaluable resource is *Linux Kernel in a Nutshell*, by Greg Kroah-Hartman, pub. O'Reilly, 2006, the full text of which is available at **http://www.kroah.com/lkn/**.

- In order to compile modules against your kernel source you need more than just a proper `.config` file. Short of running a compilation first, doing `make oldconfig`, `make prepare` and `make scripts` will take care of doing the setup for external module compilation, such as making symbolic links to the right architecture.

Step 4: Compiling and installing the new kernel.

- This involves:

  - Making the **compressed** kernel (**zImage** or **uImage**) and copying it over to the **/boot** directory with a good name.
  - Copying over the **System.map** file which is used to resolve kernel addresses mostly for logging and debugging purposes. Copying over the **vmlinux** file wich is used for debugging purposes.
  - Making modules and installing them under **/lib/modules/my-kernel-version/**.
  - Saving the kernel configuration for future reference.
  - Constructing a new **initrd** or **initramfs** image and copying it to the **/boot** directory. For ARM this step is optional.
  - Updating your boot loader configuration.

- There is a script (**/sbin/installkernel**) on most distributions which can do these steps for you, and there is also an **install** target for **make**, but we prefer to use our own script over the canned one as it requires fewer arguments and is less rigid. This script is available in the solutions under the name **DO_KERNEL.sh**.

- Thus if you want to use the canned configuration (on an x86 host), you can do everything in this manner:

```
$ tar jxvf <pathto>linux-3.0.1.tar.bz2
$ cp <pathto>config-3.0_x86_64 linux-3.0.1/.config
$ cd linux-3.0.1
$ <pathto>DO_KERNEL.sh
```

- For the ARM Kernel: To make sure we have a working config, we use a prepared kernel config. We just copy it into the current tree by:

```
cd /home/lftraining/training/linux-3.0-arm
cp /home/resources/config-3.0_arm_lab .config

armcrossmake oldconfig
armcrossmake menuconfig

armcrossmake    #  add -jN depending on the cpus of your VM

sudo armcrossmake INSTALL_MOD_PATH=/home/lftraining/targetfs modules_install

sudo cp vmlinux /home/lftraining/targetfs/vmlinux-3.0.1
sudo cp System.map /home/lftraining/targetfs/System.map
cp arch/arm/boot/zImage /tmp/zImage-3.0.1
```

We can test now our brand new kernel in an emulator! We use qemu-system-arm for this task. It is a versatile system and user-mode emulator. First we need to update the relevant image files:

```
sudo /usr/bin/mkimagefile.sh
```

This is a handmade script and creates and in-memory filesystem for usage with the emulator. We import the folders in /home/lftraining/targetfs into the root of this image. The output is written to /tmp/ramdisk.img.gz.

Next we start up the emulator:

```
qemu-system-arm -M vexpress-a9 -m 256M -kernel /tmp/zImage-3.0.1 -initrd /tmp/ramdisk.img.gz
              -append "ramdisk_size=204800 rw root=/dev/ramdisk earlyprintk
              rdinit=/simple init=/simple " -net nic,model=lan9118 -net user,restrict=n
```

- There are two steps in the kernel compilation and installing procedure which can be quite distribution-dependent.

- The first is the construction of the **initrd** or **initramfs** image. It is best to follow the procedures conventionally followed on your distribution; i.e., **mkinitrd** on older **Red Hat**-based systems, or **dracut** on newer ones; and **update-initramfs** on **Debian**-based systems including **Ubuntu**.

- The second is the updating of the boot loader configuration. On **Red Hat**-based systems this can be done either by editing manually the grub.conf file, or using the **grubby** utility. On **Debian**-based systems this is done by the **update-grub** program and the configuration files should never be edited by hand.

- Note that some recent systems used the newer **grub 2**, which has many changes; for example the configuration file is now called grub.cfg, not grub.conf, and you may have to edit the configuration file /etc/default/grub. But the same principles apply.

Chapter 3

Modules

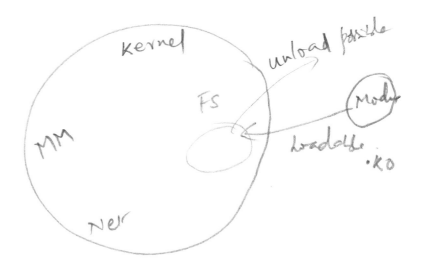

We'll begin our discussion of modularization techniques under **Linux**. We'll define what a module is and describe the command level utilities used to manipulate them. We'll discuss how to compile, load, and unload modules, and how to pass parameters to them. We'll explain how to keep track of module usage and export symbols to from one module to another, and consider module licensing.

3.1 What are Modules?

- A kernel **module** is a component that can be loaded into (and unloaded from) an already running kernel. It is a relocateable object file; i.e., it has a `.ko` extension. Once loaded a module has all the capabilities of any other part of the kernel.

- To a rough approximation, a module uses the **Linux** kernel like a shared library, linking in to it only through a list of symbols and functions which have been **exported** and thus made available to the module.

- Modules may depend on other modules and thus the order of loading and unloading may need to be done carefully.

- While many modules are **device drivers**, many others are not; i.e., a device driver may be **built-in** to the kernel and a module may have nothing to do with any hardware device.

- Many kernel components are designed so the choice of building them in or having them linked as modules is a configuration option.

- For the most part no changes are required to the source to include the modular option, and it can speed up development to leave it this way even if a facility will almost always be built-in. This permits the testing of new features and enhancements by loading and unloading modules, without a full kernel recompilation and a reboot, leading to a great savings in time.

- The **Linux** kernel is still technically a **monolithic** one, even when the use of modules is greatly deployed. This term has to do with basic architecture and whether or not there is a **microkernel**. When a module is loaded it becomes part of the monolithic kernel.

3.2   A Trivial Example

- Here is an example of a very trivial module. It does nothing but print a statement when it is loaded, and one when it is unloaded.

```
#include <linux/module.h>
#include <linux/init.h>

static int __init my_init(void)
{
        printk(KERN_INFO "Hello: module loaded at 0x%p\n", my_init);
        return 0;
}

static void __exit my_exit(void)
{
        printk(KERN_INFO "Bye: module unloaded from 0x%p\n", my_exit);
}

module_init(my_init);
module_exit(my_exit);

MODULE_AUTHOR("A GENIUS");
MODULE_LICENSE("GPL v2");
```

- Almost all modules contain callback functions for initialization and cleanup, which are specified with the module_init() and module_exit() macros. These callbacks are automatically called when the module is loaded and unloaded. A module without a cleanup function cannot be unloaded.

- In addition, use of these macros simplifies writing drivers (or other code) which can be used either as modules, or directly built into the kernel. Labeling functions with the attributes __init or __exit is a refinement to be discussed later.

- Any module which does not contain an open source license (as specified with the MODULE_LICENSE() macro) will be marked as **tainted**: it will function normally but kernel developers will be hostile to helping with any debugging.

- You will still see modules with the outdated form:

```
#include <linux/module.h>

int __init init_module(void)
{
        printk(KERN_INFO "Hello: init_module loaded at 0x%p\n", init_module);
        return 0;
}

void __exit cleanup_module(void)
{
        printk(KERN_INFO "Bye: cleanup_module loaded at 0x%p\n",
                cleanup_module);
}
```

- While direct use of the callback functions (`init_module()` and `cleanup_module()`) will still work, using them without employing the `module_init()` and `module_exit()` macros is deprecated.

- Many drivers in the kernel still use just the `init_module()`, `cleanup_module()` functions; it saves a few lines of code, especially for a driver that is always loaded as a module. While this is basically harmless, eventually use of this form will be extinguished.

3.3   Module Utilities

- The following utilities run in user-space and are part of the **module-init-tools** package. They are not directly part of the kernel source. Each has a rather complete **man** page.

- The configuration file **/etc/modprobe.conf** (as well as any files in the directory **/etc/modprobe.d**) is consulted frequently by the module utilities. Information such as paths, aliases, options to be passed to modules, commands to be processed whenever a model is loaded or unloaded, are specified therein. The possible commands are:

```
alias        wildcard modulename
options      modulename option ...
install      modulename command ...
remove       modulename command ...
include      filename
```

- The `install` and `remove` commands can be used as substitutes for the default **insmod** and **rmmod** commands.

- All **Linux** distributions prescribe a methods for the automatic loading of particular modules on system startup. However, the use of **udev** in modern **Linux** distributions usually obviates such needs.

- On **Red Hat**-based systems the file **/etc/rc.modules** will be run (if it exists) out of **/etc/rc.d/rc.sysinit**. In this file any explicit module loading can be done through the full use of the module loading commands.

- On **Debian**-based systems any modules listed in **/etc/modules** will be loaded. (Only the names of the modules go in this file, not loading commands.) on **GENTOO** systems, the same role is played by the files in **/etc/modules.autoload.d**.

- On **SUSE**-based systems the file that needs to be modified is **/etc/sysconfig/kernel**.

lsmod

- **lsmod** gives a listing of all loaded modules. The information given includes name, size, use count, and a list of referring modules. The content is the same as that in **/proc/modules**.

insmod

- **insmod** links a loadable module into the running kernel, resolving all symbols. The `-f` option will try to force loading with a version mismatch between kernel and module.

- **insmod** can be used to load parameters into modules. For example,

```
$ /sbin/insmod my_net_driver.ko irq=10
```

rmmod

- **rmmod** unloads modules from the running kernel. A list of modules may be given as in:

```
$ /sbin/rmmod my_net_driver my_char_driver
```

Note no **.ko** extension is specified.

depmod

- **depmod** creates a *Makefile*-like dependency file (**/lib/modules/KERNEL-VERSION-NUMBER /modules.dep**) based on the symbols contained in the modules explicitly mentioned on the command line, or in the default place.

- **depmod** is vital to the use of **modprobe**. It is always run during boot. Under most circumstances it should be run as

```
$ depmod -ae
```

- For **depmod** and **modprobe** to find modules they must be in prescribed places, under **/lib/modules**. The file **/etc/modprobe.conf** is consulted every time a module is loaded or when **depmod** is run.

- When modules are built in external directories and installed with the `modules_install` target, they are placed in the `extra` subdirectory.

modprobe

- **modprobe** can load (or unload with the `-r` option) a stack of modules that depend on each other, and can be used instead of **insmod**.

- It can also be used to try a list of modules, and quit whenever one is first found and successfully loaded. It is also heavily dependent on **/etc/modprobe.conf**.

- Whenever there are new modules added, or there is a change in location `depmod` should be run.

- The **modtuils** package requires use of the `.ko` extension with **insmod**, but **modprobe** and **rmmod** require no extension.

- Parameters can be passed to **modprobe** in the same way they are passed to **insmod**; i.e., you can do something like

```
$ /sbin/modprobe my_net_driver irq=10
```

3.4 Passing Parameters

- Parameters to be passed to modules must be explicitly marked as such and type checking is done. For example,

```
int irq = 12;
module_param (irq, int, 0);
```

There are a number of macros which can be used:

```
#include <linux/moduleparam.h>            Permission

module_param (name, type, perm);
module_param_named (name, value, type, perm);
module_param_array (name, type, num, perm);
module_param_string (name, string, len, perm);
```

- In the basic `module_param()` macro, `name` is the variable name, `type` can be `byte`, `short`, `ushort`, `int`, `uint`, `long`, `ulong`, `charp`, `bool`, `invbool`.

- The `perm` parameter is a permissions mask which is used for an accompanying entry in the **sysfs** filesystem. If you are not interested in **sysfs**, a value of 0 will suffice. Typically one can use the value `S_IRUGO` (0444) for read permission for all users. (See **/usr/src/linux/include/linux/stat.h** for all possibilities.) If a write permission is given, the parameter may be altered by writing to the **sysfs** filesystem entry associated with the module, but note that the module will not be notified in any way when the value changes! In this case the permission might be `S_IRUGO | S_IWUSR` (0644).

- The `module_param_named()` variation has `name` as the string used to describe the variable when loading, which does not have to be the same as `value` (which is **not** the actual value of the parameter but rather the name of the parameter as used in the module.) Note that these are macros, and neither argument has to appear within quotes.

- In the `module_param_array()` macro the integer variable `num` gives the number elements in the array which can be used as in the following example:

  ```
  $ /sbin/insmod my_project irq=3,4,5
  ```

- The `module_param_string()` macro is for passing a string directly into a `char` array.

- With this method it is possible to build your own data types; it is extensible. For more details see **http://lwn.net/Articles/22197/**.

- A feature of this method is that it still works when a driver, or other kernel facility, is compiled as built-in rather than as a module. Kernels earlier than 2.6 required use of a separate set of functions (using the `__setup()` macros) to pass parameters to the kernel on the boot command line. This makes it even easier to write code that can be used as either a module or built-in without changing the source.

- The way to pass such a parameter to the kernel as a boot parameter is to prefix its name with the name of the module and a `.`; thus the kernel boot command line might look like:

  ```
  linux root=LABEL=/ ... my_project.irq=3,4,5 ...
  ```

  A list of all known passable parameters can be found at **/usr/src/linux/Documentation/kernel-parameters.txt**.

- There are a number of related macros, defined in **/usr/src/linux/include/linux/module.h** that can be used in modules:

  ```
  MODULE_AUTHOR(name);
  MODULE_DESCRIPTION(desc);
  MODULE_SUPPORTED_DEVICE(name);
  MODULE_PARM_DESC(var,desc);
  MODULE_FIRMWARE(filename);
  MODULE_LICENSE(license);
  MODULE_VERSION(version);
  ```

- The information stored thereby is generated by running the command **modinfo**.

3.5   Compiling Modules

- In order to compile modules you must have the kernel source installed; or at least those parts of it which are required. Those should always be found under **/lib/modules/$(uname -r)/build**.

- The simple-minded way to compile a module would require specifying the right flags and options, and pointing to the correct kernel headers. However, this method has long been deprecated and in the 2.6 kernel series it has become impossible to compile completely outside the kernel source tree.

- Compilation of modules for the 2.6 kernel **requires** a kernel source which has either been through a compilation stage, or at least has been through a `make prepare`, as this is required to generate necessary configuration and dependency information. One also needs, of course a `.config` containing the kernel configuration.

- The approved approach is still to work outside the kernel source tree, but to jump into it to do the compilation. For this you'll need at least a minimal `Makefile` with at least the following in it:

  ```
  obj-m += trivial.o
  ```

  If you then type

```
$ make -C/lib/modules/$(uname -r)/build M=$PWD modules
```

it will compile your module with all the same options and flags as the kernel modules in that source location (for the currently running kernel). To compile for a kernel other than the one that is running, you just need to place the proper argument with the -C option.

- Installing the modules in the proper place so they can be automatically found by utilities such as **depmod**, requires the modules_install target:

```
$ make -C/lib/modules/$(uname -r)/build M=$PWD modules_install
```

- By default the output is brief; to make it more verbose you can set the environmental variables V=1 or KBUILD_VERBOSE=1. You could do this, for example, by typing export KBUILD_VERBOSE=1; make or make V=1 ..., etc.

- If it is necessary to split the source into more than one file, then the -r option to **ld** (which is automatically invoked by **gcc**) can be used. A simple example (for the Makefile) would be:

```
obj-m += mods.o
mods-objs := mod1.o mod2.o
```

- In the main directory of the solutions, you will find a script titled **genmake** which can automatically generate proper makefiles; it can be a great time-saver! Here is what it looks like:

```
#!/bin/bash

# Automatic kernel makefile generation
# Jerry Cooperstein, coop@linuxfoundation.org, 2/2003 - 1/2011
# Jan-Simon Moeller, jsmoeller@linuxfoundation.org, 7/2011
# License: GPLv2

OBJS=""    # list of kernel modules (.o files)
K_S=""     # list of kernel modules (.c files)
U_S=""     # list of userland programs (.c files)
U_X=""     # list of userland programs (executables)
T_S=""     # list of userland programs (.c files) that use pthreads
T_X=""     # list of userland programs (executables) that use pthreads
ALL=""     # list of all targets

CFLAGS_U_X="-O2 -Wall -pedantic"    # compile flags for user programs
CFLAGS_T_X=$CFLAGS_U_X" -pthread"   # compile flags for threaded user programs

# set the default kernel source to the running one; otherwise take from
# first command line argument

if [ "$KROOT" == "" ] ; then
    KROOT=/lib/modules/$(uname -r)/build
    [ ! -d "$KROOT" ] && KROOT=/usr/src/linux-$(uname -r)
fi

# abort if the source is not present

KMF=$KROOT/Makefile
KERNELSRC=$(grep "^KERNELSRC" $KMF | awk ' {print $3;}')

if [ "$KERNELSRC" != "" ] ; then
    echo Primary Makefile is not in $KROOT, using $KERNELSRC
```

```
        KMF=$KERNELSRC/Makefile
fi

if [ ! -d "$KROOT" ] || [ ! -f "$KMF" ] ; then
    echo kernel source directory $KROOT does not exist or has no Makefile
    exit 1
fi

if [ -d "$CROSS_COMPILE" -a ! -d "$ARCH" ] ; then
    echo CROSS_COMPILE set but no ARCH given. Check cmdline.
    exit 1
fi

if [ -d "$ARCH" -a ! -d "$CROSS_COMPILE" ] ; then
    echo ARCH set but no CROSS_COMPILE given. Check cmdline.
    exit 1
fi

# additional flags?

if [ "$KINCS"          != "" ] ; then
        CFLAGS_U_X="$CFLAGS_U_X -I$KROOT/include"
        CFLAGS_T_X="$CFLAGS_T_X -I$KROOT/include"
fi

# extract the VERSION info from the Makefile

KV=$(grep "^VERSION =" $KMF | awk ' {print $3;}')
KP=$(grep "^PATCHLEVEL =" $KMF | awk ' {print $3;}')
KS=$(grep "^SUBLEVEL =" $KMF | awk ' {print $3;}')
KE=$(grep "^EXTRAVERSION =" $KMF | awk ' {print $3;}')
KERNEL=$KV.$KP.$KS$KE

echo KERNEL=$KERNEL, KV=$KV KP=$KP KS=$KS KE=$KE

# construct lists of kernel and user sources and targets

# skip empty directories
if [ "$(find . -maxdepth 1 -name "*.c")" == "" ] ; then
    echo No need to make Makefile: no source code
    exit
fi

for names in *.c ; do

# exclude files with NOMAKE or .mod.c files

 if [ "$(grep NOMAKE $names)" ] || [ "$(grep vermagic $names)" ] ; then
     echo "$names is being skipped, it is not a module or program"
     else
     if [ "$(grep \<linux\/module.h\> $names )" ] ; then
         FILENAME_DOTO=$(basename $names .c).o
         OBJS=$OBJS" $FILENAME_DOTO"
         K_S=$K_S" $names"
     else
# is it  a pthread'ed program?
         if [ "$(grep '\<pthread.h\>' $names)" ] ; then
```

```
                FILENAME_EXE=$(basename $names .c)
                T_X=$T_X" $FILENAME_EXE"
                T_S=$T_S" $names"
            else
                U_X=$U_X" $(basename $names .c)"
                U_S=$U_S" $names"
            fi
        fi
    fi
done

CLEANSTUFF="$U_X $T_X"

# maybe there are no kernel modules

if [ "$OBJS" != "" ] ; then
    CLEANSTUFF="$CLEANSTUFF"" Module.symvers modules.order"
fi

# get ALL the targets

if [ "$U_X" != "" ] ; then ALL=$ALL" userprogs"; fi
if [ "$T_X" != "" ] ; then ALL=$ALL" threadprogs"; fi
if [ "$OBJS" != "" ] ; then ALL=$ALL"  modules" ; fi

# echo if you are curious :>

echo K_S=$K_S OBJS=$OBJS U_S=$U_S U_X=$U_X T_S=$T_S T_X=$T_X
echo ARCH=$ARCH CROSS_COMPILE=$CROSS_COMPILE

################################################################################
# We're done preparing, lets build the makefile finally!

# get rid of the old Makefile, build a new one

rm -f Makefile

echo "### Automatic Makefile generation by 'genmake' script        ####" >>Makefile
echo "### Copyright, Jerry Cooperstein, coop@linuxfoundation.org 2003-2011 ####" >>Makefile
echo "### License: GPLv2 ###"                                       >>Makefile

if [ "$K_S" != "" ] ; then
    echo -e "\nobj-m += $OBJS" >> Makefile
    echo -e "\nexport KROOT=$KROOT" >> Makefile
    if [ ! -z $ARCH ] ; then
        echo -e "\nexport ARCH=$ARCH" >> Makefile
        export xARCH="ARCH=$ARCH"
    fi
    if [ ! -z $CROSS_COMPILE ] ; then
        echo -e "\nexport CROSS_COMPILE=$CROSS_COMPILE" >> Makefile
        export xCROSSC="CROSS_COMPILE=$CROSS_COMPILE"
    fi
fi
echo -e "\nallofit: $ALL" >> Makefile

if [ "$K_S" != "" ] ; then
    echo "modules:" >> Makefile
```

```
        echo -e "\t@\$(MAKE) $xARCH $xCROSSC -C \$(KROOT) M=\$(PWD) modules" >> Makefile
        echo "modules_install:" >> Makefile
        echo -e "\t@\$(MAKE) $xARCH $xCROSSC -C \$(KROOT) M=\$(PWD) modules_install" >> Makefile
        echo "kernel_clean:" >> Makefile
        echo -e "\t@\$(MAKE) $xARCH $xCROSSC -C \$(KROOT) M=\$(PWD) clean" >> Makefile
fi

if [ "$U_X" != "" ] ; then
    echo -e "\nuserprogs:" >> Makefile
    echo -e "\t@\$(MAKE) \\" >> Makefile
    echo -e "\t\tCFLAGS=\"$CFLAGS_U_X\" \\" >> Makefile
    if [ "$LDLIBS" != "" ] ; then
        echo -e "\t\tLDLIBS=\"$LDLIBS\" \\" >> Makefile
    fi
    if [ "$CPPFLAGS" != '' ] ; then
    echo -e "\t\tCPPFLAGS=\"$CPPFLAGS\" \\" >> Makefile
    fi
    echo -e "\t$U_X" >> Makefile
fi

if [ "$T_X" != "" ] ; then
    echo -e "\nthreadprogs:" >> Makefile
    echo -e "\t@\$(MAKE) \\" >> Makefile
    echo -e "\t\tCFLAGS=\"$CFLAGS_T_X\" \\" >> Makefile
    if [ "$LDLIBS" != "" ] ; then
        echo -e "\t\tLDLIBS=\"$LDLIBS\" \\" >> Makefile
    fi
    if [ "$CPPFLAGS" != '' ] ; then
        echo -e "\t\tCPPFLAGS=\"$CPPFLAGS\" \\" >> Makefile
    fi
    echo -e "\t$T_X" >> Makefile
fi

if [ "$K_S" != "" ] ; then
    echo -e "\nclean: kernel_clean" >> Makefile
else
    echo -e "\nclean:" >> Makefile
fi
echo -e "\trm -rf $CLEANSTUFF" >> Makefile

exit


#################################################################################
```

gnmake can be used to build modules for a cross-compiled kernel. Set KROOT, ARCH and CROSS_COMPILE for this to work. In the VM there is an alias:

```
alias armgenmake='KROOT=/home/lftraining/training/linux-3.0-arm/
                  CROSS_COMPILE=$MYCROSSPREFIX ARCH=arm genmake'
```

Thus compiling labs for our ARM kernel is as easy as calling:

```
armgenmake
make
```

3.6 Role of MODULE_DEVICE_TABLE

- When the system is aware that a new device has been added or is present at boot, it is also often furnished with information describing the device. This usually includes (but is not limited to) a unique **vendor id** and **product id**.

- Drivers can specify which devices they can handle, and when modules are installed on the system, catalogues are updated. Thus, the **hot plug** facility (in user-space) is able to consult these tables and automatically load the required device driver, if it is not already present.

- For this to work the driver has to use the macro:

  ```
  MODULE_DEVICE_TABLE(type,name)
  ```

  where `type` indicates the type of driver and `name` points to an array of structures, each entry of which specifies a device. The exact structure depends on the type of device. For example:

  ```
  static const struct pci_device_id skge_id_table[] = {
  { PCI_DEVICE(PCI_VENDOR_ID_3COM, PCI_DEVICE_ID_3COM_3C940) },
  { PCI_DEVICE(PCI_VENDOR_ID_3COM, PCI_DEVICE_ID_3COM_3C940B) },
  ....
  { PCI_VENDOR_ID_LINKSYS, 0x1032, PCI_ANY_ID, 0x0015, },
  { 0 }
  };
  MODULE_DEVICE_TABLE(pci, skge_id_table);
  ```

- Note the use of the `PCI_DEVICE()` macro; each type of subsystem has such macros to aid in filling out the table of structures.

- The allowed types and the structures for them are delineated in **/usr/src/linux/include/linux/ mod_devicetable.h** and include: `pci, ieee1394, usb, hid, ccw, ap, css, acpi, pnp, pnp_card, serio, of_device_id, vio, pcmcia, input, eisa, parisc, sdio, ssb, virtio, i2c, spi, dmi,` and `platform.` Each one of these has a structure associated with it, such as `struct usb_device_id,` `struct ieee1394_device_id,` etc.

- Furthermore, when one runs the `make modules_install` step one updates the appropriate files in **/lib/modules/$(uname -r)**. such as `modules.pcimap, modules.usbmap,` etc.

- When a new device is added to the system, these files are consulted to see if it is a known device, and if so and the required driver is not already loaded, **modprobe** is run on the proper driver.

3.7 Modules vs Built-in

- Device drivers and other facilities can be loaded either as an integral part of the kernel, or as modules, and many kernel components have the capability of being used either way. Inclusion in the kernel requires kernel re-compilation of the entire kernel; modularization does not.

- At most only minor changes are necessary to the code; most often none are required. However, the kernel configuration files must deal with all three possibilities; built-in, module, or neither.

- It is possible to mark both data and functions for removal after kernel initialization. This is done with the keywords `__init` and `__initdata`. So for example, if you have

  ```
  static int some_data __initdata = 1 ;
  void __init somefunc (void) { ... }
  ```

the data and code will go into a special initialization section of the kernel and be discarded after execution. One has to be careful that the code or data is not referenced after **init** starts. You may have noticed messages to this effect during the system boot:

```
[0.841689] Freeing unused kernel memory: 424k freed
```

- The __exit macro doesn't do much except group all such labeled material together in the executable, in an area not likely to be cached.

- If you use the module_init(), module_exit() macros, you should be able to avoid using any #ifdef MODULE statements in your code.

- If MODULE is not defined, any function referenced by the module_exit() macro is dropped during compilation, since built-in drivers never get unloaded.

- In addition, the kernel arranges for automatic loading of all module_init() functions, using the following recipe:

- First, the module_init() macro in **/usr/src/linux/include/linux/module.h** will create a section in the .o file named .initcall.init This section will contain the address of the module's init function.

- Thus, when all of the .o files are linked together, the final object file will contain a section called .initcall.init which becomes, in effect, an array of pointers to all of the init functions.

- It is possible to assign priorities to initialization calls; the code which sets this up is in **/usr/src/linux/ include/linux/init.h**:

```
3.0: 194 #define pure_initcall(fn)            __define_initcall("0",fn,0)
3.0: 195
3.0: 196 #define core_initcall(fn)            __define_initcall("1",fn,1)
3.0: 197 #define core_initcall_sync(fn)       __define_initcall("1s",fn,1s)
3.0: 198 #define postcore_initcall(fn)        __define_initcall("2",fn,2)
3.0: 199 #define postcore_initcall_sync(fn)   __define_initcall("2s",fn,2s)
3.0: 200 #define arch_initcall(fn)            __define_initcall("3",fn,3)
3.0: 201 #define arch_initcall_sync(fn)       __define_initcall("3s",fn,3s)
3.0: 202 #define subsys_initcall(fn)          __define_initcall("4",fn,4)
3.0: 203 #define subsys_initcall_sync(fn)     __define_initcall("4s",fn,4s)
3.0: 204 #define fs_initcall(fn)              __define_initcall("5",fn,5)
3.0: 205 #define fs_initcall_sync(fn)         __define_initcall("5s",fn,5s)
3.0: 206 #define rootfs_initcall(fn)          __define_initcall("rootfs",fn,rootfs)
3.0: 207 #define device_initcall(fn)          __define_initcall("6",fn,6)
3.0: 208 #define device_initcall_sync(fn)     __define_initcall("6s",fn,6s)
3.0: 209 #define late_initcall(fn)            __define_initcall("7",fn,7)
3.0: 210 #define late_initcall_sync(fn)       __define_initcall("7s",fn,7s)
3.0: 211
3.0: 212 #define __initcall(fn) device_initcall(fn)
3.0: 213
3.0: 214 #define __exitcall(fn) \
3.0: 215     static exitcall_t __exitcall_##fn __exit_call = fn
3.0: 216
3.0: 217 #define console_initcall(fn) \
3.0: 218     static initcall_t __initcall_##fn \
3.0: 219     __used __section(.con_initcall.init) = fn
3.0: 220
3.0: 221 #define security_initcall(fn) \
3.0: 222     static initcall_t __initcall_##fn \
3.0: 223     __used __section(.security_initcall.init) = fn
```

so that default is priority 6. (Note that in the 2.6.19 kernel, additional sublevels such as **6s** were introduced.)

- The routine in **/usr/src/linux/init/main.c** that calls all the functions is:

```
3.0: 699 static void __init do_initcalls(void)
3.0: 700 {
3.0: 701         initcall_t *fn;
3.0: 702
3.0: 703         for (fn = __early_initcall_end; fn < __initcall_end; fn++)
3.0: 704                 do_one_initcall(*fn);
3.0: 705 }
```

- Note that in addition to using the `module_init()` macro, each driver still should use the `__init` attribute when defining the body of the init function. This places the code in the section `.text.init`, which is the section that is reclaimed.

3.8   Module Usage Count

- The kernel needs to keep track of how many times a module is being referenced by user-space processes. (This is unrelated to how many times the module is being used by other modules.) It is impossible to remove a module with a non-zero reference count.

- Once upon a time modules were expected to do most of the bookkeeping on their own, incrementing the usage count whenever a module was used by a process, and decrementing it when it was done. This procedure was difficult to accomplish without incurring errors and race conditions.

- As an improvement, module usage is now kept track of by higher levels of the kernel rather than manually. For this to work one needs to set the `owner` field in the appropriate data structure for the type of module being considered. For instance for a character device driver or a filesystem driver, this would be the `file_operations` structure. One can set this through:

```
static const struct file_operations fops = {
    .owner= THIS_MODULE,
    .open=  my_open,
    ...
}
```

Now the kernel will take care of the bookkeeping automatically. (Note for built in kernel code, `THIS_MODULE` is set to `NULL`.)

- Other examples of such structures containing tables of callback functions, or entry points, with `owner` fields include `block_device_operations` and `fb_ops`.

- If there is a need to manually modify a module's usage count (to prevent unloading while the module is being used) one can use the functions:

```
int try_module_get (struct module *module);
void module_put (struct module *module);
```

- Note that a call like `try_module_get(THIS_MODULE)` can fail if the module is in the process of being unloaded, in which case it returns 0; otherwise it returns 1. These functions are defined to have no effect when module unloading is not allowed as a kernel option during configuration.

- The reference count itself is embedded in the `module` data structure and can be obtained with the function

```
unsigned int module_refcount (struct module *mod);
```

and would usually be invoked as something like:

```
printk(KERN_INFO "Reference count= %d\n", module_refcount(THIS_MODULE));
```

3.9 Module Licensing

- Modules can be **licensed** with the MODULE_LICENSE() macro, as in:

  ```
  ....
  MODULE_DESCRIPTION("Does Everything");
  MODULE_AUTHOR("Vandals with Handles");
  MODULE_LICENSE("GPL v2");
  ....
  ```

- The following licenses are understood by the kernel:

Table 3.3: **Licenses**

License	Meaning	Tainted?
GPL	GNU Public License, V2 or later	No
GPL v2	GNU Public License, V2	No
GPL and additional rights	GNU Public License, V2 rights and more	No
Dual BSD/GPL	GNU Public License, V2 textbfor BSD license choice	No
Dual MPL/GPL	GNU Public License, V2 **or** Mozilla license choice	No
Dual MIT/GPL	GNU Public License, V2 **or** MIT license choice	No
Proprietary	Non free products (as in freedom, not free beer)	Yes

- You can see the licenses of loaded modules with a script like:

  ```
  #!/bin/bash
  for names in $(cat /proc/modules | awk ' {print $1;} ')
          do echo -ne "$names\t      \t"
          modinfo $names | grep  license
  done
  ```

- Besides the informational content, this macro has important consequences: Any other license causes the entire kernel to be **tainted**, and warning messages appear when the module is loaded. For the most part, any system problems, crashes etc. that arise while using a tainted kernel are most likely to be ignored by kernel developers. (The pseudo-file **/proc/sys/kernel/tainted** shows your kernel's status.)

- The actual value of **/proc/sys/kernel/tainted** is calculated from a bit mask of the following values defined in **/usr/src/linux/include/linux/kernel.h**:

  ```
  3.0: 352 #define TAINT_PROPRIETARY_MODULE      0
  3.0: 353 #define TAINT_FORCED_MODULE             1
  3.0: 354 #define TAINT_UNSAFE_SMP            2
  3.0: 355 #define TAINT_FORCED_RMMOD               3
  3.0: 356 #define TAINT_MACHINE_CHECK            4
  3.0: 357 #define TAINT_BAD_PAGE                        5
  ```

```
3.0: 358 #define TAINT_USER                    6
3.0: 359 #define TAINT_DIE                     7
3.0: 360 #define TAINT_OVERRIDDEN_ACPI_TABLE    8
3.0: 361 #define TAINT_WARN                    9
3.0: 362 #define TAINT_CRAP                    10
3.0: 363 #define TAINT_FIRMWARE_WORKAROUND     11
```

- A phrase sometimes heard in the **Linux** kernel developer community is:

  All binary modules are illegal.

- A thorough debate on this topic was held on the kernel mailing list in late 2006. (See **http:// lwn.net/Articles/215075** for a summary.) The main view coming out of that discussion stated that binary modules could **not** be banned, because the **GPL** controls **distribution** and not **use** of code.

- We don't want to get into a legal discussion here, but it seems clear that whether or not certain practices were accepted in the past, the future trend is that it is only going to become more difficult to get away with binary modules.

- Even if legal enforcement is not pursued vigorously, it is clear that increasing technical impediments and inefficiencies will make going proprietary more difficult and more expensive if not downright impossible.

3.10 Exporting Symbols

- In order for built-in kernel code to make a symbol (i.e., a variable or function) available for use by modules, it has to properly **export** it. If a module has symbols which are to be used by modules which are loaded after it is, it also has to export the symbol.

- This is accomplished with the use of the `EXPORT_SYMBOL()` macro:

```
int my_variable;
int my_export_fun (){ ....... };
EXPORT_SYMBOL(my_variable);
EXPORT_SYMBOL(my_export_fun);
```

- Note that the symbols will be exported even if they are declared as `static`.

- It is also possible to export symbols with the macro:

```
EXPORT_SYMBOL_GPL();
```

- Exactly how this macro should be used and interpreted has sometimes been controversial. Certainly it means quite literally the symbol can be exported only to modules which are licensed under the **GPL**; e.g., it can't be used in binary-only drivers. However, some feel it should be done only for modules which are used internally by the kernel for basic functions.

- There are some other specialized methods of exporting symbols:

```
EXPORT_PER_CPU_SYMBOL();
EXPORT_PER_CPU_SYMBOL_GPL();
EXPORT_SYMBOL_GPL_FUTURE();
EXPORT_UNUSED_SYMBOL();
EXPORT_UNUSED_SYMBOL_GPL();
```

- Kernels earlier than the 2.6 series exported all global symbols in a module **unless** they were explicitly declared as `static`; that is one reason why you see the `static` keyword so liberally used in kernel code, for the purpose of avoiding *name pollution.*

- Note that is still makes sense to declare symbols as `static`; if the code is compiled as built-in the symbols would be globally visible as the kernel is just one big program. Indeed the usual rule of thumb is that all symbols should be declared `static` unless there is a need to do otherwise.

3.11   Labs

Lab 1: Module parameters

- Write a module that can take an integer parameter when it is loaded with **insmod**. It should have a default value when none is specified.

- Load it and unload it. While the module is loaded, look at its directory in **/sys/module**, and see if you can change the value of the parameter you established.

Lab 2: Initialization and cleanup functions.

- Take any simple module, and see what happens if instead of having both initialization and cleanup functions, it has:

  - Only an initialization function.
  - Only a cleanup function.
  - Neither an initialization nor a cleanup function.

- In these cases see what happens when you try to load the module, and if that succeeds, when you try to unload it.

Lab 3: Stacked Modules

- Write a pair of modules one of which uses a function defined in the other module.

- Try loading and unloading them, using **insmod** and **modprobe**.

Lab 4: Duplicate Symbols

- Copy your first module to another file, compile and try to load both at the same time:

```
$ cp lab3_module1.c lab3_module1a.c
.... modify Makefile and compile
$ /sbin/insmod lab3_module1.ko
$ /sbin/insmod lab3_module1a.ko
```

- Does this succeed?

- Install your modules with `make modules_install`.

  See how **depmod** handles this by. analyzing the `modules.dep` file that results.

Chapter 4

Monitoring and Debugging

We'll consider various techniques used to debug kernel code. We'll consider how to trace system calls and do profiling and testing. We'll look at dissecting **oops** messages, and the use of debuggers, including **kprobes** and **SystemTap**. We'll also consider the use of **debugfs**.

4.1 Debuginfo Packages

- Many kernel debugging tools require compilation with the CONFIG_DEBUG_INFO option set, which is equivalent to using the -g option with **gcc**. In addition they also require a copy of the **uncompressed** kernel (vmlinux) rather than the compressed version which runs on the machine.

- Note that most tools (such as **crash**) do not actually require that the kernel you are running be compiled with this option set. But they do require you have a copy of a compiled kernel absolutely identical to the one you are running and want to defile or debug except for this option's inclusion.

- For kernels you compile yourself with his option, you will find vmlinux in the main kernel source directory after compilation. One should note however, that use of this options significantly increases the size of the .ko files produced.

- For distributor-supplied kernels you'll have to go to their web sites to download the **debuginfo** packages for the appropriate kernel version.

- For **Red Hat Enterprise Linux 5** one needs to go to **ftp://ftp.redhat.com:/pub/redhat/linux/ enterprise/5Server/en/os/i386/Debuginfo**, and for **CentOS 5** go to **http://debuginfo.centos.org/ 5/x86_64**. (For version 6 substitute appropriately, and for **i386** substitute for **x86_64**.)

- There are two packages to download for each kernel; the **kernel-debuginfo** and **kernel-debuginfo-common** packages. They can be installed with:

  ```
  $ rpm -Uvh kernel-debuginfo*.rpm
  ```

4.2 Tracing and Profiling

- **strace** is used to trace system calls and signals. In the simplest case you would do:

  ```
  $ strace [options] command [arguments]
  ```

- Each system call, its arguments and return value are printed. According to the man page:

- *"Arguments are printed in symbolic form with a passion."*
  and indeed they are. There are a lot of options; read the man page!

- It is possible to **profile** the kernel to identify hot spots, bottlenecks, etc., using the **oprofile** utility which can be used on the kernel as well as user applications and daemons.

- To start **oprofile**'s collection of data one does:

  ```
  $ opcontrol --init
  $ opcontrol --start --vmlinux=/usr/src/linux-3.0/vmlinux
  ```

  in which the first command loads the kernel module and the second starts accumulating data under `/var/lib/oprofile`, and points to the proper **uncompressed** kernel.

- If you are profiling a kernel which you have compiled, you can find `vmlinux` in the main kernel source directory. For a stock distributor kernel one can download the **kernel-debuginfo** and **kernel-debuginfo-common** packages from the distributor.

- The data collection is stopped with

  ```
  $ opcontrol --stop
  ```

  and flushed with `opcontrol --flush`.

- A report on all the data is obtained with

  ```
  $ opreport
  ```

  and on specific programs with something like

  ```
  $ opreport -l /usr/local/bin/myprog
  ```

- See the **man** pages for more documentation, and all the commands take a `--help` option. Detailed documentation can be found at **http://oprofile.sourceforge.net**.

- If you have the **oprofile-gui** package installed, there is an (undocumented) graphical interface that can be accessed with the command **oprof_start**.

- There are also a number of automated testing suite projects; in particular checkout the **Linux Test Project** (LTP), Full documentation as well as the source can be found at **http://ltp.sourceforge.net**.

> - A tool for identifying system latency bottlenecks can be obtained from **http://www.latencytop.org**. To make **latencytop** work `CONFIG_LATENCYTOP` must be set in the kernel configuration.
>
> - A tool for assessing power consumption can be obtained from **http://www.lesswatts.org/projects/powertop/**. To make **powertop** work `CONFIG_TIMER_STATS` must be set in the kernel configuration.

4.3   oops Messages

- **oops** messages indicate that a fault occurred in kernel mode. Depending on the nature of the fault that produced the **oops**, the fault may be fatal, serious, or inconsequential.

- If the oops occurs in process context the kernel will attempt to back out of the current task, probably killing it. If it occurs in interrupt context the kernel can't do this and will crash, as it will if it occurs in either the idle task (pid=0) or init (pid=1).

- The information provided contains a dump of the processor registers at the time of the crash and and a call trace indicating where it failed. Sometimes this is all one may need.

- Getting the most use out of **oops** messages, and almost all kernel debugging techniques, requires having at least some familiarity with assembly language. For an example of how to work through an **oops** message see **http://lkml.org/lkml/2008/1/7/406**.

- In order to cause an **oops** deliberately, one can do

```
if (disgusting_condition)
    BUG();
```

or

```
BUG_ON(disgusting_condition);
```

- One can also induce a system crash while printing out a message such as:

```
if (fatal_condition)
    panic ("I'm giving up because of task %d\n", current->pid);
```

- The website **http://www.kerneloops.org** maintains a database of current **oops** and has helped kernel developers debug successfully. Unfortunately data collection seems to have stopped with the 2.6.34 kernel.

- Here is a trivial module (`oopsit.c`) that contains a null pointer dereference that can trigger an **oops** message:

```
#include <linux/module.h>
#include <linux/init.h>

static int __init my_init(void)
{
        int *i;
```

```
        i = 0;
        printk(KERN_INFO "Hello: init_module loaded at address 0x%p\n",
                init_module);
        printk(KERN_INFO "i=%d\n", *i);
        return 0;
}

static void __exit my_exit(void)
{
        printk(KERN_INFO "Hello: cleanup_module loaded at address 0x%p\n",
                cleanup_module);
}

module_init(my_init);
module_exit(my_exit);

MODULE_LICENSE("GPL v2");
```

- We can disassemble the code with **objdump**. Doing

```
$ objdump -d oopsit.ko
```

gives

```
oopsit.ko:       file format elf64-x86-64


Disassembly of section .exit.text:

0000000000000000 <cleanup_module>:
   0:      55                        push   %rbp
   1:      48 c7 c6 00 00 00 00      mov    $0x0,%rsi
   8:      48 89 e5                  mov    %rsp,%rbp
   b:      48 c7 c7 00 00 00 00      mov    $0x0,%rdi
  12:      31 c0                     xor    %eax,%eax
  14:      e8 00 00 00 00            callq  19 <cleanup_module+0x19>
  19:      c9                        leaveq
  1a:      c3                        retq

Disassembly of section .init.text:

0000000000000000 <init_module>:
   0:      55                        push   %rbp
   1:      48 c7 c6 00 00 00 00      mov    $0x0,%rsi
   8:      48 89 e5                  mov    %rsp,%rbp
   b:      48 c7 c7 00 00 00 00      mov    $0x0,%rdi
  12:      31 c0                     xor    %eax,%eax
  14:      e8 00 00 00 00            callq  19 <init_module+0x19>
  19:      8b 34 25 00 00 00 00      mov    0x0,%esi
  20:      48 c7 c7 00 00 00 00      mov    $0x0,%rdi
  27:      31 c0                     xor    %eax,%eax
  29:      e8 00 00 00 00            callq  2e <init_module+0x2e>
  2e:      31 c0                     xor    %eax,%eax
  30:      c9                        leaveq
  31:      c3                        retq
```

- We produce the **oops** by attempting to load `oopsit.ko`; it hangs during the initialization step, and produces the following **oops** message (which gets appended to `/var/log/messages`):

```
[ 6051.467341] Hello: init_module loaded at address 0xffffffffa0026000
[ 6051.467349] BUG: unable to handle kernel NULL pointer dereference at          (null)
[ 6051.467355] IP: [<ffffffffa0026019>] my_init+0x19/0x32 [oopsit]
[ 6051.467361] PGD 37a9b067 PUD 37b14067 PMD 0
[ 6051.467367] Oops: 0000 [#1] PREEMPT SMP
[ 6051.467373] CPU 0
[ 6051.467375] Modules linked in: oopsit(+) nfsd lockd nfs_acl auth_rpcgss exportfs
               sunrpc squashfs fuse skge snd_usb_audio snd_hwdep snd_usbmidi_lib
               snd_rawmidi 8250_pnp 8250 serial_core pcspkr i2c_i801 sky2
               snd_hda_codec_analog snd_hda_intel snd_hda_codec snd_seq snd_seq_device
               snd_pcm snd_timer snd snd_page_alloc nvidia(P) i2c_core ext4 jbd2 crc16
               ahci libahci ehci_hcd uhci_hcd intel_agp intel_gtt [last unloaded:
               scsi_wait_scan]
[ 6051.467422]
[ 6051.467425] Pid: 6343, comm: insmod Tainted: P           3.0.1 #2 System manufacturer
               P5Q-E/P5Q-E
[ 6051.467432] RIP: 0010:[<ffffffffa0026019>]  [<ffffffffa0026019>] my_init+0x19/0x32
               [oopsit]
[ 6051.467438] RSP: 0018:ffff880037b2ff18  EFLAGS: 00010292
[ 6051.467441] RAX: 000000000000004d RBX: ffffffffa00240b0 RCX: 0000000000000000
[ 6051.467444] RDX: ffff880037b2ffd8 RSI: ffffffff8137dfd8 RDI: ffffffff81040fef
[ 6051.467447] RBP: ffff880037b2ff18 R08: 00000000ffffffb6 R09: ffff880037b2fdd8
[ 6051.467450] R10: 0000000000000005 R11: 0000000000000000 R12: ffffffffa0026000
[ 6051.467453] R13: 0000000000000000 R14: 0000000000603030 R15: 0000000000000003
[ 6051.467456] FS:  00007f5a3620d700(0000) GS:ffff88012fc00000(0000)
               knlGS:0000000000000000
[ 6051.467460] CS:  0010 DS: 0000 ES: 0000 CR0: 0000000080050033
[ 6051.467463] CR2: 0000000000000000 CR3: 0000000037bd6000 CR4: 00000000000006f0
[ 6051.467466] DR0: 0000000000000000 DR1: 0000000000000000 DR2: 0000000000000000
[ 6051.467469] DR3: 0000000000000000 DR6: 00000000ffff0ff0 DR7: 0000000000000400
[ 6051.467472] Process insmod (pid: 6343, threadinfo ffff880037b2e000, task
               ffff88010d4e1f20)
[ 6051.467475] Stack:
[ 6051.467477]  ffff880037b2ff48 ffffffff8100020f ffffffffa00240b0 0000000000000cd8
[ 6051.467483]  0000000000004000 0000000000603030 ffff880037b2ff78 ffffffff8107b5ce
[ 6051.467490]  0000000000603010 0000000000000cd8 00007fff87ed6756 0000000000000cd8
[ 6051.467496] Call Trace:
[ 6051.467502]  [<ffffffff8100020f>] do_one_initcall+0x7f/0x133
[ 6051.467508]  [<ffffffff8107b5ce>] sys_init_module+0x83/0x1cc
[ 6051.467517]  [<ffffffff81388187>] tracesys+0xd0/0xd5
[ 6051.467519] Code: <8b> 34 25 00 00 00 00 48 c7 c7 9f 40 02 a0 31 c0 e8 42 7f 35 e1 31
[ 6051.467549] RIP  [<ffffffffa0026019>] my_init+0x19/0x32 [oopsit]
[ 6051.467554]  RSP <ffff880037b2ff18>
[ 6051.467557] CR2: 0000000000000000
[ 6051.467560] ---[ end trace d72f19e70e06c903 ]---
```

- It contains a dump of the processor registers at the time of the crash and and a call trace indicating where it failed. We see it failed in `oopsit` at an offset of `0x19` bytes into `my_init()`. Comparing with the object dis-assembly tells us precisely what the offending line is.

4.4 Kernel Debuggers

- The first thing to understand about using debuggers on the **Linux** kernel is that Linus Torvalds **hates** them For his entertaining explanation of why, see **http://lwn.net/2000/0914/a/lt-debugger.php3**.

The short explanation for this attitude is that reliance on debuggers can encourage fixing problems with band-aids rather than brains, and leads to rotten code.

- Linus **will** tolerate (and even encourage) optional debugging aids that either check specific known errors (e.g., am I sleeping while holding a spinlock?), or require only an entry point into the kernel, and permit their work to be done through modules.

gdb

- The **gdb** debugger can be used to debug a running kernel. The execution line would be:

```
$ gdb /boot/vmlinux /proc/kcore
```
[handwritten: → Virtual dump]

where the first argument is the currently running *uncompressed* kernel. One can use **ddd** or another other graphical interfaces to **gdb**. The sections of the kernel being debugged must have been compiled with the -g option, to get much useful information. This is not for the faint-hearted. It is pretty difficult.

[handwritten: gdb - operates on snapshot.]

kgdb and kdb

- **kgdb** is interactive kernel debugger. In its fully capable mode it requires two computers to be connected through a null-modem serial cable. On the remote host system the user runs **gdb** (or a GUI wrapper to it such as **ddd**) and can then break into the kernel on the target system, setting breakpoints, examining data, etc. It is possible to stop the target machine kernel during the boot process.

- **kgdb** was incorporated in the mainline kernel with kernel version 2.6.26.

- Another interactive kernel debugger, **kdb**, existed for a long time as an out-of-tree kernel patch. It had the ability to:

  - Examine kernel memory and data structures.
  - Control operations, such as single-stepping, setting breakpoints.
  - Get stack tracebacks, do instruction dis-assembly., etc.
  - Switch CPUs in an SMP system.
  - Etc.

- **kdb** was automatically entered upon encountering an oops, a data access fault in kernel mode, using a **kdb** flag on the kernel command line, or using the **pause** key.

- The **kdb** and **kgdb** projects were finally merged together and incorporated in the 2.6.35 kernel, and there is currently a a lot of activity on extending and optimization. One can enter the debugger through using the ALT-SysRq-g key combination, or the echoing into /proc/sysrq-trigger.

- For full documentation including step-by-step instructions, see the article by Jason Wessel, the head developer on the recent integration of the two projects, at **/usr/src/linux/Documentation/DocBook/ kgdb.tmpl**, or to see it in the pdf form produced from kernel sources go to: **http://training.linuxfoundation.org/course_materials/LF339/kgdb.pdf**.

crash   *(gdb: Can not peek struct, only memory.*
           Crash tool help to peek at struct)

- The **crash** utility is probably provided by your **Linux** distribution and full documentation can be found at **http://people.redhat.com/anderson/**.

- With **crash** one can examine all critical data structures in the kernel, do source code disassembly, walk through linked lists, examine and set memory, etc. **crash** can also examine **kernel core dump** files created for example by the **kdump** or **diskdump** packages.

4.5   debugfs

- The **debugfs** filesystem first appeared in the 2.6.11 kernel. It can be used as a simpler and more modern alternative to using the **/proc** filesystem, which has an inconvenient interface and which kernel developers have lost their taste for.

- The main purpose of **debugfs** is for easy access to debugging information, and perhaps to set debugging behaviour. It is meant to be accessed like any other filesystem, which means standard reading and writing tools can be used.

- One can also use **sysfs** for the same purposes. However, **sysfs** is intended for information used in system administration, and is also meant to be based in a coherent way on the system's device tree as mapped out along the system buses.

- The code for **debugfs** was developed mainly by Greg Kroah-Hartman. The functions used are:

```
#include <linux/fs.h>
#include <linux/debugfs.h>

struct dentry *debugfs_create_dir (const char *name, struct dentry *parent)
struct dentry *debugfs_create_file (const char *name, mode_t mode, struct dentry *parent,
                                    void *data, const struct file_operations *fops);
void debugfs_remove (struct dentry *dentry);
```

- As with **/proc** you can create your own entry under the **debugfs** root directory by creating a directory with `debugfs_create_dir()`; supplying `NULL` for `parent` in the above functions places entries in the root directory. The `mode` argument is the usual filesystem permissions mask, and `data` is an optional parameter that can be used to point to a private data structure.

- The `fops` argument point to a `file_operations` structure containing a jump table of operations on the entry, just as it is used in character drivers. One probably needs to supply only the ownership field, and reading and writing entry point functions.

- For the read function one may want to take advantage of the function:

```
ssize_t simple_read_from_buffer (void __user *to, size_t count, loff_t *ppos,
                                 const void *from, size_t available);
```

which is a convenience function for getting information from the kernel buffer pointed to by `from` into the user buffer `to` (using `copy_to_read()` properly), where the position `ppos` is advanced no further than `available` bytes. An example of a read function using this:

```
static ssize_t
my_read (struct file *file, char *buf, size_t count, loff_t * ppos)
{
```

```
      int nbytes;
      nbytes=sprintf(kstring, "%d\n", val);
      return simple_read_from_buffer (buf, count, ppos, kstring, nbytes);
}
```

- Even simpler is to use are the convenience functions:

```
struct dentry *debugfs_create_u8   (const char *name, mode_t mode,
                                     struct dentry *parent, u8 *val);
struct dentry *debugfs_create_u16  (const char *name, mode_t mode,
                                     struct dentry *parent, u16 *val);
struct dentry *debugfs_create_u32  (const char *name, mode_t mode,
                                     struct dentry *parent, u32 *val);
struct dentry *debugfs_create_bool (const char *name, mode_t mode,
                                     struct dentry *parent, u32 *val);
```

- These create an entry denoted by `name`, under the parent directory, which is used to simply read in and out a variable of the proper type. Note the variable is sent back and forth as a string. Thus one can with simply one line of code (two including the header file!) create an entry!

- In order to use the **debugfs** facility you may have to mount the **debugfs** pseudo-filesystem:

```
$ mount -t debugfs none /sys/kernel/debug
```

  but all recent distributions do this automatically and you should be able to skip this step.

- Regardless of how you create your entries they **must** be removed with `debugfs_remove()` on the way out, because, as usual, the kernel does no garbage collection.

- For a review of **debugfs** and how to use it see **http://lwn.net/Articles/334546**.

4.6   kprobes and jprobes

- The **kprobes** debugging facility (originally contributed by developers at **IBM**) lets you insert breakpoints into a running kernel at any known address. One can examine as well as modify processor registers, data structures, etc.

- Up to four handlers can be installed:

  - The **pre-handler** is called just before the probed instruction is executed.
  - The **post-handler** is called just after the probed instruction is executed, if no exception is generated.
  - The **fault-handler** is called whenever an exception is generated by the probed instruction.
  - The **break-handler** is called whenever the probed instruction is being single stepped or break-pointed.

- The basic functions and data structures are defined in **/usr/src/linux/include/linux/kprobes.h** and **/usr/src/linux/kernel/kprobes.c**:

```
#include <linux/kprobes.h>

int register_kprobe(struct kprobe *p);
void unregister_kprobe(struct kprobe *p);

struct kprobe {
   struct hlist_node hlist;
```

```
        /* location of the probe point */
        kprobe_opcode_t *addr;

      /* Allow user to indicate symbol name of the probe point */
        char *symbol_name;

      /* Offset into the symbol */
        unsigned int offset;

      /* Called before addr is executed. */
        kprobe_pre_handler_t pre_handler;

      /* Called after addr is executed, unless... */
        kprobe_post_handler_t post_handler;

      /* ... called if executing addr causes a fault (eg. page fault).
       * Return 1 if it handled fault, otherwise kernel will see it. */
        kprobe_fault_handler_t fault_handler;

      /* ... called if breakpoint trap occurs in probe handler.
       * Return 1 if it handled break, otherwise kernel will see it. */
        kprobe_break_handler_t break_handler;

      /* Saved opcode (which has been replaced with breakpoint) */
        kprobe_opcode_t opcode;

      /* copy of the original instruction */
        struct arch_specific_insn ainsn;
};

typedef int (*kprobe_pre_handler_t) (struct kprobe *, struct pt_regs *);
typedef int (*kprobe_break_handler_t) (struct kprobe *, struct pt_regs *);
typedef void (*kprobe_post_handler_t) (struct kprobe *, struct pt_regs *, unsigned long flags);
typedef int (*kprobe_fault_handler_t) (struct kprobe *, struct pt_regs *, int trapnr);
```

- Note that the handler functions receive a pointer to a data structure of type `pt_regs`, which contains the contents of the processor registers. This is obviously architecture-dependent, and is detailed in **/usr/ src/linux/arch/arm/include/asm/ptrace.h.**

- The `flags` argument to the post handler can have the values:

```
KPROBE_FLAG_GONE      /* breakpoint has already gone */
KPROBE_FLAG_DISABLED  /* probe is temporarily disabled */
KPROBE_OPTIMIZED      /* probe is really optimized */
```

and is not meant to be set directly by **kprobe** users. Here optimized means on certain architectures the breakpoint instruction for interrupting execution flow can be replaced by a jump instruction, which leads to a performance boost. The `trapnr` argument to the fault handler gives which exception caused the fault.

- In order to use **kprobes**, one must:

  - Fill in the `kprobe` data structure with pointers to supplied handler functions.
  - Supply either the address (`addr`) or symbolic name (`symbol_name` with an optional `offset`) where the probe is to be inserted.
  - Call `register_kprobe()`, with a return value of 0 indicating successful probe insertion.

- When finished one uses `unregister_kprobe()`, with an obvious catastrophe being the result if one forgets to do so.

- The only remaining ingredient is to obtain the address of the probed instruction. If the symbol is exported, then you can merely point directly to it, as in

```
kp.addr = (kprobe_opcode_t *) mod_timer;
```

  Even if the symbol is not exported you can still specify the name directly with something as simple as

```
kp.symbol_name = "do_fork";
```

- One should not set **both** the address and the symbol, as that will lead to an error.

> - One can turn **kprobes** on and off dynamically, even while it is currently in use:
>
> ```
> $ ls -l /sys/kernel/debug/kprobes
> total 0
> -rw------- 1 root root 0 Jun 11 08:28 enabled
> -r--r--r-- 1 root root 0 Jun 11 01:44 list
> ```
>
> - By echoing 1 or 0 to `enabled` you can turn **kprobes** on and off. By looking at `list` you can examine all currently loaded probes.

- The additional **jprobe** facility lets you easily instrument any function in the kernel. The relevant registration and unregistration functions, and the new relevant data structure are:

```
int register_jprobe (struct jprobe *jp);
void unregister_jprobe (struct jprobe *jp);
void jprobe_return (void);

struct jprobe {
    struct kprobe kp;
    kprobe_opcode_t *entry;
}
```

- In order to use this you have to set up a structure of type `jprobe`, in which the `entry` field points to a function of the exact same prototype and arguments as the function being probed, which should be pointed in the `kp.addr` field just as for **kprobes**.

- The instrumentation function will be called every time the probed function is called and must exit with the function `jprobe_return()`. It is called **before** the probed function.

- The contents of registers and the stack are restored before the function exits. However, changing the values of arguments can make a (possibly destructive) difference.

SystemTap

- While **kprobes** is very powerful, its use requires a relatively low level kernel incursion. **SystemTap** provides an infrastructure built on top of **kprobes** that simplifies writing, compiling and installing kernel modules, and gathering up useful output. The **SystemTap** project can be found at **http://sourceware.org/systemtap/**.

4.7 Labs

Lab 1: Using kprobes

- Place a **kprobe** at an often executed place in the kernel. A good choice would be the `do_fork()` function, which is executed whenever a child process is born.

- Put in simple handler functions.

- Test the module by loading it and running simple commands which cause the probed instruction to execute, such as starting a new shell with **bash**.

Lab 2: Using jprobes

- Test the **jprobes** facility by instrumenting a commonly used kernel function.

- Keep a counter of how many times the function is called. If you print it out each time, be careful not to get overwhelmed with output.

Lab 3: Probing a module

- Take an earlier character driver module and write a new module that uses **kprobes** and **jprobes** to instrumentation the character driver.

- Does the function you are probing need to be exported to be accessible to the probe utilities?

Lab 4: Using debugfs.

- Write a module that creates entries in **debugfs**.

- First use one of the convenience functions to make just a simple one variable entry under the root **debugfs** filesystem, of whatever length you desire.

- Next create your own directory and put one or more entries in it.

Chapter 5

Crash

We describe how to use the **crash** utility to debug the kernel.

5.1   Crash

- The **crash** utility is probably provided by your **Linux** distribution and full documentation can be found at **http://people.redhat.com/anderson/**.

- With **crash** one can examine all critical data structures in the kernel, do source code disassembly, walk through linked lists, examine and set memory, etc. **crash** can also examine **kernel core dump** files created by the **kdump** or **diskdump** packages.

- In order to debug newly-released kernels you may need to obtain a newer version of **crash** than the one that has been provided by your distribution. Probably the best way to do this is to obtain the source from the website, and then compile and install it. We'll do this as a lab.

5.2   Main Commands

- **crash** has many commands and extensive inline documentation. To obtain a short list of all commands just type:

  ```
  help
  ```

  while running the program. To get help about a particular command, say **foreach**, just do:

  ```
  help foreach
  ```

- Most commands take a variety of arguments depending on intent. For example just typing:

  ```
  task
  ```

  gives information about the current task structure while typing:

  ```
  task 292
  ```

  gives the task structure for the task with **pid=292**. You can change the current task with the   **set** command.

- Here's a list of all major commands:

Table 5.1: **crash Commands**

command	meaning
foreach	execute a command for all tasks or a subset of all tasks on the system
set	point to a task, set the context
repeat	repeat a command in a loop with a delay
bt	display a task's backtrace
task	display the task_struct contents, formatted nicely
list	display contents of a linked list
struct	display structure definition
union	display information about union definitions
whatis	display information about structures, definitions, etc.
rd	read memory
wr	write memory
sym	translate a symbol to a virtual address, or vice versa
search	search user or kernel memory for a value
ptov	Convert a physical address to a kernel virtual address
vtop	Convert a user or kernel virtual address to a physical one
ptob	get the byte value of a page frame number
btop	display byte value to a page number
pte	translate a PTE into physical page address and show bit settings
vm	display virtual memory information for a task
ps	display **ps** information
kmem	display information about kernel memory
runq	display tasks on the run queue
dev	display information about devices, I/O ports, I/O memory
irq	display information about irqs, handlers, and bottom halves
timer	display information about kernel timers
waitq	display information about wait queues and tasks on them

net	display network information
swap	display swap device information
mach	display information about the computer
sys	display information about the system
mod	display information about currently loaded modules
mount	display information about mounted filesystems
log	display kernel log buffer (like **dmem**)
files	display information about open files
fuser	display information about tasks using a file descriptor or socket
sig	display signal handling information for a task
gdb	run a gdb command
p	pass arguments to the **gdb print** command
dis	dissaemble memory or functions
eval	evaluate an expression
extend	dynamically load and unload **crash extensions**.
alias	create an alias for a command
ascii	display an ascii character chart
help	get help about comands
q or **exit**	exit **crash**

5.3 Labs

Lab 1: Installing crash.

- If you have a fully functioning installation of **crash** you won't need to do this, but it never hurts to have the latest version.

- Obtain the crash source tarball, either from your instructor, or from the web site: **http://people.redhat.com/anderson/**.

- Installing it should be as simple as:

```
$ tar zxvf crash-5.0.1.tar.gz
$ cd crash-5.0.1
$ make
$ sudo make install
```

  where you should insert the proper version number and name, and only the last installation step needs to be done as a privileged user.

- You should then be able to test whether the installation succeeded by doing one of the following:

```
$ crash
$ crash /usr/src/linux-3.0/vmlinux
```

  You'll have to give the actual uncompressed kernel location in the second form if **crash** is unable to find the information on its own.

- If you get a message about the kernel not containing debugging information you'll have to recompile it with the **-g** option ("Compile the kernel with debug info" in the debugging section of the kernel configuration program.)

Lab 2: Experimenting with crash.

- Start up crash. Trying a few of the basic commands, such as **help**, **ps** etc, to verify it is working.

- Try **task** go examine the current task structure. Switch to another task by first typing **ps** and getting a process ID, and the doing **task PID**. Verify you get the same result as doing **set PID** and then **task**.

- Examine some of the main memory structures, and other quantities. Look at the list of timers, tasks on the run queue and the wait queues, etc.

- Experiment with the **foreach** command.

- To get a sense of how to examine the contents of structures, do the following. Type **task** and get the contents of the current task structure. Search down (which you can do with /) for the address of the **mm** field, which is a structure of type **mm_struct**:

```
task

PID: 5196   TASK: f1360000  CPU: 3   COMMAND: "crash"
struct task_struct {
  state = 0,
  stack = 0xf1370000,
.....
mm = 0xf2322ac0,
  active_mm = 0xf2322ac0,
  exit_state = 0,
....
```

Then get its contents by doing:

```
struct mm_struct 0xf2322ac0
```

Note the keyword `struct` is actually optional.

Chapter 6

Kernel Core Dumps

We consider **kernel core dump files**, how to produce them when the system faults, or on demand. We also briefly look at methods to examine them for debugging purposes.

6.1 Generating Kernel Core Dumps

- To generate kernel core dumps the following ingredients must be set up on your system:

  - The kernel you are running must have **kdump** (which produces the kernel core dump image) enabled, and must be compiled with the `CONFIG_DEBUG_INFO` option enabled, which keeps a full copy of the kernel symbol table in the resulting binary.

  - The **kexec-tools** package must be installed. This permits you to start a new kernel from within the presently running one. When combined with **kdump**, the **kexec** program permits you to launch into a special kernel after a crash dump is generated which can be used to analyze the core dump.

  - The **kdump** system service must be turned on.

  - Your **grub** configuration file must be set up to reserve memory for the **kdump/kexec** facility.

  - An **uncompressed** copy of the kernel (`vmlinux`, not `vmlinuz`) is required for analysis of the core dump image.

  - The **crash** utility is used to analyze the core dump image

- **Note:** The last two ingredients are not needed to produce the core dump image, only to analyze it.

6.2   kexec

- Rebooting a system can take a long time, as you have to go through the entire **BIOS** startup routine, boot loader (such as **grub**) etc. Furthermore, if you are toying with a new kernel you'll have to configure the boot loader configuration files.

- The **kexec** mechanism makes it possible to short circuit the entire process by launching a new kernel from inside the old one, and avoiding all the **BIOS** and boot loader rigmarole.

- Because the hardware does not have to be reset, the reboot may actually be more reliable, and even quite a bit faster in the **Linux** stages. On the other hand, because the hardware does not have to be reset, it may be less reliable as the state of various devices may not be clean and they might do well with a reset.

- The fast reboot mechanism is non-trivial for a number of reasons. One is that the new kernel would normally occupy the same memory locations as the currently running one. Thus the replacement kernel cannot be loaded until the current one has shut down. But once this is done it is no longer capable of loading a new one.

- First **kexec** puts a copy of the new kernel in memory, in a buffer containing not necessarily contiguous pages. It also sets aside a small piece of memory to be a **reboot code buffer**.

- Rebooting involves:

  - Shutting the kernel down, putting devices in a stable known state. Filesystems are **not** unmounted and processes are **not** killed; it is expected to be done through the normal user-space shutdown procedure.

  - A small program, (compiled from assembly language) is copied into the reboot code buffer. This program copies the new kernel from its buffer into the desired location, overwriting the old kernel.

  - Executes the new kernel.

- There are a variety of uses for **kexec**. One need not reconfigure **grub** in order to test a new kernel. One can just save a lot of time during reboots. When coupled with **kdump** it can be used for debugging, and a special debugging kernel can be loaded, and a kernel crash dump image can be saved and then analysed.

- Before rebooting into a new kernel one first has to load the new kernel image into the currently running kernel. This is done with the -l option, as in:

```
$ kexec -l --initrd=/boot/initrd-3.0.0.img --command-line="ro root=LABEL=/ rhgb" \
        /boot/vmlinuz-3.0.0
```

- If you want to use the same kernel you are running, with the same command line options, you could use a little script like:

```
#!/bin/bash -x

KV=$(uname -r)
INITRD=/boot/initrd-"$KV".img
if [ ! -f $INITRD ] ; then
INITRD=/boot/initrd.img-"$KV"
fi
KERNEL=/boot/vmlinuz-$KV
CMDLINE=$(cat /proc/cmdline)

kexec -l --initrd=$INITRD --command-line="$CMDLINE"  $KERNEL
```

- Now that the replacement kernel is loaded, you could do a simple `reboot` command to do a normal shutdown and then the system will reboot **without** going through the normal **BIOS** route.

- You can cause an **immediate** reboot by doing

  ```
  $ kexec -e
  ```

  but of course your filesystems will not be cleanly unmounted, etc.

- If you do:

  ```
  $ kexec --help
  ```

  you'll get a complete list of options, including architecture-dependent ones.

6.3   Setting Up Kernel Core Dumps

- First you have to make sure **kexec** is installed with:

  ```
  $ sudo yum install kexec-tools
  ```

  on **Red Hat**-based systems, and

  ```
  $ apt-get install kexec-tools
  ```

  on **Debian**-based systems.

- Next you have to ensure that your system is **kdump**-enabled. On **Red Hat**-derived systems you can do this with:

  ```
  $ sudo service kdump status
  ```

  If this doesn't give a result indicating you are **kdump**-enabled, try:

  ```
  $ sudo service kdump start
  ```

- On **Debian**-based systems there are a number of methods to do the equivalent steps such as:

  ```
  $ sudo /etc/init.d kdump status
  $ sudo /etc/init.d kdump start
  ```

- If this fails you'll have to investigate what the problem is. First of all make sure that your **/boot/grub/ grub.conf** file has the `crashkernel` parameter set for the kernel you are running, as in:

  ```
  kernel /vmlinuz-2.6.18-194.32.1.el5PAE ro root=LABEL=RHEL5-32 rhgb quiet crashkernel=128M@16M
  ```

  If it doesn't have this parameter, edit the file accordingly and then you'll have to reboot.

6.4   Labs

Lab 1: Using kexec.

- First make sure **kexec** is installed by doing `which kexec`. If it is not found, do on Red Hat-derived systems:

  ```
  $ yum install kexec-tools
  ```

  On Debian-based systems:

  ```
  $ sudo apt-get install kexec-tools
  ```

  - **Note:** Change your VM settings to a single core configuration. Otherwise **kexec** might not work properly!

- Next try to a clean reboot of your system by loading a replacement kernel with `kexec -l ...`, and then doing a normal reboot. Do this with the following script:

  ```
  #!/bin/bash -x

  KV=$(uname -r)
  INITRD=/boot/initrd-"$KV".img
  if [ ! -f $INITRD ] ; then
  INITRD=/boot/initrd.img-"$KV"
  fi
  KERNEL=/boot/vmlinuz-$KV
  CMDLINE=$(cat /proc/cmdline)

  kexec -l --initrd=$INITRD --command-line="$CMDLINE"  $KERNEL
  ```

- Then try an immediate reboot with `kexec -e`. You'll probably want to do a `umount -a` and a `sync` first to make the filesystems as clean as possible before reboot.

Lab 2: Producing a Kernel Core Dump

- It's probably a good idea to make sure your system is up to date. If you haven't done so yet, do:

  ```
  $ yum update
  ```

- Before rebooting, to make sure **kdump** gets loaded you have to edit the file **/boot/grub/grub.conf** to append the following to the kernel command line:

  ```
  crashkernel=128M@16M
  ```

  so that the entry looks like:

  ```
  title CentOS (2.6.18-194.32.1.el5)
          root (hd0,0)
          kernel /vmlinuz-2.6.18-194.32.1.el5 ro root=LABEL=/ rhgb quiet crashkernel=128M@16M
          initrd /initrd-2.6.18-194.32.1.el5.img
  ```

On Ubuntu with grub2 edit the file **/etc/default/grub** and add the parameter there. Don't forget to run `sudo update-grub`.

- Make sure the **kdump** service will be running when the system reboots:

  `$ chkconfig kdump on`

- Now reboot the system.

> - **Note:** At present **kdump** will only work properly on a single CPU system!

- After the reboot completes, make sure **kdump** is running with:

  `$ service kdump status`

- To pre-load the kdump kernel run the following script:

```
#!/bin/bash -x

KV=$(uname -r)
INITRD=/boot/initrd-"$KV".img
KERNEL=/boot/vmlinuz-$KV
CMDLINE=$(cat /proc/cmdline)

kexec -p --initrd=$INITRD --command-line="$CMDLINE"  $KERNEL
```

- To trigger a core dump and reboot cycle you can do:

  `$ echo c > /proc/sysrq-trigger`

- When you have rebooted, you should find your core dump file under **/var/crash**.

- Hint: you may want to do:

  `telinit 3`

  before triggering the crash dump, as you will see more output on the screen.

Lab 3: Analyzing a Kernel Core Dump

- Next you'll have to obtain the **debuginfo** packages for your kernel and install them.

- Note: Rather than going on the Internet to get these packages you should be able to obtain them from the instructor in the classroom, to save bandwidth and time, and then just run the installation step.

- To analyze the core dump you have to do:

  `$ crash /usr/lib/debug/lib/modules/$(uname -r)/vmlinux /var/crash/[timestamp]/vmcore`

  where the `[timestamp]` field indicates which core dump to analyze.

Chapter 7

Device Drivers

We'll discuss how device drivers are used and consider the different types of devices; i.e., character, block and network. We'll discuss the difference between mechanism and policy. We'll consider the disadvantages of loading binary blobs. We will then take a quick tour of how applications interface with device drivers and make system calls. We'll see how errors are defined, and how to obtain kernel output using `printk()`. We'll consider all this in detail later.

7.1 Types of Devices

- A **device driver** is the lowest level of software as it is directly bound to the hardware features of the device. The kernel can be considered an application running on top of device drivers; each driver manages one or more piece of hardware while the kernel handles process scheduling, filesystem access, interrupts, etc.

- Drivers may be integrated directly into the kernel, or can be designed as loadable **modules**. Not all modules are device drivers. A driver can be designed as either a modular or a built-in part of the kernel, with little or no change of the source.

- In the usual device taxonomy there are three main types:

Character Devices

- Can be written to and read from a byte at a time.

- Well represented as **streams**.

- Usually permit only sequential access.

- Can be considered as files.

- Implement **open, close, read,** and **write** functions.

- Serial/parallel ports, console (monitor and keyboard), etc.

- Examples: `/dev/tty0, /dev/ttyS0, /dev/dsp0, /dev/lp1`

Block Devices

- Can be written to and read from only in block-size multiples; access is usually **cached**.

- Permit random access.

- Filesystems can be mounted on these devices.

- In **Linux** block devices can behave like character devices, transferring any number of bytes at a time.

- Hard drives, cdroms, etc.

- Examples: `/dev/sda1, /dev/fd0`

Network Devices

- Transfer packets of data. Device sees the packets, not the streams.

- Most often accessed via the BSD socket interface.

- Instead of **read, write**, the kernel calls packet reception and transmission functions.

- Network interfaces are not mapped to the filesystem; they are identified by a name.

- Examples: `eth0, ppp0`

Device Types and User-Hardware Connection

- What differentiates the types of drivers is the methods they use to connect the kernel with user-space. Most of the time the connection passes through the **VFS** (**V**irtual **F**ile **S**ystem), and then what methods are invoked depends on whether the access is to a character device node, block device node, or a socket.

- Character drivers may or may not work on character streams; the essential thing is they are most directly connected to the user and to the hardware.

- Block drivers are connected to the hardware, and to the user through the filesystem, caching, and the Virtual File System (VFS).

- Network drivers are connected to the hardware and to the user through various kinds of protocol stacks.

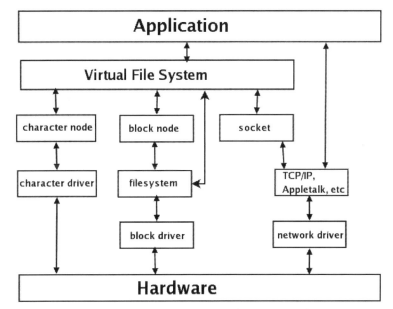

Figure 7.1: **From Application to Device**

Devices with Core and Controller API's

- There are devices which have another degree of freedom in addition to the the character/block/network division (although functionally they can be used for any of these three generic classes of peripherals.)

    - **SCSI** (**S**mall **C**omputers **S**ystems **I**nterconnect) devices share an underlying protocol regardless of function. Hard work goes into writing the driver for the controller hardware which may run many devices.

    - **USB** (**U**niversal **S**erial **B**us) devices also share an underlying protocol. Once again there is a lower layer of drivers tied to the controller hardware, and then device-specific drivers for the various peripherals connected to the bus.

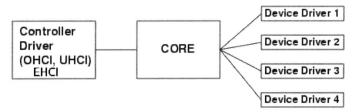

Figure 7.2: **USB: Controller, Core and Device**

User Space Devices

- **User-space drivers**, such as the video drivers incorporated into **X.Org** (**http://www.x.org**), reside in user-space but are given privileges to directly address hardware. They use the **ioperm()** and **iopl()** functions to accomplish this, which we'll discuss when we discuss reading and writing to I/O ports.

7.2   Mechanism vs. Policy

- Device drivers should maintain a clear distinction between **mechanism** and **policy**.

- By **mechanism**, we mean providing flexibly the abilities that the device itself can capably perform. By **policy**, we mean controlling how those capabilities are used.

- In other words it is not up to the driver to enforce certain decisions (unless there is a hardware limitation) such as:

  - How many processes can use the device at once.
  - Whether I/O is blocking or non-blocking, synchronous or asynchronous, etc.
  - Whether certain combinations of parameters can never occur even if they are unwise.

- Often a driver may come with a user-space control program, or daemon, which has the capability of controlling device policy. As such, it should provide methods of setting parameters and modifying behaviour, perhaps through the use of **ioctl**'s, **/proc**, **/sys** etc.

- A driver which fails to distinguish between mechanism and policy is a driver destined for trouble. Tomorrow's user may have quite different needs than today's. Being human, the driver developer may even forget why a narrowing of choices was made. One should never underestimate the likelihood of a user behaving in an unexpected fashion.

7.3   Avoiding Binary Blobs

- There is a method of deploying a **Linux** device driver which has been promoted by certain vendors, with which we strongly disagree.

- The essence of this method is to separate the driver into two parts:

  - A binary blob, for which the source is not given. This blob may contain all or part of the driver from another operating system (usually from you-know-who.)
  - An open-source glue layer, which calls into the binary blob as well as the kernel API.

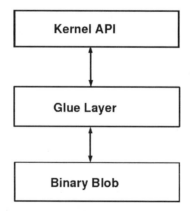

Figure 7.3: **Using Binary Blobs in drivers**

- Well known examples of this method are employed by the **Nvidia** graphics drivers and **ndiswrapper** wireless and NIC drivers.

- With this method the driver writer can contain in the binary blob whatever code has been ported in from another operating system, or whatever code is wished to remain private; the first reason may be legal under **Linux** licensing, while the second is definitely not.

- When such a driver is loaded the kernel becomes **tainted** which means it is impossible to debug properly because there is not source available for all the running code.

- We strongly disapprove of this method for many reasons, but two are sufficient:

  - Loading arbitrary binary code into the kernel is a recipe for disaster.
  - Manufacturers promote this as **Linux** support and don't support the development of genuine open-source drivers.

- Thus, we won't teach this method and we discourage even the use of such drivers, much less their development.

- Use of binary **firmware** is not the same as the methods described above. This firmware is data that could have been put in memory on the card, but vendors find it cheaper to have the operating system load it. Use of firmware does not cause tainting.

- The line between firmware and binary blobs is gray, and there are **Linux** distributions which have problems distributing drivers with require binary firmware, or which don't distribute the binary firmware itself.

7.4 How Applications Use Device Drivers

- The **Unix** philosophy is to use a number of elementary methods connected through both piping and nesting to accomplish complex tasks.

- User applications (and daemons) interact with peripheral devices using the same basic system calls irrespective of the specific nature of the device.

- For the moment we'll leave networking device drivers out of the mix since they are not reached through filesystem entries; we'll concentrate on character drivers which have thinner layers between the applications and the device driver, and between the hardware and the device driver.

- For each one of the limited number of these system calls, there is a corresponding **entry point** in the driver. The main ones for character drivers are:

  `open(), release(), read(), write(), lseek(), ioctl(), mmap()`

- Strictly speaking, the name of the system call and the entry point may differ, but in the above list the only one that does is the system call `close()` which becomes `release()` as an entry point. However, the return type of the system call as well as the arguments can be quite different than that of the entry point.

- Note that there are other kinds of callback functions that may exist in a driver, which are **not** directly reached by user system calls:

- Loading and unloading the driver cause initializing and shutting down callbacks to get invoked.

- Higher layers of the kernel may call functions in the driver for such things as power management.

- The driver may execute a deferred task, such as after a given amount of time has elapsed, or a condition has become true.

- Interrupts may cause asynchronous execution of driver code, if the driver is registered to handle particular interrupts.

- Once a device driver is loaded, therefore, its methods are all registered with the kernel, and it is event-driven; it responds to direct entries (which can be multiple and simultaneous) from user applications, and it executes code as requested by other kernel layers and in response to hardware provocation.

7.5 Walking Through a System Call

- Let's see what actually happens when an application attempts to read from a device which has already been opened. The application will open and then read with:

```
. . . .
char *buf = malloc(nbytes);
fd = open ("/dev/mydriver", O_RDWR);
nread = read (fd, buf, nbytes);
. . . .
```

(Of course we are giving only code fragments and being sloppy about error checking and all that!)

- Let's concentrate on the `read()` call, which is simpler to trace than the `open()`. The `read()` is inter-cepted by **libc**, which knows how to make system calls, and the kernel is entered through the function `sys_read()`, which is in **/usr/src/linux/fs/read_write.c**:

```
3.0: 402 SYSCALL_DEFINE3(read, unsigned int, fd, char __user *, buf, size_t, count)
3.0: 403 {
3.0: 404     struct file *file;
3.0: 405     ssize_t ret = -EBADF;
3.0: 406     int fput_needed;
3.0: 407
3.0: 408     file = fget_light(fd, &fput_needed);
3.0: 409     if (file) {
3.0: 410         loff_t pos = file_pos_read(file);
3.0: 411         ret = vfs_read(file, buf, count, &pos);
3.0: 412         file_pos_write(file, pos);
3.0: 413         fput_light(file, fput_needed);
3.0: 414     }
3.0: 415
3.0: 416     return ret;
3.0: 417 }
```

The `SYSCALL_DEFINE3()` macro is complicated, but among other things it changes the name of the function to `sys_read()`.

- This function associates a `file` kernel data structure with `fd`, the user application file descriptor; the kernel works in terms of these structures, not file descriptors. It then passes off the work to `vfs_read()`:

```
3.0: 306 ssize_t vfs_read(struct file *file, char __user *buf, size_t count, loff_t
                              *pos)
3.0: 307 {
```

```
3.0: 308        ssize_t ret;
3.0: 309
3.0: 310        if (!(file->f_mode & FMODE_READ))
3.0: 311                return -EBADF;
3.0: 312        if (!file->f_op || (!file->f_op->read && !file->f_op->aio_read))
3.0: 313                return -EINVAL;
3.0: 314        if (unlikely(!access_ok(VERIFY_WRITE, buf, count)))
3.0: 315                return -EFAULT;
3.0: 316
3.0: 317        ret = rw_verify_area(READ, file, pos, count);
3.0: 318        if (ret >= 0) {
3.0: 319                count = ret;
3.0: 320                if (file->f_op->read)
3.0: 321                        ret = file->f_op->read(file, buf, count, pos);
3.0: 322                else
3.0: 323                        ret = do_sync_read(file, buf, count, pos);
3.0: 324                if (ret > 0) {
3.0: 325                        fsnotify_access(file);
3.0: 326                        add_rchar(current, ret);
3.0: 327                }
3.0: 328                inc_syscr(current);
3.0: 329        }
3.0: 330
3.0: 331        return ret;
3.0: 332 }
```

- After checking to see if the file has been opened with permission for reading, and making other security checks, this function looks at the `file_operations` structure embedded in this structure (`file->f_op`) and if it has a read method defined (`file->f_op->read`), just passes the read request through to it. It then brings the return value of the read back to user-space.

- Note that the functions `fget()`, `fput()` also increment and decrement a reference count of the file descriptor; the "light" version of these functions is faster for files already being used by a process.

- None of the above is actually specific to device drivers; if we had opened a normal file, the method returned would have been that for the particular filesystem involved. Because our filesystem entry pointed to a device, we got device-specific methods instead.

- Similar kinds of walk throughs can be performed for any of the entry points.

7.6 Error Numbers

- Standard error numbers are defined in header files included from `linux/errno.h`. The first bunch come from **/usr/src/linux/include/asm-generic/errno-base.h**:

```
....
3.0:  4 #define EPERM       1  /* Operation not permitted */
3.0:  5 #define ENOENT      2  /* No such file or directory */
3.0:  6 #define ESRCH       3  /* No such process */
3.0:  7 #define EINTR       4  /* Interrupted system call */
3.0:  8 #define EIO         5  /* I/O error */
3.0:  9 #define ENXIO       6  /* No such device or address */
3.0: 10 #define E2BIG       7  /* Argument list too long */
3.0: 11 #define ENOEXEC     8  /* Exec format error */
3.0: 12 #define EBADF       9  /* Bad file number */
```

```
3.0:    13 #define ECHILD      10  /* No child processes */
3.0:    14 #define EAGAIN      11  /* Try again */
3.0:    15 #define ENOMEM      12  /* Out of memory */
3.0:    16 #define EACCES      13  /* Permission denied */
3.0:    17 #define EFAULT      14  /* Bad address */
....
```

- Usually one returns -ERROR, while the error return for system calls is almost always -1, with the actual error code being stored in the thread-local variable errno in user-space.

- Thus, in user-space a typical code fragment would be:

```
#include <errno.h>

if ( ioctl(fd, CMD, arg) < 0 ){
    perror("MY_DRIVER_IOCTL_CALL");
    return (errno);
}
```

- Remember, it is up to **you** to provide the proper error returns from your kernel entry points, which will cause errno to be set appropriately.

- Usually one can check the status of a function that has a pointer return value by simply checking for NULL. However, it doesn't make clear the cause of the error and the **Linux** kernel permits encoding the error code in the return value. The simple functions that deal with this situation are:

```
void *ERR_PTR (long error);
long IS_ERR (const void *ptr);
long PTR_ERR (const void *ptr);
```

where ERR_PTR() encodes the error, IS_ERR() checks for the presence of an error, and PTR_ERR() extracts the actual error code.

7.7 printk()

- printk() is similar to the standard **C** function printf(), but has some important differences. A typical invocation might be:

```
printk(KERN_INFO "Your device driver was opened with Major Number = %d\n", major_number);
```

- printk() has no floating point format support.

- Every message in a printk() has a "loglevel" (if not explicitly given, a default level is applied). These levels are defined in **/usr/src/linux/include/linux/printk.h**, and are:

```
3.0:     9 #define KERN_EMERG      "<0>"   /* system is unusable              */
3.0:    10 #define KERN_ALERT      "<1>"   /* action must be taken immediately */
3.0:    11 #define KERN_CRIT       "<2>"   /* critical conditions             */
3.0:    12 #define KERN_ERR        "<3>"   /* error conditions                */
```

```
3.0:   13 #define KERN_WARNING    "<4>"    /* warning conditions              */
3.0:   14 #define KERN_NOTICE     "<5>"    /* normal but significant condition */
3.0:   15 #define KERN_INFO       "<6>"    /* informational                   */
3.0:   16 #define KERN_DEBUG      "<7>"    /* debug-level messages            */
```

- The loglevel (or priority) forces an informational string to be pre-pended to your print statement.

- The pseudo-file `/proc/sys/kernel/printk` lists the log levels set on the system: On most systems you'll get the numbers:

  6   4   1   7

which have the following meanings respectively:

Table 7.3: **printk() logging levels**

Value	Meaning
console_loglevel	Messages with a higher priority than this will be printed to the console.
default_message_loglevel	Messages without an explicit priority will be printed with this priority.
minimum_console_level	Minimum (highest) value to which the console_loglevel can be set.
default_console_loglevel	Default value for console_loglevel.

- Note that a higher priority means a lower loglevel and processes can dynamically alter the `console_loglevel`; in particular a kernel fault raises it to 15.

- Messages go into a circular log buffer, with a default length of 128 KB which can be adjusted during kernel compilation. The contents can be viewed with the **dmesg** utility; the file `/var/log/dmesg` contains the buffer's contents at system boot.

- The default size of the buffer can be overwritten during system initialization, by setting the parameter `log_buf_len=n` on the kernel command line, where **n** must be a power of two.

- Where the messages go depends on whether or not **syslogd** and **klogd** are running and how they are configured. If they are not you can simply do `cat /proc/kmsg`. Generally they will go to `/var/log/messages` (although on some recent **Ubuntu** systems they go to `/var/log/syslog`) but if you are running **X** you can't see them trivially. A good way to see them is to open a terminal window, and in that window type `tailf /var/log/messages`. On a **Gnome** desktop you can also access the messages by clicking on `System->Administration->System Log` or `Applications->System Tools->Log File Viewer` in your Desktop menus.

- Ultimate control of kernel logging is in the hands of the daemons **syslogd** and **klogd**. These can control all aspects of the behaviour, including default levels and message destinations, directed by source and severity. There is actually a **man** page for **syslog** which also gives the **C**-language interface from within the kernel.

- Note you can alter the various log levels through parameters to **syslogd**, but an even easier method is to exploit the `/proc` filesystem, by writing to it. The command

```
echo 8 > /proc/sys/kernel/printk
```

will cause all messages to appear on the console.

- If the same line of output is repeatedly printed out, the logging programs are smart enough to compress the output, so if you do something like:

```
for (j=0; j<100; j++)
    printk(KERN_INFO "A message\n");
printk(KERN_INFO "another message\n");
```

what you will get out will be:

```
Dec 18 15:51:54 p3 kernel: A message
Dec 18 15:51:54 p3 last message repeated 99 times
Dec 18 15:51:54 p3 kernel: another message
```

Also you should note that you can only be assured that `printk()` will flush its output if the line ends with a `"\n"`.

- It is pretty easy to get overwhelmed with messages, and it is possible to limit the number of times a messages gets printed. The function for doing this is:

```
int printk_ratelimit (void);
```

and a typical use would be

```
if (printk_ratelimit())
    printk (KERN_WARNING "The device is failing\n");
```

Under normal circumstances you'll just get the normal printout. However, if the threshold is exceeded `printk_ratelimit()` will start returning zero and messages will fall on the floor.

- The threshold can be controlled with modifying **/proc/sys/kernel/printk_ratelimit** and **/proc/sys/kernel/printk_ratelimit_burst**. The first parameter gives the minimum time (in jiffies) between messages, and the second the number of messages to send before rate-limiting kicks in.

- An optional timestamp that can be printed with each line handled by `printk()` can be turned on by setting `CONFIG_PRINTK_TIME` in the configuration file. The time is printed out in seconds as in:

```
Jun 30 07:54:36 localhost kernel: [  707.921716] Hello: module loaded
Jun 30 07:54:36 localhost kernel: [  707.921765] Jiffies=1102136
Jun 30 07:54:43 localhost kernel: [  714.537416] Bye: module unloaded
Jun 30 07:54:43 localhost kernel: [  714.537422] Jiffies=1108757
```

- This feature can be turned on and off at system initialization by setting the parameter `printk.time=[1/Y/y]|[0/N/n]`.

7.8   Labs

Lab 1: Installing a Basic Character Driver

- In this exercise we are going to compile, load (and unload) and test a sample character driver (provided). In subsequent sections we will discuss each of these steps in detail.

- **Compiling:** First you have to make sure you have the installed kernel source for the kernel you are running You can verify this by doing:

```
$ ls -l /lib/modules/$(uname -r)/build
```

and make sure it points to a non-empty directory. If it doesn't your instructor will help you fix this, or ask you to reboot into a different kernel which has the appropriate files installed on your system.

- We will discuss in depth how to construct **Makefile**s for for compiling external kernel modules shortly, but for now use the **genmake** script provided with the solutions; just do:

```
$ ../genmake
```

and then compile the kernel module with:

```
$ make
```

. which will compile your module with all the same options and flags as the kernel modules in that source location.

- **Monitoring Output:** If you are working at a virtual terminal or in non-graphical mode, you'll see the output of your module appear on your screen. Otherwise you'll have to keep an eye on the file /var/log/messages, to which the system logging daemons direct kernel print messages. The best way to do this is to open a terminal window, and in it type:

```
$ tailf /var/log/messages
```

- **Loading and Unloading:** The easiest way to load and unload the module is with:

```
$ /sbin/insmod lab1_chrdrv.ko
$ /sbin/rmmod lab1_chrdrv
```

Try and load and unload the module. If you look at **/proc/devices** you should see your driver registered, and if you look at **/proc/modules** (or type **lsmod**) you should see that your module is loaded.

- **Creating a Device Node:** Before you can actually use the module, you'll have to create the device node with which applications interact. You do this with the **mknod** command:

```
$ mknod /dev/mycdrv c 700 0
```

Note that the **name** of the device node (/dev/mycdrv) is irrelevant; the kernel identifies which driver should handle the system calls only by the **major number** (700 in this case.) The **minor number** (0 in this case) is generally used only within the driver.

- **Using the Module**: You should be able to test the module with simple commands like:

```
$ echo Some Input > /dev/mycdrv
$ cat somefile > /dev/mycdrv
$ dd if=/dev/zero of=/dev/mycdrv count=1
$ dd if=/dev/mycdrv count=1
```

We've only skimmed the surface; later we will consider the details of each of these steps.

Chapter 8

A Driver Example

We'll step through the **tsc2007** touchscreen driver to get a feel for a simple but well-constructed device driver.

8.1 The tsc2007 Touchscreen Driver

- We'll examine a small driver to get an overview before we dive into detail on device drivers.

- This will be done using the tsc2007 touchscreen driver, the full source of which can be found at: **/usr/ src/linux/drivers/input/touchscreen/tsc2007.c**.

- We'll start from the bottom:

```
3.0: 384 static int __init tsc2007_init(void)
3.0: 385 {
3.0: 386         return i2c_add_driver(&tsc2007_driver);
3.0: 387 }
3.0: 388
3.0: 389 static void __exit tsc2007_exit(void)
3.0: 390 {
3.0: 391         i2c_del_driver(&tsc2007_driver);
3.0: 392 }
3.0: 393
3.0: 394 module_init(tsc2007_init);
3.0: 395 module_exit(tsc2007_exit);
3.0: 396
3.0: 397 MODULE_AUTHOR("Kwangwoo Lee <kwlee@mtekvision.com>");
3.0: 398 MODULE_DESCRIPTION("TSC2007 TouchScreen Driver");
3.0: 399 MODULE_LICENSE("GPL");
```

- These are the standard **init** and **exit** definitions to register with the **i2c** subsystem, and are invoked when the driver is loaded or unloaded.

- The `tsc2007_driver` structure and its device table are defined as:

```
3.0: 367 static const struct i2c_device_id tsc2007_idtable[] = {
3.0: 368         { "tsc2007", 0 },
3.0: 369         { }
3.0: 370 };
3.0: 371
3.0: 372 MODULE_DEVICE_TABLE(i2c, tsc2007_idtable);
3.0: 373
3.0: 374 static struct i2c_driver tsc2007_driver = {
3.0: 375         .driver = {
3.0: 376                 .owner        = THIS_MODULE,
3.0: 377                 .name         = "tsc2007"
3.0: 378         },
3.0: 379         .id_table        = tsc2007_idtable,
3.0: 380         .probe           = tsc2007_probe,
3.0: 381         .remove          = __devexit_p(tsc2007_remove),
3.0: 382 };
3.0: 383
```

- In the i2c_driver structure, tsc2007_driver, we set the probe() and remove() callback functions calls. These are given by:

```
3.0: 266 static int __devinit tsc2007_probe(struct i2c_client *client,
3.0: 267                                    const struct i2c_device_id *id)
3.0: 268 {
3.0: 269         struct tsc2007 *ts;
3.0: 270         struct tsc2007_platform_data *pdata = client->dev.platform_data;
3.0: 271         struct input_dev *input_dev;
3.0: 272         int err;
3.0: 273
3.0: 274         if (!pdata) {
3.0: 275                 dev_err(&client->dev, "platform data is required!\n");
3.0: 276                 return -EINVAL;
3.0: 277         }
3.0: 278
3.0: 279         if (!i2c_check_functionality(client->adapter,
3.0: 280                                 I2C_FUNC_SMBUS_READ_WORD_DATA))
3.0: 281                 return -EIO;
3.0: 282
3.0: 283         ts = kzalloc(sizeof(struct tsc2007), GFP_KERNEL);
3.0: 284         input_dev = input_allocate_device();
3.0: 285         if (!ts || !input_dev) {
3.0: 286                 err = -ENOMEM;
3.0: 287                 goto err_free_mem;
3.0: 288         }
3.0: 289
3.0: 290         ts->client = client;
3.0: 291         ts->irq = client->irq;
3.0: 292         ts->input = input_dev;
3.0: 293         INIT_DELAYED_WORK(&ts->work, tsc2007_work);
3.0: 294
3.0: 295         ts->model         = pdata->model;
3.0: 296         ts->x_plate_ohms  = pdata->x_plate_ohms;
3.0: 297         ts->max_rt        = pdata->max_rt ? : MAX_12BIT;
```

```
3.0: 298            ts->poll_delay        = pdata->poll_delay ? : 1;
3.0: 299            ts->poll_period       = pdata->poll_period ? : 1;
3.0: 300            ts->get_pendown_state = pdata->get_pendown_state;
3.0: 301            ts->clear_penirq      = pdata->clear_penirq;
3.0: 302
3.0: 303            snprintf(ts->phys, sizeof(ts->phys),
3.0: 304                        "%s/input0", dev_name(&client->dev));
3.0: 305
3.0: 306            input_dev->name = "TSC2007 Touchscreen";
3.0: 307            input_dev->phys = ts->phys;
3.0: 308            input_dev->id.bustype = BUS_I2C;
3.0: 309
3.0: 310            input_dev->evbit[0] = BIT_MASK(EV_KEY) | BIT_MASK(EV_ABS);
3.0: 311            input_dev->keybit[BIT_WORD(BTN_TOUCH)] = BIT_MASK(BTN_TOUCH);
3.0: 312
3.0: 313            input_set_abs_params(input_dev, ABS_X, 0, MAX_12BIT, pdata->fuzzx, 0);
3.0: 314            input_set_abs_params(input_dev, ABS_Y, 0, MAX_12BIT, pdata->fuzzy, 0);
3.0: 315            input_set_abs_params(input_dev, ABS_PRESSURE, 0, MAX_12BIT,
3.0: 316                            pdata->fuzzz, 0);
3.0: 317
3.0: 318            if (pdata->init_platform_hw)
3.0: 319                    pdata->init_platform_hw();
3.0: 320
3.0: 321            err = request_irq(ts->irq, tsc2007_irq, 0,
3.0: 322                            client->dev.driver->name, ts);
3.0: 323            if (err < 0) {
3.0: 324                    dev_err(&client->dev, "irq %d busy?\n", ts->irq);
3.0: 325                    goto err_free_mem;
3.0: 326            }
3.0: 327
3.0: 328            /* Prepare for touch readings - power down ADC and enable PENIRQ */
3.0: 329            err = tsc2007_xfer(ts, PWRDOWN);
3.0: 330            if (err < 0)
3.0: 331                    goto err_free_irq;
3.0: 332
3.0: 333            err = input_register_device(input_dev);
3.0: 334            if (err)
3.0: 335                    goto err_free_irq;
3.0: 336
3.0: 337            i2c_set_clientdata(client, ts);
3.0: 338
3.0: 339            return 0;
3.0: 340
3.0: 341  err_free_irq:
3.0: 342            tsc2007_free_irq(ts);
3.0: 343            if (pdata->exit_platform_hw)
3.0: 344                    pdata->exit_platform_hw();
3.0: 345  err_free_mem:
3.0: 346            input_free_device(input_dev);
3.0: 347            kfree(ts);
3.0: 348            return err;
3.0: 349  }
3.0: 350
3.0: 351  static int __devexit tsc2007_remove(struct i2c_client *client)
3.0: 352  {
3.0: 353            struct tsc2007          *ts = i2c_get_clientdata(client);
3.0: 354            struct tsc2007_platform_data *pdata = client->dev.platform_data;
```

```
3.0: 355
3.0: 356          tsc2007_free_irq(ts);
3.0: 357
3.0: 358          if (pdata->exit_platform_hw)
3.0: 359                  pdata->exit_platform_hw();
3.0: 360
3.0: 361          input_unregister_device(ts->input);
3.0: 362          kfree(ts);
3.0: 363
3.0: 364          return 0;
3.0: 365 }
3.0: 366
```

- Note that in the probe() function, the INIT_DELAYED_WORK(&ts->work, tsc2007_work) macro sets up the call to the worker function:

```
3.0: 155 static void tsc2007_work(struct work_struct *work)
3.0: 156 {
3.0: 157          struct tsc2007 *ts =
3.0: 158                  container_of(to_delayed_work(work), struct tsc2007, work);
3.0: 159          bool debounced = false;
3.0: 160          struct ts_event tc;
3.0: 161          u32 rt;
3.0: 162
3.0: 163          /*
3.0: 164           * NOTE: We can't rely on the pressure to determine the pen down
3.0: 165           * state, even though this controller has a pressure sensor.
3.0: 166           * The pressure value can fluctuate for quite a while after
3.0: 167           * lifting the pen and in some cases may not even settle at the
3.0: 168           * expected value.
3.0: 169           *
3.0: 170           * The only safe way to check for the pen up condition is in the
3.0: 171           * work function by reading the pen signal state (it's a GPIO
3.0: 172           * and IRQ). Unfortunately such callback is not always available,
3.0: 173           * in that case we have rely on the pressure anyway.
3.0: 174           */
3.0: 175          if (ts->get_pendown_state) {
3.0: 176                  if (unlikely(!ts->get_pendown_state())) {
3.0: 177                          tsc2007_send_up_event(ts);
3.0: 178                          ts->pendown = false;
3.0: 179                          goto out;
3.0: 180                  }
3.0: 181
3.0: 182                  dev_dbg(&ts->client->dev, "pen is still down\n");
3.0: 183          }
3.0: 184
3.0: 185          tsc2007_read_values(ts, &tc);
3.0: 186
3.0: 187          rt = tsc2007_calculate_pressure(ts, &tc);
3.0: 188          if (rt > ts->max_rt) {
3.0: 189                  /*
3.0: 190                   * Sample found inconsistent by debouncing or pressure is
3.0: 191                   * beyond the maximum. Don't report it to user space,
3.0: 192                   * repeat at least once more the measurement.
3.0: 193                   */
3.0: 194                  dev_dbg(&ts->client->dev, "ignored pressure %d\n", rt);
3.0: 195                  debounced = true;
```

```
3.0: 196                        goto out;
3.0: 197
3.0: 198                }
3.0: 199
3.0: 200        if (rt) {
3.0: 201                struct input_dev *input = ts->input;
3.0: 202
3.0: 203                if (!ts->pendown) {
3.0: 204                        dev_dbg(&ts->client->dev, "DOWN\n");
3.0: 205
3.0: 206                        input_report_key(input, BTN_TOUCH, 1);
3.0: 207                        ts->pendown = true;
3.0: 208                }
3.0: 209
3.0: 210                input_report_abs(input, ABS_X, tc.x);
3.0: 211                input_report_abs(input, ABS_Y, tc.y);
3.0: 212                input_report_abs(input, ABS_PRESSURE, rt);
3.0: 213
3.0: 214                input_sync(input);
3.0: 215
3.0: 216                dev_dbg(&ts->client->dev, "point(%4d,%4d), pressure (%4u)\n",
3.0: 217                        tc.x, tc.y, rt);
3.0: 218
3.0: 219        } else if (!ts->get_pendown_state && ts->pendown) {
3.0: 220                /*
3.0: 221                 * We don't have callback to check pendown state, so we
3.0: 222                 * have to assume that since pressure reported is 0 the
3.0: 223                 * pen was lifted up.
3.0: 224                 */
3.0: 225                tsc2007_send_up_event(ts);
3.0: 226                ts->pendown = false;
3.0: 227        }
3.0: 228
3.0: 229 out:
3.0: 230        if (ts->pendown || debounced)
3.0: 231                schedule_delayed_work(&ts->work,
3.0: 232                                msecs_to_jiffies(ts->poll_period));
3.0: 233        else
3.0: 234                enable_irq(ts->irq);
3.0: 235 }
```

- Here we call tsc2007_read_values(), tsc2007_calculate_pressure() and tsc2007_send_up_events(), which are defined as:

```
3.0: 108 static void tsc2007_read_values(struct tsc2007 *tsc, struct ts_event *tc)
3.0: 109 {
3.0: 110        /* y- still on; turn on only y+ (and ADC) */
3.0: 111        tc->y = tsc2007_xfer(tsc, READ_Y);
3.0: 112
3.0: 113        /* turn y- off, x+ on, then leave in lowpower */
3.0: 114        tc->x = tsc2007_xfer(tsc, READ_X);
3.0: 115
3.0: 116        /* turn y+ off, x- on; we'll use formula #1 */
3.0: 117        tc->z1 = tsc2007_xfer(tsc, READ_Z1);
3.0: 118        tc->z2 = tsc2007_xfer(tsc, READ_Z2);
3.0: 119
3.0: 120        /* Prepare for next touch reading - power down ADC, enable PENIRQ */
```

```
3.0: 121          tsc2007_xfer(tsc, PWRDOWN);
3.0: 122 }
3.0: 123
3.0: 124 static u32 tsc2007_calculate_pressure(struct tsc2007 *tsc, struct ts_event *tc)
3.0: 125 {
3.0: 126          u32 rt = 0;
3.0: 127
3.0: 128          /* range filtering */
3.0: 129          if (tc->x == MAX_12BIT)
3.0: 130                  tc->x = 0;
3.0: 131
3.0: 132          if (likely(tc->x && tc->z1)) {
3.0: 133                  /* compute touch pressure resistance using equation #1 */
3.0: 134                  rt = tc->z2 - tc->z1;
3.0: 135                  rt *= tc->x;
3.0: 136                  rt *= tsc->x_plate_ohms;
3.0: 137                  rt /= tc->z1;
3.0: 138                  rt = (rt + 2047) >> 12;
3.0: 139          }
3.0: 140
3.0: 141          return rt;
3.0: 142 }
3.0: 143
3.0: 144 static void tsc2007_send_up_event(struct tsc2007 *tsc)
3.0: 145 {
3.0: 146          struct input_dev *input = tsc->input;
3.0: 147
3.0: 148          dev_dbg(&tsc->client->dev, "UP\n");
3.0: 149
3.0: 150          input_report_key(input, BTN_TOUCH, 0);
3.0: 151          input_report_abs(input, ABS_PRESSURE, 0);
3.0: 152          input_sync(input);
3.0: 153 }
3.0: 154
```

- Now we're only missing the definitions of the inline function `tsc2007_xfer()` and the `tsc2007` and `ts_event` data structures:

```
3.0:  60 struct ts_event {
3.0:  61          u16       x;
3.0:  62          u16       y;
3.0:  63          u16       z1, z2;
3.0:  64 };
3.0:  65
3.0:  65
3.0:  66 struct tsc2007 {
3.0:  67          struct input_dev      *input;
3.0:  68          char                  phys[32];
3.0:  69          struct delayed_work   work;
3.0:  70
3.0:  71          struct i2c_client     *client;
3.0:  72
3.0:  73          u16                   model;
3.0:  74          u16                   x_plate_ohms;
3.0:  75          u16                   max_rt;
3.0:  76          unsigned long         poll_delay;
3.0:  77          unsigned long         poll_period;
```

```
3.0:  78
3.0:  79          bool                            pendown;
3.0:  80          int                             irq;
3.0:  81
3.0:  82          int                       (*get_pendown_state)(void);
3.0:  83          void                      (*clear_penirq)(void);
3.0:  84 };
3.0:  85
3.0:  86 static inline int tsc2007_xfer(struct tsc2007 *tsc, u8 cmd)
3.0:  87 {
3.0:  88          s32 data;
3.0:  89          u16 val;
3.0:  90
3.0:  91          data = i2c_smbus_read_word_data(tsc->client, cmd);
3.0:  92          if (data < 0) {
3.0:  93                  dev_err(&tsc->client->dev, "i2c io error: %d\n", data);
3.0:  94                  return data;
3.0:  95          }
3.0:  96
3.0:  97          /* The protocol and raw data format from i2c interface:
3.0:  98           * S Addr Wr [A] Comm [A] S Addr Rd [A] [DataLow] A [DataHigh] NA P
3.0:  99           * Where DataLow has [D11-D4], DataHigh has [D3-D0 << 4 | Dummy 4bit].
3.0: 100           */
3.0: 101          val = swab16(data) >> 4;
3.0: 102
3.0: 103          dev_dbg(&tsc->client->dev, "data: 0x%x, val: 0x%x\n", data, val);
3.0: 104
3.0: 105          return val;
3.0: 106 }
3.0: 107
```

- Last but not least, the includes and macros used:

```
3.0:  23 #include <linux/module.h>
3.0:  24 #include <linux/slab.h>
3.0:  25 #include <linux/input.h>
3.0:  26 #include <linux/interrupt.h>
3.0:  27 #include <linux/i2c.h>
3.0:  28 #include <linux/i2c/tsc2007.h>
3.0:  29
3.0:  30 #define TSC2007_MEASURE_TEMP0              (0x0 << 4)
3.0:  31 #define TSC2007_MEASURE_AUX               (0x2 << 4)
3.0:  32 #define TSC2007_MEASURE_TEMP1             (0x4 << 4)
3.0:  33 #define TSC2007_ACTIVATE_XN               (0x8 << 4)
3.0:  34 #define TSC2007_ACTIVATE_YN               (0x9 << 4)
3.0:  35 #define TSC2007_ACTIVATE_YP_XN            (0xa << 4)
3.0:  36 #define TSC2007_SETUP                     (0xb << 4)
3.0:  37 #define TSC2007_MEASURE_X             (0xc << 4)
3.0:  38 #define TSC2007_MEASURE_Y             (0xd << 4)
3.0:  39 #define TSC2007_MEASURE_Z1           (0xe << 4)
3.0:  40 #define TSC2007_MEASURE_Z2           (0xf << 4)
3.0:  41
3.0:  42 #define TSC2007_POWER_OFF_IRQ_EN     (0x0 << 2)
3.0:  43 #define TSC2007_ADC_ON_IRQ_DIS0           (0x1 << 2)
3.0:  44 #define TSC2007_ADC_OFF_IRQ_EN            (0x2 << 2)
3.0:  45 #define TSC2007_ADC_ON_IRQ_DIS1           (0x3 << 2)
3.0:  46
3.0:  47 #define TSC2007_12BIT                     (0x0 << 1)
```

```
3.0:   48 #define TSC2007_8BIT                            (0x1 << 1)
3.0:   49
3.0:   50 #define        MAX_12BIT                        ((1 << 12) - 1)
3.0:   51
3.0:   52 #define ADC_ON_12BIT          (TSC2007_12BIT | TSC2007_ADC_ON_IRQ_DIS0)
3.0:   53
3.0:   54 #define READ_Y               (ADC_ON_12BIT | TSC2007_MEASURE_Y)
3.0:   55 #define READ_Z1              (ADC_ON_12BIT | TSC2007_MEASURE_Z1)
3.0:   56 #define READ_Z2              (ADC_ON_12BIT | TSC2007_MEASURE_Z2)
3.0:   57 #define READ_X               (ADC_ON_12BIT | TSC2007_MEASURE_X)
3.0:   58 #define PWRDOWN              (TSC2007_12BIT | TSC2007_POWER_OFF_IRQ_EN)
3.0:   59
```

- As seen in this example, while reading the driver source bottom-up, we move from registering the driver within the subsystem down to the communication with the real hardware.

Chapter 9

Character Devices

We'll begin our detailed discussion of building character device drivers. We'll talk about device nodes, how to create them, access them, and register them with the kernel. We'll discuss the **udev/HAL** interface. Then we'll describe in detail the important `file_operations` data structure and itemize in detail the driver entry points it points to. Two other important data structures, the `file` and `inode` structures are also considered. Finally we show how modules keep track of their usage count, and discuss **miscellaneous** character drivers.

9.1 Device Nodes

- Character and block devices have filesystem entries associated with them. These **nodes** can be used by user-level programs to communicate with the device, whose driver can manage more than one device node.

- Examples of device nodes:

```
lrwxrwxrwx  1 root root              3 Dec 28 06:30 cdrom -> sr0
lrwxrwxrwx  1 root root              3 Dec 28 06:30 dvdrw -> sr0
crw-rw----  1 root root         10, 228 Dec 28 00:30 hpet
crw-r-----  1 root kmem          1,   2 Dec 28 00:30 kmem
brw-rw----  1 root disk          7,   0 Dec 28 10:58 loop0
brw-rw----  1 root disk          7,   1 Dec 28 06:30 loop1
crw-rw----  1 root lp            6,   0 Dec 28 00:30 lp0
crw-rw----  1 root lp            6,   1 Dec 28 00:30 lp1
brw-rw----  1 root disk          8,   0 Dec 28 06:30 sda
brw-rw----  1 root disk          8,   1 Dec 28 06:30 sda1
brw-rw----  1 root disk          8,  18 Dec 28 06:30 sdb2
brw-rw----+ 1 root cdrom        11,   0 Dec 28 06:30 sr0
lrwxrwxrwx  1 root root             15 Dec 28 00:30 stderr -> /proc/self/fd/2
lrwxrwxrwx  1 root root             15 Dec 28 00:30 stdin -> /proc/self/fd/0
lrwxrwxrwx  1 root root             15 Dec 28 00:30 stdout -> /proc/self/fd/1
crw-rw----  1 root dialout       4,  64 Dec 28 06:30 ttyS0
crw-rw----  1 root dialout       4,  65 Dec 28 06:30 ttyS1
crw-rw-rw-  1 root root          1,   5 Dec 28 00:30 zero
```

- Device nodes are made with:

  ```
  $ mknod [-m mode] /dev/name <type> <major> <minor>
  ```

  e.g., `mknod -m 666 /dev/mycdrv c 254 1`

  or from the `mknod()` system call.

9.2   Major and Minor Numbers

- The **major** and **minor** numbers identify the driver associated with the device.

- The **minor** number is used **only** within the device driver to either differentiate between instances of the same kind of device, (such as the first and second sound card, or hard disk partition) or alternate modes of operation of a given device (such as different density floppy drive media.)

- The major and minor numbers are stored together in a variable of type `dev_t`, which has 32 bits, with 12 bits reserved for the major number, and 20 bits for the minor number.

- One should always use the following macros to construct (or deconstruct) major and minor numbers from a `dev_t` structure:

Table 9.1: **Device Node Macros**

Macro	Meaning
`MAJOR(dev_t dev);`	Extract the major number.
`MINOR(dev_t dev);`	Extract the minor number.
`MKDEV(int major, int minor);`	Return a `dev_t` built from major and minor numbers

- One can also use the inline convenience functions:

```
unsigned iminor(struct inode *inode); /* = MINOR(inode->i_rdev) */
unsigned imajor(struct inode *inode); /* = MAJOR(inode->i_rdev) */
```

when one needs to work with `inode` structures.

 Kernel Version Note Kernel Version Note

- In the 2.4 kernel, device numbers were packed in the `kdev_t` type, which was limited to 16 effective bits, even divided between minor and major numbers, so that each was limited to the range 0 – 255.

- In the 2.4 kernel once a driver registered a major number, no other driver could be registered with the same major number, and all minor numbers belonged to the driver.

- In the 2.6 kernel, however, one registers a **range** of minor numbers which can be less than all available, and indeed two concurrently loaded drivers can have the same major number, as long as they have distinct minor number ranges.

- A list of the major and minor numbers pre-associated with devices can be found in **/usr/src/linux/ Documentation/devices.txt**. (Note the major numbers 42, 120-127 and 240-254 are reserved for local and experimental use.) Symbolic names for assigned major numbers can be found in **/usr/src/linux/ include/linux/major.h**. Any further requesting of device number reservations is now prohibited, as more modern methods use **dynamical allocation**.

- Note that device numbers have meaning in user-space as well; in fact some **Posix** system calls such as `mknod()` and `stat()` have arguments with the `dev_t` data type, or utilize structures that do. For example:

```
$ stat /boot/64/vmlinuz-2.6.35-rc3

  File: '/boot/64/vmlinuz-2.6.35-rc3'
  Size: 3705936          Blocks: 7272        IO Block: 1024    regular file
Device: 802h/2050d       Inode: 18506        Links: 1
Access: (0644/-rw-r--r--) Uid: (    0/    root) Gid: (    0/    root)
Access: 2010-06-13 08:21:00.000000000 -0500
Modify: 2010-06-13 08:21:00.000000000 -0500
Change: 2010-06-13 08:21:00.000000000 -0500
```

shows the file resides on the disk partition with major number 8 and minor number 2 (/dev/sda2), which is listed at **802h** (hexadecimal) or **2050d** (decimal).

9.3 Reserving Major/Minor Numbers

- Adding a new driver to the system (i.e., registering it) means assigning a major number to it, usually during the device's initialization routine. For a character driver one calls:

```
#include <linux/fs.h>

int register_chrdev_region (dev_t first, unsigned int count, char *name);
```

where `first` is the first device number being requested, of a range of `count` contiguous numbers; usually the minor number part of `first` would be 0, but that is not required.

- `name` is the device name, as it will appear when examining /**proc/devices**. Note it is **not** the same as the node name in `/dev` that your driver will use. (The kernel decides which driver to invoke based on the major/minor number combination, not the name.)

- A return value of 0 indicates success; negative values indicate failure and the requested region of device numbers will not be available. Note that **mknod** will still have to be run to create the appropriate device node(s).

- It is important when undoing the registration to remove the association with device numbers, once they are no longer needed. This is most often done in the device cleanup function with:

```
void unregister_chrdev_region (dev_t first, unsigned int count);
```

Note that this will **not** remove the node itself.

- If you fail to unregister a device, you'll get a segmentation fault the next time you do `cat /proc/devices`. It is pretty hard (although not impossible) to recover from this kind of error without a system reboot.

Kernel Version Note **Kernel Version Note**

- In the 2.4 kernel only 8-bit major and minor numbers were available, and the functions for registering and de-registering were:

  ```
  #include <linux/fs.h>

  int register_chrdev (unsigned int major, const char *name,
                       const struct file_operations *fops);
  int unregister_chrdev (unsigned int major, const char *name);
  ```

- Dynamic allocation was accomplished by specifying 0 as a a major number; the return value gave the supplied major number which was obtained by decreasing from 254 until an unused number was found. (When dynamic allocation was not requested, the return value upon success was 0, which was confusing.)

- We'll discuss the `struct file_operations` pointer argument shortly, which delineates the methods used by the driver.

- Only one device driver could use a given major number at at a time; in the 2.6 kernel it is required that only major/minor number set is unique.

- This interface, while more limited that the new one, is used in some old device drivers and there is no great rush to eliminate it. However, any new drivers should always use the more modern methods.

Dynamic Allocation of Major Numbers

- Choosing a unique major number may be difficult: dynamic allocation of the device numbers is used to avoid collisions. This is accomplished with the function:

  ```
  #include <linux/fs.h>

  int alloc_chrdev_region (dev_t *first, unsigned int firstminor, unsigned int count,
                           char *name);
  ```

  where `first` is now passed by address as it will be filled in by the function. The new argument, `firstminor` is obviously the first requested minor number, (usually 0.) The de-registration of the device numbers is the same with this method.

- The disadvantage of dynamic allocation is that the proper node can not be made until the driver is loaded. Furthermore, one usually needs to remove the node upon unloading of the driver module. Thus some scripting is required around both the module loading and unloading steps.

- While it would be possible to have a module do an `exec()` call to `mknod` and jump out to user-space, this is never done; kernel developers feel strongly that making nodes belongs in user-land, not the kernel.

- Even better, you can use the **udev** facility to create a node from within your module. We'll show you how to do this later.

9.4   Accessing the Device Node

- Under **Unix**-like operating systems, such as **Linux**, applications access peripheral devices using the same functions as they would for ordinary files. This is an essential part of the *everything is a file* philosophy. For example, listening to a sound would involve **reading** from the device node associated with the sound card (generally /dev/audio).

- There are a limited number of **entry points** into device drivers, and in most cases there is a one to one mapping of the **system calls** applications make and the entry point in the driver which is exercised when the call is made.

- For a given class of devices, such as **character** or **block**, the entry points are the same irrespective of the actual device itself. In the case of character drivers, the mapping is relatively direct; in the case of block drivers there is more indirection; i.e., several layers of the kernel may intercede between the system call and the entry point; a read would involve the virtual filesystem, the actual filesystem, and cache layers before requests to get blocks of data on or off a device are made to the driver through a read() or write() system call.

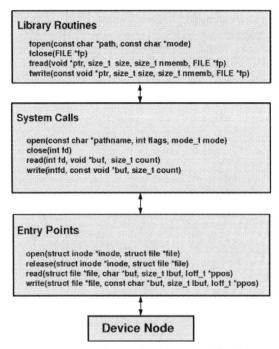

Figure 9.1: **Accessing Device Nodes**

- The following are the main operations that can be performed on character device nodes by programs in user-space:

```
int     open  (const char *pathname, int flags);
int     close (int fd);
ssize_t read  (int fd, void *buf, size_t count);
ssize_t write (int fd, const void *buf, size_t count);
int     ioctl (int fd, int request, ...);
off_t   lseek (int fd, off_t offset, int whence);
void    *mmap (void *start, size_t length, int prot, int flags, int fd, off_t offset);
int poll (struct pollfd *fds, nfds_t nfds, int timeout);
```

These entry points all have **man** pages associated with them.

- The device driver has entry points corresponding to these functions; however names and arguments may differ. In the above list, for example, the system call `close()` will lead to the entry point `release()`.

- Remember that applications can exert these system calls indirectly; for instance by using the standard I/O library functions, `fopen()`, `fclose()`, `fread()`, `fwrite()`, and `fseek()`.

9.5   Registering the Device

- So far all we have done is reserve a range of device numbers for the exclusive use of our driver. More work has to be done before the device can be used.

- Character devices are associated with a `cdev` structure, as defined in **/usr/src/linux/include/linux/cdev.h**:

```
struct cdev {
        struct kobject kobj;
        struct module *owner;
        const struct file_operations *ops;
        struct list_head list;
        dev_t dev;
        unsigned int count;
};
```

- Normally you won't work directly with the internals of this structure, but reach it through various utility functions. In particular we'll see how the `owner` and `ops` pointers are used.

- A number of related functions which are needed to work with character devices are:

```
#include <linux/cdev.h>

struct cdev *cdev_alloc (void);
void cdev_init (struct cdev *p, const struct file_operations *fops);
void cdev_put (struct cdev *p);
struct kobject *cdev_get (struct cdev *p);
int cdev_add (struct cdev *p, dev_t first, unsigned count);
void cdev_del (struct cdev *p);
```

- These structures should always be allocated dynamically, and then initialized with code like:

```
struct cdev *mycdev = cdev_alloc ();
cdev_init (mycdev, &fops);
```

This code allocates memory for the structure, initializes it, and sets the `owner` and `ops` fields to point to the current module, and the proper `file_operations` table.

- The driver will go **live** when one calls:

  ```
  cdev_add (mycdev, first, count);
  ```

  This function should not be called until the driver is ready to handle anything that comes its way. The inverse function is

  ```
  cdev_del (mycdev)
  ```

  and after this is called the device is removed from the system and the `cdev` structure should never be accessed after this point.

9.6   udev and HAL

- The methods of managing device nodes became clumsy and difficult as **Linux** evolved. The number of device nodes lying in **/dev** and its subdirectories reached numbers in the 15,000 - 20,000 range in most installations during the 2.4 kernel series. Nodes for all kinds of devices which would never be used on most installations were still created by default, as distributors could never be sure exactly which hardware would be needed.

- Of course many developers and system administrators trimmed the list to what was actually needed, especially in embedded configurations, but this was essentially a manual and potentially error-prone task.

- Note that while device nodes are not normal files and don't take up significant space on the filesystem, having huge directories slowed down access to device nodes, especially upon first usage. Furthermore, exhaustion of available major and minor numbers required a more modern and dynamic approach to the creation and maintenance of device nodes.

- Ideally, one would like to register devices by name, However, major and minor numbers can not be gotten rid of altogether, as **Posix** requires them.

- The **udev** method creates device nodes on the fly as they are needed. There is no need to maintain a ton of device nodes that will never be used. The **u** in **udev** stands for **user**, and indicates that most of the work of creating, removing, and modifying devices nodes is done in user-space.

- **udev** handles the dynamical generation of device nodes but it does not handle the discovery of devices or management of them. This requires the **Hardware Abstraction Layer**, or **HAL**, which is a project of **freedesktop.org** (**http://www.freedesktop.org/wiki/Software/hal**).

- **HAL** uses the **D-BUS** (device bus) infrastructure, as provided by the **HAL** daemon (**haldaemon**). It maintains a dynamic database of all connected hardware devices and is closely coupled to the hotplug facility. The command `lshal` will dump out all the information that **HAL** currently has in its database. There are a number of configuration files on the system (in **/usr/share/hal** and **/etc/hal**) which control behaviour and set exceptions.

- The cleanest way to use **udev** is to have a pure system; the **/dev** directory is empty upon the initial kernel boot, and then is populated with device nodes as they are needed. When used this way, one must boot using an **initrd** or **initramfs** image, which may contain a set of preliminary device nodes as well as the **udev** program itself.

- As devices are added or removed from the system, working with the hotplug subsystem, **udev** acts upon notification of events to create and remove device nodes. The information necessary to create them with the right names, major and minor numbers, permissions, etc, are gathered by examination of information already registered in the **sysfs** pseudo-filesystem (mounted at **/sys**) and a set of configuration files.

- The main configuration file is **/etc/udev/udev.conf**. It contains information such as where to place device nodes, default permissions and ownership etc. By default rules for device naming are located in the **/etc/udev/rules.d** directory. By reading the **man** page for **udev** one can get a lot of specific information about how to set up rules for common situations.

- Creation and removal of a device node dynamically, from within the driver using **udev**, is done by the use of the following functions defined in **/usr/src/linux/include/linux/device.h**:

```
#include <linux/device.h>

struct class  *class_create  (struct module *owner, const char *name);
struct device *device_create (struct class *cls, struct device *parent, dev_t devt,
                              void *drvdata, const char *fmt, ...);
void device_destroy (struct class *cls, dev_t dev);
void class_destroy (struct class *cls);
```

Generally, the `parent` is `NULL` which means the class is created at the top level of the hierarchy. A code fragment serves to show the use of these functions:

```
static struct class *foo_class;

/* create node in the init function */
    foo_class = class_create (THIS_MODULE, "my_class");
    device_create (foo_class, NULL, first, NULL, "%s%d", "mycdrv", 1);

/* remove node in the exit function */
    device_destroy (foo_class,first);
    class_destroy (foo_class);
```

- One has to be careful to do whatever is necessary to make the device usable before the device node is created, to avoid race conditions.

9.7   file_operations Structure

- The `file_operations` structure is defined in **/usr/src/linux/include/linux/fs.h**, and looks like:

```
3.0:1546 struct file_operations {
3.0:1547         struct module *owner;
3.0:1548         loff_t (*llseek) (struct file *, loff_t, int);
3.0:1549         ssize_t (*read) (struct file *, char __user *, size_t, loff_t *);
3.0:1550         ssize_t (*write) (struct file *, const char __user *, size_t, loff_t *);
3.0:1551         ssize_t (*aio_read) (struct kiocb *, const struct iovec *, unsigned long,
                                     loff_t);
3.0:1552         ssize_t (*aio_write) (struct kiocb *, const struct iovec *, unsigned long,
                                      loff_t);
3.0:1553         int (*readdir) (struct file *, void *, filldir_t);
3.0:1554         unsigned int (*poll) (struct file *, struct poll_table_struct *);
3.0:1555         long (*unlocked_ioctl) (struct file *, unsigned int, unsigned long);
3.0:1556         long (*compat_ioctl) (struct file *, unsigned int, unsigned long);
3.0:1557         int (*mmap) (struct file *, struct vm_area_struct *);
3.0:1558         int (*open) (struct inode *, struct file *);
3.0:1559         int (*flush) (struct file *, fl_owner_t id);
3.0:1560         int (*release) (struct inode *, struct file *);
3.0:1561         int (*fsync) (struct file *, int datasync);
```

```
3.0:1562        int (*aio_fsync) (struct kiocb *, int datasync);
3.0:1563        int (*fasync) (int, struct file *, int);
3.0:1564        int (*lock) (struct file *, int, struct file_lock *);
3.0:1565        ssize_t (*sendpage) (struct file *, struct page *, int, size_t, loff_t *, int);
3.0:1566        unsigned long (*get_unmapped_area)(struct file *, unsigned long, unsigned long,
                                unsigned long, unsigned long);
3.0:1567        int (*check_flags)(int);
3.0:1568        int (*flock) (struct file *, int, struct file_lock *);
3.0:1569        ssize_t (*splice_write)(struct pipe_inode_info *, struct file *, loff_t *,
                                size_t, unsigned int);
3.0:1570        ssize_t (*splice_read)(struct file *, loff_t *, struct pipe_inode_info *, size_t,
                                unsigned int);
3.0:1571        int (*setlease)(struct file *, long, struct file_lock **);
3.0:1572        long (*fallocate)(struct file *file, int mode, loff_t offset,
                                loff_t len);
3.0:1574 };
```

and is a **jump table** of **driver entry points**, with the exception of the first field, `owner`, which is used for module reference counting.

- This structure is used for purposes other than character drivers, such as with filesystems, and so some of the entries won't be used in this arena. The same is true with the `file` and `inode` structures to be discussed shortly.

- The file operations structure is initialized with code like:

```
struct file_operations fops = {
        .owner   = THIS_MODULE,
        .open    = my_open,
        .release = my_close,
        .read    = my_read,
        .write   = my_write,
        .unlocked_ioctl  = my_unlocked_ioctl,
};
```

- According to the C99 language standard, the order in which fields are initialized is irrelevant, and any unspecified elements are `NULL`-ed.

- These operations are associated with the device with the `cdev_init()` function, which places a pointer to the `file_operations` structure in the proper `cdev` structure. Whenever a corresponding system call is made on a device node owned by the device, the work is passed through to the driver; e.g., a call to `open` on the device node causes the `my_open()` method to be called in the above example.

- If no method is supplied in the `file_operations` structure, there are two possibilities for what will occur if the method is invoked through a system call:

  - The method will fail: An example is `mmap()`.
  - A generic default method will be invoked: An example is `llseek()`. Sometimes this means the method will always succeed: Examples are `open()` and `release()`.

9.8 Driver Entry Points

- `struct module *owner;`

  The only field in the structure that is not a method. Points to the module that owns the structure and is used in reference counting and avoiding race conditions such as removing the module while the driver is being used. Usually set to the value `THIS_MODULE`.

- `loff_t (*llseek) (struct file *filp, loff_t offset, int whence);`

  changes the current read/write position in a file, returning the new position. Note that `loff_t` is 64-bit even on 32-bit architectures.

  If one wants to inhibit seeking on the device (as on a pipe), one can unset the `FMODE_LSEEK` bit in file `file` structure (probably during the `open()` method) as in:

  ```
  file->f_mode = file->f_mode & ~FMODE_LSEEK;
  ```

- `ssize_t (*read) (struct file *filp, char __user *buff, size_t size, loff_t *offset);`

  reads data from the device, returning the number of bytes read. An error is a negative value; zero may mean end of device and is not an error. You may also choose to block if data is not yet ready and the process hasn't set the non-blocking flag.

- A simple `read()` entry point might look like:

  ```
  static ssize_t mycdrv_read (struct file *file, char __user *buf, size_t lbuf, loff_t * ppos)
  {
      int nbytes = lbuf - copy_to_user (buf, kbuf + *ppos, lbuf);
      *ppos += nbytes;
      printk (KERN_INFO "\n READING function, nbytes=%d, pos=%d\n", nbytes, (int) *ppos);
      return nbytes;
  }
  ```

  In this simple case a read merely copies from a buffer in kernel-space (kbuf) to a buffer in user-space (buf.) But one can not use `memcpy()` to perform this because it is improper to de-reference user pointers in kernel-space; the address referred to may not point to a valid page of memory at the current time, either because it hasn't been allocated yet or it has been swapped out.

- Instead one must use the `copy_to_user()` and `copy_from_user()` functions (depending on direction) which take care of these problems. (We'll see later there are more advanced techniques for avoiding the extra copy, including memory mapping, raw I/O, etc.)

- The kernel buffer will probably be dynamically allocated, since the in-kernel per-task stack is very limited. This might be done with:

  ```
  #include <linux/slab.h>
  char *kbuf = kmalloc (kbuf_size, GFP_KERNEL);
  ....
  kfree (kbuf);
  ```

  where the limit is 1024 pages (4 MB on **x86**).

- If using the `GFP_KERNEL` flag, memory allocation may block until resources are available; if `GFP_ATOMIC` is used the request is non blocking. We will discuss memory allocation in detail later.

- The position in the device is updated by modifying the value of *ppos which points to the current value. The return value is the number of bytes successfully read; this is a case where a positive return value is still success.

- `ssize_t (*write) (struct file *filp, const char __user *buff, size_t size, loff_t *offset);`

  writes data to the device, returning the number of bytes written. An error is a negative value; zero may mean end of device and is not an error. You may also choose to block if the device is not yet ready and the process hasn't set the non-blocking flag.

  The same considerations apply about not directly using user-space pointers. Here one should use

  ```
  int nbytes = lbuf - copy_from_user (kbuf + *ppos, buf, lbuf);
  ```

  for the same reason

- `int (*readdir) (struct file *filp, void *, filldir_t filldir);`

  should be `NULL` for device nodes; used only for directories, and is used by filesystem drivers, which use the same `file_operations` structure.

- `unsigned int (*poll) (struct file *filp, struct poll_table_struct *ptab);`

  checks to see if a device is readable, writable, or in some special state. In user-space this is accessed with both the `poll()` and `select()` calls. Returns a bit mask describing device status.

- `int (*ioctl) (struct inode *inode, struct file *filp, unsigned int, unsigned long);`

  is the interface for issuing device-specific commands. Note that some `ioctl` commands are not device-specific and are intercepted by the kernel without referencing your entry point.

- `long (*unlocked_ioctl) (struct file *filp, unsigned int, unsigned long);`

  Unlike the normal `ioctl()` entry point, the big kernel lock is not taken before and released after calling. New code should use this entry point; if present the old one will be ignored.

- `int (*mmap) (struct file *filp, struct vm_area_struct *vm);`

  requests a mapping of device memory to a process's memory. If you don't implement this method, the system call will return `-ENODEV`.

- `int (*open) (struct inode *inode, struct file *filp);`

  opens a device. If set to `NULL` opening the device always succeeds, but the driver is not notified. The `open()` method should:

  - Check for hardware problems like the device not being ready.
  - Initialize the device if it is the first time it is being opened.
  - If required, note the minor number.
  - Set up any data structure being used in `private_data` field of the `file` data structure.

- `int (*flush) (struct file *filp);`

  is used when a driver closes its copy of a file descriptor for a device. It executes and waits for any outstanding operations on a device. Rarely used. Using `NULL` is safe.

- `int (*release) (struct inode *inode, struct file *filp);`

  closes the node. Note when a process terminates all open file descriptors are closed, even under abnormal exit, so this entry may be called implicitly. The `release()` method should reverse the operations of `open()`:

  - Free any resources allocated by `open`.
  - If it is the last usage of the device, take any shutdown steps that might be necessary.

- `int (*fsync) (struct file *filp, struct dentry *dentry, int datasync);`

  is used to flush any pending data.

- `int (*fasync) (int, struct file *filp, int);`

  checks the devices `FASYNC` flag, for *asynchronous* notification. Use `NULL` unless your driver supports asynchronous notification.

- `int (*lock) (struct file *filp, int, struct file_lock *lock);`

  is used to implement file locking; generally not used by device drivers, only files.

- `ssize_t (*aio_read) (struct kiocb *iocb, const struct iovec *iov, unsigned long niov, loff_t pos);`

- `ssize_t (*aio_write)(struct kiocb *iocb, const struct iovec *iov, unsigned long niov, loff_t pos);`

- `int (*aio_fsync) (struct kiocb *, int datasync);`

  These implement **asynchronous** methods for I/O. If not supplied, the kernel will always use the corresponding synchronous methods.

- `ssize_t (*sendfile) (struct file *filp, loff_t *offset, size_t, read_actor_t, void *);`

  Implements copying from one file descriptor to another without separate read and write operations, minimizing copying and the number of system calls made. Used only when copying a file through a socket. Unused by device drivers.

- `ssize_t (*sendpage) (struct file *filp, struct page *, int, size_t, loff_t *offset, int);`

  Inverse of `sendfile()`; used to send data (a page at a time) to a file. Unused by device drivers.

- `unsigned long (*get_unmapped_area) (struct file *filp, unsigned long, unsigned long, unsigned long, unsigned long);`

  Find an address region in the process's address space that can be used to map in a memory segment from the device. Not normally used in device drivers.

- `int (*check_flags)(int);`

  A method for parsing the flags sent to a driver through `fcntl()`.

- `int (*dir_notify) (struct file *filp, unsigned long arg);`

  Invoked when `fcntl()` is called to request directory change notifications. Not used in device drivers.

- `int (*flock) (struct file *, int, struct file_lock *);`

  Used for file locking; Not used in device drivers.

9.9 The file and inode Structures

- The `file` and `inode` data structures are defined in **/usr/src/linux/include/linux/fs.h**. Both are important in controlling both device nodes and normal files.

- The `file` structure has nothing to do with the `FILE` data structure used in the standard **C** library; it never appears in user-space programs.

- A new `file` structure is created whenever the `open()` call is invoked on the device, and gets passed to all functions that use the device node. This means there can be multiple `file` structures associated with a device simultaneously, as most devices permit multiple opens. The structure is released and the memory associated with it is freed during the `release()` call.

- Some important structure members:

Table 9.5: **file Structure Elements**

Field	Meaning
`struct path f_path`	Gives information about the file directory entry, including a pointer to the inode.
`const struct file_operations f_op`	Operations associated with the file. Can be changed when the method is invoked again.
`f_mode_t f_mode`	Identified by the bits `FMODE_READ` and `FMODE_WRITE`. Note the kernel checks permissions before invoking the driver.
`loff_t f_pos`	Current position in the file; a 64-bit value. While the final argument to the `read()` and `write()` entry points usually points to this, the `llseek()` entry should update `f_pos`, but the `read()` and `write()` entry points should update the argument. (Use of `f_pos` for this purpose is incorrect because the `pread()`, `pwrite()` system calls use the same read and write methods but do not have this linkage.)
`unsigned int f_flags`	`O_RDONLY`, `O_NONBLOCK`, `O_SYNC`, etc. Needs to be checked for non-blocking operations.
`void * private_data`	Can be used to point to allocated data. Can be used to preserve state information across system calls. The pointer to this is set to `NULL` before the `open()` call, so your driver can use this to point to whatever it wants, such as an allocated data structure. In this case you must remember to free the memory upon `release()`. Note there will be a unique instance of this structure for each time your device is opened.

- Note that a pointer to the `file_operations` structures lies inside the structure. To obtain a pointer to the `inode` structure you have to descend through the `f_path` element which is a structure of type:

```
struct path {
    struct vfsmount *mnt;
    struct dentry *dentry;
};
```

with the `inode` field contained in the `dentry` structure. So you'll often see references like:

```
struct file *f;
f->f_path.dentry->d_inode
```

- Unlike the `file` structure, there will only be one `inode` structure pointing to a given device node; each open descriptor (and corresponding internal `file` structure representation) on the device node will in turn to point to that same `inode` structure.

- While the `inode` structure contains all sorts of information about the file it points to, here it happens to be a device node, and very few of the fields are of interest for character drivers. Two of importance are:

Table 9.6: **inode structure elements**

Field	Meaning
dev_t i_rdev	Contains the actual device number from with the major and minor numbers can be extracted.
dev_t i_cdev	Points back to the basic character driver structure.

9.10 Miscellaneous Character Drivers

- For most simple character drivers it makes more sense to take advantage of the **misc** (for miscellaneous) character driver **API** which takes fewer lines of code and automatically interfaces with the **udev** system to create device nodes on the fly. Inventing your own class is rendered unnecessary.

- All misc drivers share the same major number (10) and can either request a specific minor number, or have one generated dynamically. The registration and de-registration functions, and the relevant data structure are defined in **/usr/src/linux/include/linux/miscdevice.h**:

```
#include <linux/miscdevice.h>

int misc_register(struct miscdevice * misc);
int misc_deregister(struct miscdevice *misc);

struct miscdevice  {
        int minor;
        const char *name;
        const struct file_operations *fops;
        struct list_head list;
        struct device *parent;
        struct device *this_device;
        const char *nodename;
        mode_t mode;
};
```

- One fills in the `miscdevice` structure and then calls the registration function when the device is loaded and the de-registration function when it is unloaded. Both of these functions return 0 on success and error codes on failure.

- Normally only three fields in the `miscdevice` structure are ever filled in as in:

```
static struct miscdevice my_misc_device = {
        .minor = MISC_DYNAMIC_MINOR,
        .name = MYDEV_NAME,
        .fops = &mycdrv_fops,
};
```

where by using `MISC_DYNAMIC_MINOR` we are asking the kernel to assign us a minor number, the `name` field gives our device node name (which will appear under the /dev directory) and `fops` is our usual file operations table.

- This is all a lot easier than filling out a full character driver.

9.11   Labs

Lab 1: Improving the Basic Character Driver

- Starting from **sample_driver.c**, extend it to:

    - Keep track of the number of times it has been opened since loading, and print out the counter every time the device is opened.

    - Print the major and minor numbers when the device is opened.

- To exercise your driver, write a program to read (and/or write) from the node, using the standard **Unix** I/O functions (`open()`, `read()`, `write()`, `close()`).

    After loading the module with **insmod** use this program to access the node.

- Track usage of the module by using **lsmod** (which is equivalent to typing `cat /proc/modules`.)

Lab 2: Private Data for Each Open

- Modify the previous driver so that each opening of the device allocates its own data area, which is freed upon release. Thus data will not be persistent across multiple opens.

Lab 3: Seeking and the End of the Device.

- Adapt one of the previous drivers to have the read and write entries watch out for going off the end of the device.

- Implement a `lseek()` entry point. See the **man** page for `lseek()` to see how return values and error codes should be specified.

- For an extra exercise, unset the `FMODE_LSEEK` bit to make any attempt to seek result in an error.

Lab 4: Dynamical Node Creation (I)

- Adapt one of the previous drivers to allocate the device major number dynamically.

- Write loading and unloading scripts that ascertain the major number assigned and make and remove the node as required.

Lab 5: Dynamical Node Creation (II)

- Adapt the previous dynamic registration driver to use **udev** to create the device node on the fly.

- A second solution is given which includes a header file (`lab_header.h`) which will be used to simplify the coding in subsequent character drivers we will write.

Lab 6: Using the misc API

- Implement your fullest driver from above with the **misc** API.

- Once again a second solution is given which includes the same header file previously used.

Chapter 10

Kernel Features

We'll profile the major components of the kernel, such as process and memory management, the handling of filesystems, device management and networking. We'll consider the differences between user and kernel modes. We'll consider the important task structure and review scheduling algorithms. Finally we'll consider the differences between when the kernel is in process context and when it is not.

10.1 Components of the Kernel

Process Management

- Creating and destroying processes.

- Input and output to processes.

- Inter-process communication (IPC) and signals and pipes.

- Scheduling.

Memory Management

- Build up a virtual addressing space for all processes.

KERNEL

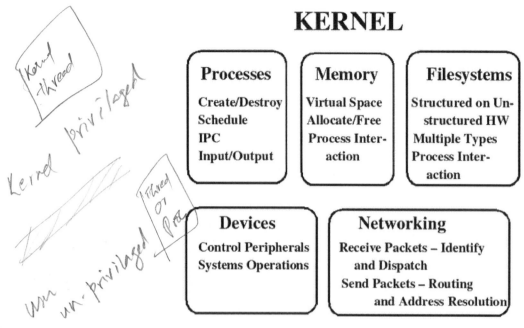

Figure 10.1: **Main Kernel Tasks**

- Allocating and freeing up memory.

- Process interaction with memory.

Filesystems

- Build structured filesystems on top of unstructured hardware.

- Use multiple filesystem types.

- Process interaction with filesystems.

Device Management

- Systems operations map to physical devices.

- **device drivers** control operations for virtually every peripheral and hardware component.

Networking

- Networking operations are not process specific; must be handled by the operating system.

- Incoming packets are asynchronous; must be collected, identified, dispatched.

- Processes must be put to sleep and wake for network data.

- The kernel also has to address routing and address resolution issues.

10.2 User-Space vs. Kernel-Space

Execution modes

- **user** mode

  Applications and daemons execute with limited privileges. (**Ring 3** on **x86**.) This is true even if the application has **root** privileges.

- **kernel** mode

  Kernel has direct, privileged access to hardware and memory. (**Ring 0** on **x86**.) Drivers (and modules) have kernel privileges.

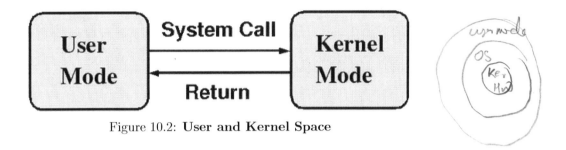

Figure 10.2: **User and Kernel Space**

- Execution is transferred from user mode (space) to kernel mode (space) through system calls (which are implemented using synchronous interrupts, or exceptions) and hardware interrupts (or asynchronous interrupts).

- The mode is a state of **each CPU** in a multi-processor system rather than the kernel itself, as each processor may be in a different execution mode.

- When running **virtualization** kernels the **hypervisor** runs in Ring 0, while the guest (client) kernels may run in Ring 0 or Ring 1 depending on the type of virtualization.

- If it is Ring 1 a certain amount of trickery and/or emulation is required to accomplish this.

10.3 Scheduling Algorithms and Task Structures

- **Scheduling** is arguably the most important work the kernel does.

- Tasks constantly switch back and forth between kernel mode and user mode (where they have lesser privileges.) Scheduling doesn't directly control these mode switches, but it does have to handle the context switching between different tasks.

- Under **Linux**, a task by itself can not **preempt** a current running task and take over; it must wait its turn for a *time-slice*. However, the scheduler can preempt one task to allow another to run.

- Tasks run until one of the following occurs:

- They need to wait for some system event to complete (such as reading a file.)

- The amount of time in their time-slice expires.

- The scheduler is invoked and finds a more deserving task to run.

- Additionally, the 2.6 kernel has compile-time options for a **preemptible** kernel; when configured this way even a single-processor system can behave much like a multi-processor one, and lower latency and preempt code even when it is in kernel mode. Thus all code which can be preempted this way must be fully re-entrant.

- A task's `task_struct` is the critical data structure under **Linux**, and contains all information the kernel knows about a task, and everything it needs to switch it in and out. It is sometimes called a **process descriptor**. It is defined in **/usr/src/linux/include/linux/sched.h**.

- The data structure of the current task (on the current CPU) can be referred to with the `current` macro; e.g., `current->tgid` is the current process ID and `current->pid` is the current task ID. (These can differ; for a multiple-threaded task each thread shares the same process ID but has a unique task (thread) ID.) This data structure contains information about signal handling, memory areas used by the process, parent and children tasks, etc.

- Within the kernel schedulable processes (or more precisely tasks, or threads) that run either in user or kernel-space are identified by pointers to a `task_struct`, not by a **pid**. One can always obtain such a pointer from a **pid** with:

  `struct task_struct *t = pid_task(find_vpid(pid),PIDTYPE_PID);`

  (Note that in a multi-threaded process this macro will locate the master thread, whose process identifier and thread identifier match.)

- One generally doesn't need to obtain this information from a module and race conditions can be a problem as **pid**'s can change during the lifetime of a process.

- While the `schedule()` function may be called directly (from kernel code, not user code), it is more likely reached through an indirect call such as: when the current task goes to sleep and is placed onto a **wait queue**; when a system call returns; just before a task returns to user mode from kernel mode; or after an interrupt is handled.

- When the scheduler runs it determines which task should occupy the CPU, and if it is a different task than the current one, arranges the context switch. It tries to keep tasks on the same CPU (to minimize cache thrashing). When a new task is chosen to run, the state of the current task is saved in its `task_struct` and then the new task is switched in and made the current one.

- The scheduler used before the 2.6.23 kernel was called the **O(1)** scheduler; the time required to make a scheduling decision was independent of the number of running tasks. It was designed to scale particularly well with **SMP** systems and those with many tasks. Separate queues were maintained for each CPU; these queues were kept in a priority-ordered fashion, so rather than having to tediously search through all tasks for the right task to run, the decision could be made through a quick bit-map consultation.

- The 2.6.23 kernel saw replacement of the **O(1)** scheduler with an entirely new algorithm, which drives the **CFS** (**C**ompletely **F**air **S**cheduler) scheduler.

- The completely fair time is the amount of time the task has been waiting to run, divided by the number of running tasks (with some weighting for varying priorities.) This time is compared with the actual time the task has received to determine the next task.

- **CFS** also includes hierarchical **scheduler modules**, each of which can be called in turn.

[handwritten notes in top margin: "tgid = thread group ID"; "parent .tgid = 6000 .pid = 6000"; "child .tgid = 6000 .pid = 6010"]

10.4 Process Context

- When the kernel executes code it always has full kernel privileges, and is obviously in kernel mode. However, there are distinct contexts it can be in.

- In **process context** the kernel is executing code on behalf of a process. Most likely, a **system call** has been invoked and caused entry into the kernel, at one of a finite number of entry points. Examples would be:

  - An application (or daemon) has issued a `read()` or `write()` request, either on a special device file, such as a serial port, or on a normal file residing on hardware to which the kernel has access to.

  - A request for memory has been made from user-space. Once again only the kernel can handle such a request.

  - A user process has made a system call like `getpriority()` to examine, or set, its priority, or `getpid()` to find out its process ID.

- When not in process context, the kernel is not working on behalf of any particular user process. Examples would be:

  - The kernel is servicing an **interrupt**. Requests to do so arrive on an **IRQ** line, usually in response to data arriving or being ready to send. For example a mouse click generates three or four interrupts. It is up to the kernel to decide what process may desire the data and it may have to wake it up to process the data.

  - The kernel is executing a task which has been scheduled to run at either a specific time or when convenient. Such a function may be queued up through a kernel timer, a tasklet or another kind of **softirq**.

  - The kernel is initializing, shutting down, or running the scheduler.

- At such times the process context is not defined; although references to the `current task_struct` may not yield obvious errors, they are meaningless. Sometimes this situation is called **interrupt** context, but as we have seen it can arise even when no interrupts are involved.

- The kernel context has a **lighter weight** than that of a user process; swapping in and out between kernel threads is significantly easier and faster than it is for full weight processes.

- **Linux** also deploys many so-called **kernel processes**, which are much like user processes but which are run directly by the kernel.

- Such pseudo-processes are used to execute management threads, such as the ones maintaining the buffer and page caches, which have to synchronize the contents of files on disk with memory areas. Other examples are the **ksoftirqd** and **kjournald** threads; do `ps aux` and look at processes whose names are surrounded by square brackets.

- These processes are scheduled like normal processes and are allowed to sleep. However, they do not have a true process context and thus can not transfer data back and forth with user-space. In fact they all share the same memory space and switching between them is relatively fast.

- You can examine what context you are in with the macros:

```
in_irq();       /* in hardware interrupt context    */
in_softirq();   /* in software interrupt context (bh)*/
in_interrupt(); /* in either hard/soft irq context  */
in_atomic();    /* in preemption-disabled context   */
```

- Sleeping is disallowed if any of these macros evaluate as true.

10.5   Labs

Lab 1: Using strace.

- **strace** is used to trace system calls and signals. In the simplest case you would do:

  ```
  $ strace [options] command [arguments]
  ```

- Each system call, its arguments and return value are printed. According to the man page:

- *"Arguments are printed in symbolic form with a passion."*

  and indeed they are. There are a lot of options; read the man page!

- As an example, try

  ```
  $ strace ls -lRF / 2>&1 | less
  ```

  You need the complicated redirection because **strace** puts its output on `stderr` unless you use the `-o` option to redirect it to a file.

- While this is running (paused under **less**), you can examine more details about the **ls** process, by examining the **/proc** filesystem. Do

  ```
  $ ps aux | grep ls
  ```

  to find out the process ID associated with the process. Then you can look at the pseudo-files

  ```
  /proc/<pid>/fd/*
  ```

  to see how the file descriptors are mapped to the underlying files (or pipes), etc.

IRQ Actions:
Disable processing IRQ's:] *short*
Enable processing IRQ's:

Chapter 11

Interrupts and Exceptions

We'll take a detailed look at how the **Linux** kernel handles synchronous interrupts (exceptions) and asynchronous interrupts. We'll consider message-signalled interrupts (**MSI**). We'll show how to enable/disable interrupts. We'll have a discussion of what you can and can not do when in interrupt context. We'll consider the main data structures associated with interrupts and show how to install an interrupt handler, or service routine. Finally we'll discuss in detail what has to be done in the top and bottom halves of such functions.

11.1 What are Interrupts and Exceptions?

- An **interrupt** alters (interrupts) the instruction sequence followed by a processor. It is always connected with an electrical signal stemming from either inside or outside the processor.

- When an interrupt arrives the kernel must suspend the thread it is currently executing, deal with it by invoking one or more **service routines** (**ISR**) (or **handlers**) assigned to the specific interrupt, and then return to the suspended thread, or service another interrupt.

- Under **Linux**, interrupts should never be lost; the service routines may be delayed according to various locking mechanisms and priorities, but will be invoked eventually. However, interrupts are not queued up; only one interrupt of a given type will be serviced, although if another interrupt of the same type arrives while it is being serviced, it too will be serviced in turn.

- There are two distinct kinds of interrupts:

  - **Synchronous** interrupts, often called **exceptions**, are generated by the CPU.
  - **Asynchronous** interrupts, often just called **interrupts**, are generated by other hardware devices, and are generally fed through the **APIC** (**A**dvanced **P**rogrammable **I**nterrupt **C**ontroller.)

- **Exceptions** may be caused by run time errors such as division by zero, or by special conditions such as a page fault. They may also be caused by certain instructions, such as the one a system call can make to request the CPU enter kernel mode to service a request from user-land. They may occur in or out of process context. They often cause a signal to be sent to one or more processes.

- **Interrupts** generally arise from relatively random events such as a mouse click, keyboard press, a packet of data arriving on a network card, etc, or more regular events such as a timer interrupt. They are never associated with a process context.

- Interrupts are very similar to signals; one might say interrupts are hardware signals, or signals are software interrupts. The general lessons of efficient and safe signal handling apply equally well to interrupts.

- Handling interrupts is one of the most difficult tasks incurred by device drivers. It requires careful design to avoid race conditions and problems with non-reentrant code.

- Under **Linux** interrupts may be shared, and when an interrupt is shared, all handlers for that interrupt must agree to share. Each of them will receive the interrupt in turn; i.e., there is no **consumption** of the interrupt by one of the handlers.

11.2   Asynchronous Interrupts

- There are two kind of asynchronous interrupts:

  - **Maskable** interrupts are sent to the **INTR** microprocessor pin. They can be disabled by appropriate flags set in the **eflags** register.
  - **Nonmaskable** interrupts are sent to the **NMI** microprocessor pin. They can not be disabled and when they occur there is usually a critical hardware failure.

- Any device which issues interrupts has an **IRQ** (**I**nterrupt **ReQ**uest) line, which is connected to an **APIC** (**A**dvanced **P**rogrammable **I**nterrupt **C**ircuit.)

- On the **x86** architecture one has a **Local APIC** integrated into each CPU. Additionally one has an **I/O APIC** used through the system's peripheral buses.

- On **ARM** there are **IRQ** and **FIQ** (**F**ast **IRQ**) lines. The **IRQ** line is typically extended by an interrupt controller: e.g. **GIC** (**G**eneric **I**nterrupt **C**ontroller) **http://infocenter.arm.com/help/index.jsp?topic=/com.arm.doc.ihi0048b/index.html**.

- On **ARM** processors (e.g. **Cortex-A8**) there is a fixed priority system for exceptions (see **http://infocenter.arm.com/help/topic/com.arm.doc.ddi0344k/Beigaeaj.html**.)

- The **I/O APIC** routes interrupts to individual **Local APIC**s, according to a redirection table that it keeps.

- The **Local APIC** constantly monitors the IRQ lines it is responsible for and when it finds a signal has been raised:

- Notes which **IRQ** is involved.

- Stores it in an I/O port it owns so it can be read on the data bus.

- Issues an interrupt by sending a signal to its INTR pin.

- When the CPU acknowledges the IRQ by writing back into a controller I/O port it clears the INTR pin.

- Goes back to waiting for a new interrupt to arrive.

- A list of currently installed IRQ handlers can be obtained from the command cat **/proc/interrupts**, which gives something like:

```
         CPU0    CPU1    CPU2    CPU3
   0:     129       1       2       1   IO-APIC-edge      timer
   1:     722      12      40      32   IO-APIC-edge      i8042
   8:       0       0       0       1   IO-APIC-edge      rtc0
   9:       0       0       0       0   IO-APIC-fasteoi   acpi
  16:    1546     948     102      90   IO-APIC-fasteoi   uhci_hcd:usb3, pata_marvell, nvidia
  18:   16287      10      14   18141   IO-APIC-fasteoi   eth0, ehci_hcd:usb1, uhci_hcd:usb5,
                                                         uhci_hcd:usb8
  19:       2       1       1       0   IO-APIC-fasteoi   uhci_hcd:usb7, ohci1394
  21:       0       0       0       0   IO-APIC-fasteoi   uhci_hcd:usb4
  22:     534     151    4510    2284   IO-APIC-fasteoi   HDA Intel
  23:   44436   38789    4644    4122   IO-APIC-fasteoi   ehci_hcd:usb2, uhci_hcd:usb6
  28:       0       0       1       0   PCI-MSI-edge      eth1
  29:   17358    2567   18150   17191   PCI-MSI-edge      ahci
 NMI:       0       0       0       0   Non-maskable interrupts
 LOC:  255559   16184  147985  131046   Local timer interrupts
 SPU:       0       0       0       0   Spurious interrupts
 RES:    1849    1183    1520    1158   Rescheduling interrupts
 CAL:     340     475     475     450   Function call interrupts
 TLB:    1773    2734    1720    2689   TLB shootdowns
 TRM:       0       0       0       0   Thermal event interrupts
 THR:       0       0       0       0   Threshold APIC interrupts
 ERR:       0
 MIS:       0
```

- Note that the numbers here are the number of times the interrupt line has fired since boot. Only currently installed handlers are listed. If a handler is unregistered (say through unloading a module) and then it or another handler is later re-registered, the number will not be zeroed in the process.

- You will also notice two types of interrupts:

  - **Level**-triggered interrupts respond to an electrical signal (generally a voltage) having a certain value.

  - **Edge**-triggered interrupts respond to a change in electrical signal, which can be either up or down.

  In principle one could miss a level-triggered interrupt if it is cleared somehow before the change in condition is noticed.

- On **SMP** systems interrupts may be serviced on any available CPU (although affinities can be mandated), but only one CPU will handle an interrupt of a certain kind at the same time.

- It is sometimes advantageous to set **IRQ**-affinity; to force particular interrupts to be dealt with only some subset of all the CPUs, rather than being distributed roughly equally.

- This is done by accessing /proc/irq/IRQ#/smp_affinity. One can not turn off all CPUs in the mask, and won't work if the physical **IRQ** controller doesn't have the capability to support an affinity selection.

- The **irqbalance** daemon dynamically adjusts the **IRQ** affinity in response to system conditions. It takes into account performance (latency and cache coherence) and power consumption (keeping **CPUs** no more active than necessary when system load is light.)

- There was also an in-kernel **IRQ**-balancing option, but this was deprecated and finally removed in kernel version 2.6.29 in favor of the user-space solution. Full documentation about the daemon method can be found at **http://www.irqbalance.org**.

11.3   MSI

- In pre-**PCI-e** (PCI-express) buses interrupts are **line-based** and are now considered as legacy technology. The external pins that signal interrupts are wired separately from the bus main lines, producing **out of band** signalling.

- **PCI-e** maintains compatibility with older software by emulating this legacy behaviour with **in-band** methods, but these are still limited to only four lines and often require sharing of interrupts among devices.

- The **PCI** 2.2 standard added a new mechanism known as **MSI** (for Message-Signalled Interrupts), which was further enhanced in the **PCI** 3.0 standard to become **MSI-X**, which is backward compatible with **MSI**.

- Under **MSI** devices send 16-bit **messages** to specified memory addresses by sending an inbound memory write to the front side bus (**FSB**). The message value is opaque to the device but delivery generates an interrupt. The message is not acknowledged, and thus we get an edge-triggered interrupt.

- Under **MSI** each device can use up to 32 addresses and thus interrupts, although the operating system may not be able to use them all. The address is the same for each message, but they are distinguished by modifying low bits of the message data.

- Under **MSI-X** the messages become 32-bit and up to 2048 individual messages can be sent for each device. Each **MSI-X** interrupt uses a different address and data value (unlike in **MSI**).

- There are important advantages of using message-signalled interrupts. First, the device no longer has to compete for a limited number of **IRQ** lines; thus there is no need to share. Interrupt latency is therefore potentially reduced and getting rid of sharing also makes behaviour more predictable and less variable.

- **MSI** is optional for **PCI** 2.3 compliant devices and mandatory for PCI-Express devices. Support for **MSI** and **MSI-X** must be configured in the kernel to use them; only one standard can be used in a particular driver at a time.

- Details about the **Linux** implementation are given in **/usr/src/linux/Documentation/PCI/MSI-HOWTO.txt**, which contains details about the **API** and enumerates important considerations.

11.4   Enabling/Disabling Interrupts

- Sometimes it is useful for a driver to enable and disable interrupt reporting for an IRQ line. The functions for doing this are:

```
#include <asm/irq.h>
#include <linux/interrupt.h>

void disable_irq (int irq);
void disable_irq_nosync (int irq);
void enable_irq (int irq);
```

These actions are effective only for the CPU on which they are called; other processors continue to process the disabled interrupt.

- Because the kernel automatically disables an interrupt before calling its service routine and enables it again when done, it makes no sense to use these functions within the handler servicing a particular IRQ.

- Calling `disable_irq()` ensures any presently executing interrupt handler completes before the disabling occurs, while `disable_irq_nosync()` will return instantly. While this is faster, race conditions may result. The first form is safe from within IRQ context; the second form is dangerous. However, the first form can lead to deadlock if it is used while a resource is being held that the handler may need; the second form may permit the resource to be freed.

- It is important to notice that the enable/disable functions have a depth; if `disable_irq()` has been called twice, `enable_irq()` will have to be called twice before interrupts are handled again.

- It is also possible to disable/enable all interrupts, in order to protect critical sections of code. This is best done with the appropriate **spinlock** functions:

```
unsigned long flags;
spinlock_t my_lock;
spinlock_init (&my_lock);
...
spin_lock_irqsave(&my_lock,flags);
...... critical code ........
spin_unlock_irqrestore(&my_lock,flags);
```

- You should be very careful with the use of these functions as you can paralyze the system.

11.5   What You Cannot Do at Interrupt Time

- Interrupts do not run in process context. Thus you cannot refer to `current` to access the fields of the `task_struct` as they are ill-defined at best. Usually `current` will point to whatever process was running when the interrupt service routine was entered, which has no *a priori* connection to the IRQ.

- Anything which blocks can cause a kernel freeze, at least on the processor that blocks. In particular you cannot call `schedule()` or use any of the **sleep** functions, directly or indirectly. Indirect usage would happen for instance if you try to allocate memory with the flag `GFP_KERNEL` which can block if memory is not currently available, so you have to use `GFP_ATOMIC` instead.

- You can neither take out nor release a **mutex**.

- You cannot do a `down()` call on a **semaphore** as it can block while waiting for a resource. However, you can do an `up()` or any kind of `wake_up()` call.

- You cannot request loading a module with `request_module()`.

- You cannot transfer any data to or from a process's address space; i.e., no use of the `get_user()`, `put_user()`, `copy_to_user()`, `copy_from_user()` functions. Not only do these functions have the potential to go to sleep, but because there is no real user context one also can not transfer data to and from user-space using these functions.

11.6   IRQ Data Structures

- The basic data structures involving IRQ's are defined in **/usr/src/linux/include/linux/irqdesc.h**
  and **/usr/src/linux/include/linux/interrupt.h**.

- For each IRQ there is a **descriptor** defined as:

```
3.0:  39 struct irq_desc {
3.0:  40         struct irq_data          irq_data;
3.0:  41         struct timer_rand_state *timer_rand_state;
3.0:  42         unsigned int __percpu   *kstat_irqs;
3.0:  43         irq_flow_handler_t       handle_irq;
3.0:  44 #ifdef CONFIG_IRQ_PREFLOW_FASTEOI
3.0:  45         irq_preflow_handler_t    preflow_handler;
3.0:  46 #endif
3.0:  47         struct irqaction        *action;         /* IRQ action list */
3.0:  48         unsigned int             status_use_accessors;
3.0:  49         unsigned int             core_internal_state__do_not_mess_with_it;
3.0:  50         unsigned int             depth;          /* nested irq disables */
3.0:  51         unsigned int             wake_depth;     /* nested wake enables */
3.0:  52         unsigned int             irq_count;      /* For detecting broken IRQs */
3.0:  53         unsigned long            last_unhandled; /* Aging timer for unhandled count */
3.0:  54         unsigned int             irqs_unhandled;
3.0:  55         raw_spinlock_t           lock;
3.0:  56 #ifdef CONFIG_SMP
3.0:  57         const struct cpumask    *affinity_hint;
3.0:  58         struct irq_affinity_notify *affinity_notify;
3.0:  59 #ifdef CONFIG_GENERIC_PENDING_IRQ
3.0:  60         cpumask_var_t            pending_mask;
3.0:  61 #endif
3.0:  62 #endif
3.0:  63         unsigned long            threads_oneshot;
3.0:  64         atomic_t                 threads_active;
3.0:  65         wait_queue_head_t        wait_for_threads;
3.0:  66 #ifdef CONFIG_PROC_FS
3.0:  67         struct proc_dir_entry   *dir;
3.0:  68 #endif
3.0:  69         const char              *name;
3.0:  70 } ____cacheline_internodealigned_in_smp;
```

- status can be one of the following values:

Table 11.1: **IRQ Status Values**

Value	Meaning
IRQ_INPROGRESS	The handler for this IRQ handler is currently being executed.
IRQ_DISABLED	The IRQ line has been disabled.
IRQ_PENDING	An IRQ has occurred and been acknowledged, but not yet serviced.
IRQ_REPLAY	The IRQ line has been disabled but the previous occurrence on this line has not yet been acknowledged.
IRQ_AUTODETECT	The kernel is trying auto-detection on this IRQ line.
IRQ_WAITING	The kernel is trying auto-detection on this IRQ line and no interrupts have yet been detected.
IRQ_LEVEL	The IRQ line is level-triggered.
IRQ_MASKED	The IRQ line is masked and shouldn't be seen again.

IRQ_PER_CPU	The IRQ is per CPU.

- `action` lists the service routines associated with the IRQ; the element points to the first `irqaction` structure in the list. We'll describe this structure in detail.

- `depth` is 0 if the IRQ line is enabled. A positive value indicates how many times it has been disabled. Each `disable_irq()` increments the counter and each `enable_irq()` decrements it until it reaches 0 at which point it enables it. Thus this counter is used as a semaphore.

- `lock` is used to prevent race conditions.

- The `irqaction` structure looks like:

```
3.0: 106 struct irqaction {
3.0: 107     irq_handler_t handler;
3.0: 108     unsigned long flags;
3.0: 109     void *dev_id;
3.0: 110     struct irqaction *next;
3.0: 111     int irq;
3.0: 112     irq_handler_t thread_fn;
3.0: 113     struct task_struct *thread;
3.0: 114     unsigned long thread_flags;
3.0: 115     unsigned long thread_mask;
3.0: 116     const char *name;
3.0: 117     struct proc_dir_entry *dir;
3.0: 118 } ____cacheline_internodealigned_in_smp;
```

- `handler` points to the interrupt service routine, or handler, that is triggered when the interrupt arrives. We'll discuss the arguments later.

- `flags` is a mask of the following main values:

Table 11.2: **IRQ Handler Flags**

Flag	Meaning
IRQF_DISABLED	The handler runs with interrupts disabled; i.e., it is a **fast** handler.
IRQF_SHARED	The IRQ may be shared with other devices, if they **all** mutually agree to it.
IRQF_SAMPLE_RANDOM	The IRQ line may contribute to the **entropy pool** which the system uses to generate random numbers which are used for purposes like encryption. This should not be turned on for interrupts which arrive at predictable times.
IRQF_PROBE_SHARED	Set when sharing mismatches are expected to occur.
IRQF_TIMER	Set to indicate this is a timer interrupt handler.
IRQF_NOBALANCING	Set to exclude this interrupt from irq balancing.
IRQF_IRQPOLL	Interrupt is used for polling (only the interrupt that is registered first in an shared interrupt is considered for performance reasons)

(There are some other possibilities; see **/usr/src/linux/include/linux/interrupt.h**.)

- Note that if the IRQ line is being shared, the `IRQF_DISABLED` flag will be effective only if it is specified on the first handler registered for that IRQ line.

- `mask` indicates which interrupts are blocked while running.

- `name` points to the identifier that will appear in **/proc/interrupts**.

- `dev_id` points to a unique identifier in the address space of the device driver (or kernel subsystem) that has registered the IRQ. It is used as a **cookie** to distinguish among handlers for shared IRQ's and is important for making sure the right handler is deregistered when a request is made. Device drivers often have it point to a data structure which the handler routine will have access to. If the IRQ is not being shared, `NULL` can be used.

- `next` points to the next `irqaction` structure in the chain that are sharing the same IRQ.

Kernel Version Note

Kernel Version Note

- The `IRQF_DISABLED` flag has been deprecated for quite a while and as of kernel 2.6.35 it no longer has any effect.

11.7   Installing an Interrupt Handler

- Normally device drivers do not directly access the data structures we just described. Instead they use the following functions to install and uninstall interrupt handlers:

```
#include <linux/interrupt.h>

int request_irq (unsigned int irq,
    irqreturn_t (*handler)(int irq, void *dev_id),
    unsigned long flags,
    const char *device,
    void *dev_id);
void synchronize_irq (unsigned int irq);
void free_irq (unsigned int irq, void *dev_id);
```

- `irq` is the interrupt number.

- `handler()` is the handler to be installed.

- `flags` is the same bit-mask of options we described before; i.e., `IRQF_DISABLED` etc. Requesting sharing when the IRQ has been already registered as non-sharing may generate verbose but harmless debugging messages.

- **device** is the same as the **name** field in the **irqaction** structure; it sets the identifier appearing in **/proc/interrupts**:

- **dev_id** is the same unique identifier used for shared IRQ lines that appeared in the **irqaction** structure. It is often used as a private data area to be passed to the handler routine.

- The **handler()** function has two arguments:

  - **irq** is useful if more than one IRQ is being serviced.
  - **dev_id** is used for shared interrupts and can also be used as a private data pointer.

Kernel Version Note   Kernel Version Note

- Kernels earlier than 2.6.19 contained a third argument, a data structure of type **pt_regs**, which holds a snapshot of the processor's context before the interrupt. It is used mostly for debugging, and for restoring the register state after the interrupt is handled. The precise definition of this structure is CPU-dependent; see **/usr/src/linux/arch/arm/include/asm/ptrace.h**.

- The **pt_regs** argument was removed in the 2.6.19 kernel, as it was rarely used in drivers, and eliminating it saved stack space and code, and boosted performance somewhat.

- If access to this structure should happen to be needed, the inline function **struct pt_regs *regs = get_irq_regs()**; can be used.

- **request_irq()** can be called either upon device initialization or when the device is first used (**open()**). Before the introduction of **udev** it often was better to do it in **open()** when the device was first used. However, with **udev** one doesn't tend to pre-load devices. This function should be called **before** the device is sent an instruction to enable generation of interrupts.

- **free_irq()** can be called either during cleanup or **release()** (close). This function should be called only after the device is instructed not to interrupt the CPU anymore.

- Before calling **free_irq()** one should call **synchronize_irq()** which ensures that all handlers for this particular **IRQ** are finished running before the free request is made. One should be careful that this function does not block.

- The interrupt handler returns a value of type **irqreturn_t**. The three possible return values and a convenience macro are:

Table 11.5: **IRQ Handler Return Values**

Return Value	Meaning
IRQ_NONE	The handler didn't recognize the event; i.e., it was due to some other device sharing the interrupt, or it was spurious.
IRQ_HANDLED	The handler recognized the event and did whatever was required.
IRQ_WAKE_THREAD	Used for **threaded interrupt handlers**, to be discussed later.
IRQ_RETVAL(x)	Evaluates as IRQ_HANDLED if the argument is non-zero; IRQ_NONE otherwise.

- If no registered handler returns IRQ_HANDLED for a given IRQ, it is assumed to be spurious and a warning messaged is printed. Note that there is still no **consumption** of interrupts; all registered handlers are still called for a given IRQ line, even if one or more of them claims to have handled the event.

11.8   Labs

Lab 1: Shared Interrupts

- Write a module that shares its IRQ with your network card. You can generate some network interrupts either by browsing or pinging. (If you have trouble with the network driver, try using the mouse interrupt.)

- Check /proc/interrupts while it is loaded.

- Have the module keep track of the number of times the interrupt handler gets called.

Lab 2: Sharing All Interrupts

- Extend the previous solution to construct a character driver that shares every possible interrupt with already installed handlers.

- The highest interrupt number you have to consider will depend on your kernel and platform; look at **/proc/interrupts** to ascertain what is necessary.

- Take particular care when you call free_irq() as it is very easy to freeze your system if you are not careful.

- The character driver can be very simple; for instance if no open() and release() methods are specified, success is the default.

- A read() on the device should return a brief report on the total number of interrupts handled for each **IRQ**.

- To do this you'll also have to write a short application to retrieve and print out the data. (Don't forget to create the device node before you run the application.)

Chapter 12

Timing and Timers

We'll consider the various methods **Linux** uses to manage time. We'll see how **jiffies** are defined and used, and how delays and timing are implemented. We'll discuss **kernel timers**, showing how they are used and how they are implemented in the **Linux** kernel. We'll also discuss the **hrtimers** feature and its high resolution implementation.

12.1 Jiffies

- A coarse time measurement is given by the variable `unsigned long volatile jiffies` defined in **/usr/src/linux/include/linux/jiffies.h**

- Before kernel 2.6.21 `jiffies` was simply a counter that is incremented with every timer interrupt. However, with the the incorporation of `tickless` kernels one need not keep processing timer interrupts when the system is idle. (For full details, see **http://www.lesswatts.org/projects/tickless**.)

- The default frequency is `HZ = 1000` on the **x86**, but is configurable at compile time, within a range of `HZ=100` to `HZ=1000`. Thus we obtain a resolution between 10 and 1 milliseconds for the `jiffies` value.

- On **ARM** the default timer frequency varies for different **SoC**'s. **OMAP2plus** has `HZ` set to 128, **DOVE** to 100 and **EXYNOS4** to 200.

- With `HZ=1000` jiffies will overflow (and wrap) at about 50 days of uptime; if someone has been sloppy, what will happen then is unpredictable. However, if you are writing kernel code it is unlikely you will reach that long an uptime.

- To help avoid any potential problems, the `jiffies` value is set during boot to `INITIAL_JIFFIES = -300 HZ`, which causes the value to wrap after five minutes. As a side effect you may notice that the value of `jiffies` differs from the number of timer interrupts read from `/proc/interrupts` by the same value. (Tickless kernels also break this equality.)

- Useful macros to compare relative `jiffies` values are:

```
time_after(a,b)
time_before(a,b)
time_after_eq(a,b)
time_before_eq(a,b)
```

  where the first one is true if time `a` is after time `b`, and the second one is the inverse macro. The other two macros also check for equality.

- Note that there exists a variable named `jiffies_64`. On 64-bit platforms this is the same as `jiffies`; on 32-bit platforms `jiffies` points to its lower 32 bits. Since `jiffies_64` won't wrap for almost 600 million years (with `HZ=1000`), one need not worry about it doing so.

- One has to be careful when using the 64-bit counter (on 32-bit platforms) as access to the value is not atomic; to do so one needs to use

```
u64 get_jiffies_64(void);
```

  to read the value. (Note you never **set** a value of course.)

- A number of macros are provided to convert `jiffies` back and forth to other ways of specifying time:

```
#include <linux/jiffies.h>

unsigned long timespec_to_jiffies (struct timespec *val);
void jiffies_to_timespec (unsigned long jiffies, struct timespec *val);

unsigned long timeval_to_jiffies (struct timeval *val);
void jiffies_to_timeval (unsigned long jiffies, struct timeval *val);

unsigned int  jiffies_to_msecs (const unsigned long j);
unsigned int  jiffies_to_usecs (const unsigned long j);
unsigned long msecs_to_jiffies (const unsigned int m);
unsigned long usecs_to_jiffies (const unsigned int u);
```

  where the `timeval` and `timespec` structures should be familiar from user-space:

```
struct timeval {
  long    tv_sec;  /* seconds */
  long    tv_usec; /* microseconds */
};
struct timespec {
  long    tv_sec;  /* seconds */
  long    tv_nsec; /* nanoseconds */
};
```

- The use of `jiffies` is gradually becoming less and less with the view that time is better expressed in actual time units such as seconds, milliseconds, nanoseconds, etc.

12.2 Inserting Delays

- While **jiffies** can be used to introduce busy waiting, e.g.,

```
#include <linux/sched.h>

jifdone = jiffies + delay * HZ;
while ( time_before(jiffies,jifdone) )
  {
    /* do nothing */
  }
```

this is an idiotic thing to do; because `jiffies` is volatile, it is reread every time it is accessed. Thus this loop locks the CPU during the delay (except that interrupts may be serviced.)

- For short delays, one can use the following functions:

```
#include <linux/delay.h>

void ndelay(unsigned long nanoseconds);
void udelay(unsigned long microseconds);
void mdelay(unsigned long milliseconds);
```

One should not expect true nanosecond resolution for `ndelay()`; depending on the hardware it will probably be closer to microseconds.

- Another delaying method which does not involve busy waiting is to use the functions:

```
void msleep (unsigned int milliseconds);
unsigned long msleep_interruptible (unsigned int milliseconds);
```

If `msleep_interruptible()` returns before the sleep has finished (because of a signal) it returns the number of milliseconds left in the requested sleep period.

12.3 What are Dynamic Timers?

- **Dynamic timers** (also known as **kernel timers**) are used to delay a function's execution until a specified time interval has elapsed. The function will be run on the CPU on which it is submitted.

- Because a CPU may not be immediately available when it is time to execute the function, you are guaranteed only that the function will not run before the timer expires; practically speaking this means it should occur at most a clock tick afterwards, unless some greedy high latency task has been suspending interrupts.

- While an explicit periodic scheduling function does not exist, it is trivial to make a timer function re-install itself recursively.

- The function will not be run in a process context; it will run as a **softirq** in an atomic context. Thus one cannot do anything which can not be done at **interrupt time**; i.e., no transfer of data back and forth with user-space, no memory allocation with GFP_KERNEL, no use of semaphores, etc., as these methods can go to sleep.

12.4 Timer Functions

- The important data structure and functions used by kernel timers are:

```
#include <linux/timer.h>

struct timer_list {
    struct list_head entry;
    unsigned long expires;
    void (*function)(unsigned long);
    unsigned long data;
    struct tvec_t_base_s *base;
};

void init_timer (struct timer_list *timer);
void add_timer  (struct timer_list *timer);
void mod_timer  (struct timer_list *timer, unsigned long expires);
int  del_timer  (struct timer_list *timer);
int  del_timer_sync (struct timer_list *timer);
```

- In this structure **entry** points to the doubly-linked circular list of kernel timers; it should never be touched directly. The **expires** field in measured in **jiffies** and is an absolute value, not a relative one. The function to be run is passed as **function()** and data can be passed to it through the pointer argument **data**.

- The **init_timer()** function zeroes the previous and next pointers in the linked list and must be called before a timer is queued up.

- The **add_timer()** function inserts the timer into the global timer list; The **mod_timer()** function can be used to reset the time at which a timer expires.

- **del_timer()** can remove a timer before it expires. It returns 1 if it deletes the timer, or 0 if it's too late because the timer function has already started executing. It is not necessary to call **del_timer()** if the timer expires on its own.

- **del_timer_sync()** makes sure that upon return the timer function is not running on another CPU, and helps avoid race conditions and is usually preferable.

- A timer can reinstall itself to set up a periodic timer. This can be done in either of two ways:

```
....
init_timer(&t);
t.expires= jiffies + delay;
add_timer(&t);
```

or

```
....
mod_timer(&t, jiffies+delay);
```

which is often done as a more compact form. Note that it is very important to reinitialize the timer when reinstalling; `mod_timer()` does this under the hood.

Example:

```
static struct timer_list my_timer;

init_timer(&my_timer);
my_timer.function = my_function;
my_timer.expires = jiffies+ticks;
my_timer.data = &my_data;

add_timer(&my_timer);
....
del_timer(&my_timer);
....
void my_function(unsigned long var){ };
```

12.5   Timer Implementation

- The implementation of dynamic timers has to take care of two distinct tasks:

  - Functions have to be inserted in and removed from the list of timers, or have the expiration times modified.
  - Functions have to be executed at the proper time.

- The simplest implementation would be to maintain one linked list of kernel timers, and add the newly requested timer function into the list either at the tail, or in some kind of sorted fashion, and then when the kernel decides to run any scheduled timer functions, scan the list and run those whose time value has expired.

- However, this would be quite inefficient. There may be many, even thousands, of functions whose expiration times might need to be scanned, and the kernel would be strangled by this task. Sorting might help the scanning process, but it would be paid for by expensive insertion and deletion operations.

- **Linux** has implemented a very clever method in which it actually maintains 512 doubly-linked circular lists, so that the `next` and `prev` fields in the `timer_list` struct point only within one of the lists at any given time. Which list depends on the value of the `expires` field.

- These lists are further partitioned into 5 groups:

Table 12.2: **Timer Groups**

Group	Ticks	Time (for HZ=1000)
tv1	< 256	$< .256$ secs
tv2	$< 2^{14}$	< 16.4 secs
tv3	$< 2^{20}$	< 17.5 mins
tv4	$< 2^{26}$	18.6 hrs
tv5	$< \infty$	$< \infty$

- The **tv1** group has a vector of 256 doubly-linked lists, set up so those in the first list will expire in the next timer tick, those in the second group will expire on the tick after that, and so on. Likewise, the **tv2-5** groups each have a vector of 64 doubly-linked lists, ordered in time groups.

- Each time there is a timer tick, an index into the **tv1** list of vectors is incremented by one, and the timer functions which need to be launched are all in one doubly-linked list. When this index reaches 256, the function cascade_timers() gets called, which brings the first group of **tv2** in to replenish **tv1**, the first group of **tv3** in to replenish **tv2**, etc.

12.6   High Resolution Timers

- The **Linux** kernel approach to dynamic timer implementation, while being quite clever and efficient, received a great enhancement with the addition of a new approach, gradually introduced since the 2.6.16 kernel

- We begin with the observation that there are really two kind of dynamic timers:

  - **Timeout** functions, found primarily in networking code and device drivers, used to signal when an event does not happen within a specified window of time, and either a task should be dropped or a recovery action initiated.

  - **Timer** functions, expected to actually run within a specified latency and sequence.

- Timeout functions tend to be far more numerous than timer ones, and thus in the present dynamic timer implementation, removal of a timer before it runs is far more frequent than actually running the function.

- Timeout functions generally have only a weak precision requirement, while (in principle at least) timer functions may have more stringent needs.

- The original implementation works very well for timeout functions, particularly because it does such a rapid job of timer removal, since only an index look up is required, and jiffies-level accuracy is generally fine.

- The **hrtimers** (High Resolution Timers) **API** is designed for dynamic timers actually expected to execute.

- Rather than having a complex set of lists, there is only one list (per CPU) sorted by time of expiration, using a red-black tree algorithm. While insertion and removal may be somewhat slower than in the original method, there will be no need for a cascade operation and there are fewer elements in the list.

- Expiration periods for the **hrtimers** are be expressed in nanoseconds rather than jiffies.

12.7 Using High Resolution Timers

- The **hrtimers** feature required introduction of a new (and opaque) `ktime_t` which measures time with nanosecond resolution if the particular architecture can support it. The internal representation of `ktime_t` is quite different on 64-bit and 32-bit platforms and should not be monkeyed with.

- Functions for dealing with this new time variable are contained in **/usr/src/linux/include/linux/ ktime.h** and don't require much explanation:

```
#include <linux/ktime.h>

ktime_t ktime_set (const long secs, const unsigned long nsecs);
ktime_t ktime_add (const ktime_t kt1, const ktime_t kt2);
ktime_t ktime_sub (const ktime_t kt1, const ktime_t kt2);
ktime_t ktime_add_ns (const ktime_t kt, u64 ns);
ktime_t ktime_get (void) /* monotonic time */
ktime_t ktime_get_real (void) /* real (wall) time */

ktime_t timespec_to_ktime (const struct timespec tspec);
ktime_t timeval_to_ktime (const struct timeval tval);
struct timespec ktime_to_timespec (const ktime_t kt);
struct timeval ktime_to_timeval (const ktime_t kt);
u64 ktime_to_ns (const ktime_t kt);
```

- The high resolution timers are controlled with the functions defined in **/usr/src/linux/include/linux/ hrtimer.h**:

```
#include <linux/hrtimer.h>

void hrtimer_init    (struct hrtimer *timer, clockid_t which_clock, enum hrtimer_mode mode);
int hrtimer_start    (struct hrtimer *timer, ktime_t time, enum hrtimer_mode mode);
unsigned long hrtimer_forward(struct hrtimer *timer, ktime_t now, ktime_t interval);

int hrtimer_cancel        (struct hrtimer *timer);
int hrtimer_try_to_cancel (struct hrtimer *timer);

int hrtimer_restart(struct hrtimer *timer);

ktime_t hrtimer_get_remaining (const struct hrtimer *timer);
int hrtimer_active (const struct hrtimer *timer);
int hrtimer_get_res (const clockid_t which_clock, struct timespec *tp);
```

- The only field in the data structure:

```
struct hrtimer {
    struct rb_node        node;
    ktime_t               expires;
    enum hrtimer_restart  (*function)(struct hrtimer *);
    struct hrtimer_base   *base;
};
```

that needs to be set by the user is `function()`.

- The earliest implementation of the API had a void argument to the function and also a data field in the structure. With the current API, one will probably want to embed the timer structure in a data structure that can be used to pass data into the function.

- This can be done with the `container_of()` macro as such:

```
static struct my_data {
    struct hrtimer timer;
    unsigned long data ;
    ....
}
struct hrtimer *my_timer;
struct my_data *dat = container_of (my_timer, struct my_data, timer);
```

where the first argument is a pointer to the timer structure, the second the type of structure it is contained in, and the third is the name of the timer structure in the data structure.

- The return value of the function should be `HRTIMER_NORESTART` for a one-shot timer, and `HRTIMER_RESTART` for a recurring timer.

- For the recurring case, the function `hrtimer_forward()` should be called to reset a new expiration time before the callback function returns. The `now` argument should be the current time. It can be obtained with:

```
struct hrtimer *timer;
....
ktime_t now = timer->base->get_time();
```

- A hrtimer is initialized by `hrtimer_init()` and is bound to the type of clock specified by `which_clock` which can be `CLOCK_MONOTONIC` or `CLOCK_REALTIME` which matches current real-world time, and can differ if the system time is altered, such as by network time protocol daemons.

- Once initialized the timer is launched with `hrtimer_start()`. If `mode` = `HRTIMER_MODE_ABS` the argument `time` is absolute; if `mode` = `HRTIMER_MODE_REL` it is relative.

- The function `hrtimer_cancel()` will wait until the timer is no longer active, and its function is not running on any CPU, returning 0 if the timer has already expired and 1 if it was successfully canceled. The `hrtimer_try_to_cancel()` function differs but won't wait if the function is currently running, and will return -1 in that case. A canceled timer can be restarted by calling `hrtimer_restart()`.

- The remaining functions return the remaining time before expiration, whether the timer is currently on the queue, and ascertain the clock resolution in nanoseconds.

- Here's an example of simple high resolution timer:

```
#include <linux/module.h>
#include <linux/timer.h>
#include <linux/init.h>
#include <linux/version.h>
#include <linux/ktime.h>
#include <linux/hrtimer.h>

static struct kt_data {
        struct hrtimer timer;
        ktime_t period;
} *data;

static enum hrtimer_restart ktfun(struct hrtimer *var)
{
        ktime_t now = var->base->get_time();
        printk(KERN_INFO "timer running at jiffies=%ld\n", jiffies);
        hrtimer_forward(var, now, data->period);
        return HRTIMER_RESTART;
```

```
        }

        static int __init my_init(void)
        {
                data = kmalloc(sizeof(*data), GFP_KERNEL);
                data->period = ktime_set(1, 0);          /* short period, 1 second */
                hrtimer_init(&data->timer, CLOCK_REALTIME, HRTIMER_MODE_REL);
                data->timer.function = ktfun;
                hrtimer_start(&data->timer, data->period, HRTIMER_MODE_REL);

                return 0;
        }

        static void __exit my_exit(void)
        {
                hrtimer_cancel(&data->timer);
                kfree(data);
        }

        module_init(my_init);
        module_exit(my_exit);
        MODULE_LICENSE("GPL v2");
```

12.8 Labs

Lab 1: Kernel Timers from a Character Driver

- Write a driver that puts launches a kernel timer whenever a `write()` to the device takes place.

- Pass some data to the driver and have it print out.

- Have it print out the `current->pid` field when the timer function is scheduled, and then again when the function is executed.

Lab 2: Multiple Kernel Timers

- Make the period in the first lab long enough so you can issue multiple writes before the timer function run. (Hint: you may want to save your data before running this lab.)

- How many times does the function get run?

- Fix the solution so multiple timers work properly.

Lab 3: Periodic Kernel Timers

- Write a module that launches a periodic kernel timer function; i.e., it should re-install itself.

Lab 4: Multiple Periodic Kernel Timers

- Write a module that launches two periodic kernel timer functions; i.e., they should re-install themselves.

- One periodic sequence should be for less than 256 ticks (so it falls in the `tv1` vector), and the other should be for less than 16 K ticks (so it falls in the `tv2` vector.)

- Each time the timer functions execute, print out the total elapsed time since the module was loaded (in jiffies).

Lab 5: High Resolution Timers

- Do the same things as in the previous exercise, setting up two periodic timers, but this time use the **hrtimer** interface.

Lab 6: Using kprobes to get statistics.

- Using **kprobes**, find out how often kernel timers are deleted before they are run.

- Examination of the kernel source discloses that timers are started with either `add_timer()` or `mod_timer()`.

- You can see how often timers are deleted by monitoring `del_timer()` and `del_timer_sync()`; however, on single processor systems, `del_timer_sync()` is not defined.

- Timers are frequent so you'll probably won't want to print out every time they are scheduled or deleted, but say every 100 times plus final statistics.

- Is it possible that timer deletion can be more frequent than timer scheduling?

Chapter 13

Race Conditions and Synchronization Methods

We'll consider some of the methods the kernel uses to syncrhronize and avoid race conditions. We'll discuss atomic functions and bit operations, the use of **spinlocks**, **mutexes**, **semaphores**, and **completion functions**. Finally we'll see how the kernel maintains reference counts.

13.1 Concurrency and Synchronization Methods

- Kernel execution is asynchronous and unpredictable; interrupts occur at any time, system calls can be entered from many different processes, and kernel threads of execution will also occupy the CPUs.

- Many kernel resources can be modified in one place while being used in another. In some cases the code paths are distinct, while in others the same code is being executed more than once simultaneously. Either way data corruption is a danger as are potential race conditions including deadlock.

- Such **concurrency** can be of two types:

  - **True concurrency** occurs on **SMP** systems, when two threads of execution on different processors simultaneously access a resource.

  - **Pseudo-concurrency** occurs even on single processor systems, when one thread is pre-empted or interrupted and another accesses an open resource.

- A variety of mechanisms can be used to ensure integrity of shared resources; let's consider the various methods in order of **increasing** overhead.

- The simplest method is the use of **atomic functions**, which work on specially typed variables which are essentially integers and include the use of **atomic bit operations**. Atomic functions:

  - Execute in one single instruction; i.e., they can not be interrupted in mid-stream, and if two operations are requested simultaneously one must complete before the second can proceed.

  - Can be used either in or out of process context.

  - Can never go to sleep.

  - Do not suspend interrupts while executing.

- If more than one operation needs to be performed, one can use **spinlocks**; these get their name because if one attempts to take out a spinlock which is already held, the code will **spin**; i.e., do a busy wait, until the lock is available. The spinlock functions:

  - Can be used either in or out of process context, but if used in interrupts, the forms which temporarily block interrupts should be used when the same spinlock is referenced in process context.

  - Can block but do not go to sleep; i.e., another process can not be scheduled in.

  - Can suspend interrupts while being used.

  - Have supplemental **read** and **write** forms for the case in which one wants to permit simultaneous readers, and writes are relatively rare.

- If one wants the ability to go to sleep if the resource is not available (to call the scheduler and have it yield the CPU to another process) one can use either **mutexes** (for which the basic operations are `mutex_lock()` and `mutex_unlock()`) or **semaphores**, (for which the basic operations are `up()` and `down()`.) Whenever possible mutexes should be used rather than semaphores in new code.

- One should note:

  - One can use `mutex_lock()` and `down()` only in process context; `mutex_unlock()` should not be used from an interrupt context, while the `up()` functions can be be used at any time.

  - The `mutex_lock()` and `down()` functions can sleep. The sleep may or may not be interruptible by signals, depending on the form used.

  - Interrupts are not suspended by these functions.

  - Like spinlocks, the semaphore functions also have supplemental **read** and **write** forms for the case in which one wants to permit simultaneous readers when writing is relatively rare.

- As an alternative, **completion** functions can be used in place of semaphores in the case where contention is expected to be high.

- The kernel also employs the **seqlock()** mechanism, used when one often has to read a value which is rarely changed, and for which speed is essential.

- Another method for similar situations is **RCU** (for Read-Copy-Update), which can lead to great performance boosts.

- Exactly which mechanism should be used depends on:

  - Whether contention is expected to be high or low.
  - Whether one is in or out of process context.
  - How many operations have to be performed while the lock is held.
  - Whether sleeping is permissible.
  - How often the lock needs to be taken.

- For frequent operations, one would generally pick the one with the lowest overhead which fits the other requirements.

- For an extremely comprehensive overview of the challenges of parallel programming, download Paul McKenney's opus at: **http://kernel.org/pub/linux/kernel/people/paulmck/perfbook/perfbook.2011.01.02a.pdf**. *perfbook –*

- All major locking and synchronization mechanisms are discussed from a very experienced perspective.

13.2 Atomic Operations

- **Atomic** functions (many of which are macros) are completed as one single instruction and work on a variable of type `atomic_t`, which is a structure defined as

```
typedef struct {
    volatile int counter;
} atomic_t;
```

Using a structure helps prevent mixing up atomic variables with normal integers as you can't use atomic functions on integers and vice versa without explicit casting.

- These in-line macros and functions are **SMP**-safe and depend on the architecture:

```
#include <asm/atomic.h>

#define ATOMIC_INIT(i)    { (i) }
#define atomic_read(v)    ((v)->counter)
#define atomic_set(v,i)   (((v)->counter) = (i))

void atomic_add (int i, atomic_t *v);
void atomic_sub (int i, atomic_t *v);
void atomic_inc (atomic_t *v);
void atomic_dec (atomic_t *v);

int atomic_dec_and_test (atomic_t *v);
int atomic_inc_and_test_greater_zero (atomic_t *v);
int atomic_sub_and_test (int i, atomic_t *v);
int atomic_add_negative (int i, atomic_t *v);
int atomic_sub_return (int i, atomic_t *v);
int atomic_add_return (int i, atomic_t *v);
```

```
int atomic_inc_return (int i, atomic_t *v);
int atomic_dec_return (int i, atomic_t *v);
```

- Note that the `ATOMIC_INIT()`, `atomic_read()`, and `atomic_set()` macros are automatically atomic since they just read a value.

- On 64-bit platforms there are also a 64-bit atomic type and associated functions, such as `void atomic64_inc(atomic64_t *v)`. You can see the appropriate header file for details.

13.3   Bit Operations

- In order to examine and modify individual bits in various flag and lock variables there are a number of atomic **bit** operation functions provided by the kernel.

- These are accomplished through a single machine operation and thus are very fast; on most platforms this can be done without disabling interrupts.

- The functions, not surprisingly, differ somewhat according to architecture.   They are defined in **/usr/src/linux/arch/arm/include/asm/bitops.h**:

```
#include <asm/bitops.h>

void set_bit            (int nr, volatile unsigned long *addr);
void clear_bit          (int nr, volatile unsigned long *addr);
void change_bit         (int nr, volatile unsigned long *addr);

int test_bit            (int nr, volatile unsigned long *addr);
int test_and_set_bit    (int nr, volatile unsigned long *addr);
int test_and_clear_bit  (int nr, volatile unsigned long *addr);
int test_and_change_bit (int nr, volatile unsigned long *addr);

long find_first_zero_bit (const unsigned long *addr, unsigned long size);
long find_next_zero_bit (const unsigned long *addr, long size, long offset);
long find_first_bit ( const unsigned long *addr, unsigned long size);

unsigned long ffz (unsigned long word);
unsigned long ffs (int x);
unsigned long fls (int x);
```

- In these functions the type of `nr` depends on the architecture; for 32-bit **x86** and **ARM** it is just an integer, while for the **alpha** it is an `unsigned long`. The second argument points to the variable in which bits are going to be examined or modified. It's type varies among architectures, usually being `volatile unsigned long`.

- The `test_` functions give the previous bit value as their return value.

- Note that `ffz()`, `ffs()` and `fls()` find the first zero bit, first set bit and last set bit in a word (integer), while the functions `find_first_zero_bit()`, `find_next_zero_bit()` and `find_first_bit()` work on a bit mask of variable length.

- There also exist a set of **non-atomic** bit functions, which differ from the above by being prefixed with `__`; e.g., `__set_bit()`. These can be used when locks are already taken out and integrity is assured, and are somewhat faster than the atomic versions.

13.4 Spinlocks

- A **spinlock** is a mechanism for protecting critical sections of code. It will *spin* while waiting for a resource to be available, and not go to sleep.

- One can protect the same code section from executing on more than one CPU, but more generally one protects simultaneous access to the same resource, which may be touched by differing code paths, which in addition, may be in or out of process context.

- Spinlocks were important only on multi-processor systems before kernel preemption was included. This was because on **SMP** systems two CPUs can try to access a critical section of code simultaneously. Thus before kernel preemption was incorporated in the 2.6 kernel, on single processor systems, spinlocks were defined as no-ops. However, with a preemptible, hyper-threaded, or multi-core system, spinlocks are always operative.

- The macros in **/usr/src/linux/arch/arm/include/asm/spinlock.h** (included from **/usr/src/linux/include/linux/spinlock.h**, when on an **SMP** system) contain the basic code for spinlocks.

  In the simplest invocation you have something like:

  ```
  spinlock_t my_lock;
  spin_lock_init (&my_lock);

  spin_lock (&my_lock);
  ...... critical code ........
  spin_unlock (&my_lock);
  ```

  This guarantees the code touching the critical resource can't be run on more than one processor simultaneously, and does nothing on a single processor system with a non-preemptable kernel. However, the above functions should not be used out of process context (i.e., in interrupt handlers) as they may cause deadlocks in that case. (See **/usr/src/linux/Documentation/spinlocks.txt** for some further explanation.)

- Often one wants to suspend, or disable, interrupt handling at the same time. In this case one does:

  ```
  unsigned long flags;
  spinlock_t my_lock;

  spin_lock_init (&my_lock);

  spin_lock_irqsave (&my_lock,flags);
  ...... critical code ........
  spin_unlock_irqrestore (&my_lock,flags);
  ```

  On single processor systems, this is not a no-op, as the interrupt disabling and restoring still goes on, and as mentioned these functions should be used when out of process-context. These functions take more time than the above "irq-less" versions.

- Note that the disabling of interrupts occurs **only** on the current processor; other CPUs are free to handle interrupts while the lock is held.

- There also exists the somewhat faster functions:

  ```
  spin_lock_irq (&my_lock);
  spin_unlock_irq (&my_lock);
  ```

the difference being that the original mask of enabled interrupts is not saved, and all interrupts are restored in the unlocking operation. This is dangerous (an interrupt may have been disabled) and generally these functions should not be used.

- There are also reader and writer spinlock functions; with these there can be more than one reader in a critical region, but in order to make changes an exclusive write lock must be invoked. In other words, read lock blocks only a write lock, while a write lock blocks everyone. Examples would be:

```
unsigned long flags;
rwlock_t my_lock;
rw_lock_init (&my_lock);
....
read_lock_irqsave (&my_lock,flags);
...... critical code , reads only ..........
read_unlock_irqrestore (&my_lock,flags);

write_lock_irqsave (&my_lock,flags);
...... critical code , exclusive read and write access ....
write_unlock_irqrestore (&my_lock,flags);
```

- There are also faster "irq-less" versions of these calls for non-interrupt contexts.

- These locks favor readers over writers; i.e., if a writer is waiting for a lock and more readers come they will get first access. This can cause **writer starvation** and helped motivate the development and use of **seqlocks**.

- There are a few other spinlock functions:

```
spin_unlock_wait (spinlock_t *lock);
int spin_is_locked (spinlock_t *lock);
int spin_trylock (spinlock_t *lock);
```

- `spin_unlock_wait()` waits until the spinlock is free.

- `spin_is_locked()` returns 1 if the spinlock is set.

- `spin_trylock()` returns 1 if it got the lock; otherwise it returns with 0; i.e., it is a non-blocking call.

13.5   Big Kernel Lock

- One locking mechanism that was used abundantly throughout the **Linux** kernel is the so-called **Big Kernel Lock**, or **BKL**. It could be invoked simply with

```
lock_kernel();
....
critical code
....
unlock_kernel();
```

- The **BKL** was originally a normal spinlock with widespread usage, and as such a relic of earlier times when locking was very coarse-grained.

- However, in the 2.6.11 kernel the **BKL** was converted to a semaphore and really should have been renamed the **Big Kernel Semaphore**. As a result it differed in two ways from other locking mechanisms:

  - Recursive application could be used within a given thread.

– Sleeping is permitted while holding the **BKL**; it is released when sleep begins and grabbed again upon awakening.

- Furthermore, with kernel preemption turned on it was possible to also turn on **BKL** preemption as a kernel configuration option through kernel version 2.6.24; after that it was automatically done.

- Newcomers are sometimes confused by code like:

```
lock_kernel();
....
spin_lock (&my_lock);
....
spin_unlock (&my_lock);
....
unlock_kernel();
```

in which a finer-grained lock is nested within the **BKL**. The confusion arises because of not understanding that all spinlocks are **advisory**; i.e., they only are effective when code examines a lock status. They are not **mandatory** locks.

- There is an ongoing effort to exterminate almost all instances of the **BKL**, as its promiscuous use led to a lot of bottlenecks when code that in no way interacts with other code took out the **BKL** and suspended the other code.

- Minimizing the use of the **BKL** has been tedious. Each removal requires careful examination and testing against unanticipated side effects, but it is a necessary chore to accomplish on the way to fully fine-grained locking. Removal involves replacing it with appropriate and narrow locking mechanisms for each particular purpose.

- The 2.6.37 kernel offers complete removal of the **BKL** as a kernel compilation option; in the 2.6.39 kernel it was completely removed.

- Any references to **lock_kernel()** and `unlock_kernel()` will fail to compile as will in any to the header file `smp_lock.h`.

13.6 Mutexes

- A **mutex** (**mut**ual **ex**clusion object) is a basic kind of sleepable locking mechanism. While **spinlocks** are also a kind of mutex, they do not permit sleeping.

- The elementary data structure is defined in **/usr/src/linux/include/linux/mutex.h**:

```
#include <linux/mutex.h>

struct mutex {
    atomic_t         count;
    spinlock_t       wait_lock;
    struct list_head wait_list;
};
```

and is meant to be used opaquely. If `count` is 1, the mutex is free, if it is 0 it is locked, and if it is negative, it is locked and processes are waiting.

- Mutexes are initialized in an unlocked state with

  ```
  DEFINE_MUTEX (name);
  ```

  at compile time or

  ```
  void mutex_init (struct mutex *lock);
  ```

  at run time.

- The locking primitives come in uninterruptible and interruptible forms but with only one unlocking function:

  ```
  void mutex_lock (struct mutex *lock);
  int mutex_lock_interruptible (struct mutex *lock);
  int mutex_lock_killable (struct mutex *lock);

  void mutex_unlock (struct mutex *lock);
  ```

- Any signal will break a lock taken out with `mutex_lock_interruptible()` while only a fatal signal will break one taken out with `mutex_lock_killable()`. Locks taken out by `mutex_lock()` are not affected by signals.

- There are some important restrictions on the use of mutexes:

  - The mutex must be released by the original owner.
  - The mutex can not be applied recursively.
  - The mutex can not be locked or unlocked from interrupt context.

- Note however, that violation of these restrictions will not be detected without mutex debugging configured into the kernel.

- The **owner** of the mutex is the task in whose context the mutex is taken out. If that task is no longer active another task may release the mutex without triggering debugging warnings.

- A non-blocking attempt to get the lock can be made with

  ```
  int mutex_trylock (struct mutex *lock);
  ```

  and

  ```
  int mutex_is_locked (struct mutex *lock);
  ```

  checks the state of the lock.

- Note that `mutex_trylock()` returns 1 if it obtains the lock, akin to `spin_trylock()` and unlike `down_trylock()`.

- There are no special reader/writer mutexes such as there are for other exclusion devices such as semaphores and spinlocks.

13.7   Semaphores

- It is also possible to use counting **semaphores** to protect critical sections of code. These work on data structures of type `semaphore` and `rw_semaphore`.

- The basic functions (defined as macros) can be found in **/usr/src/linux/include/linux/semaphore.h**, and **/usr/src/linux/include/linux/rwsem.h**:

```
#include <linux/semaphore.h>

void down (struct semaphore *sem);
int down_interruptible (struct semaphore *sem);
int down_trylock (struct semaphore *sem);
void up (struct semaphore *sem);

void down_read (struct rw_semaphore *sem);
void down_write (struct rw_semaphore *sem);
void up_read (struct rw_semaphore *sem);
void up_write (struct rw_semaphore *sem);

struct semaphore {
        unsigned int count;
        int sleepers;
        wait_queue_head_t wait;
};
struct rw_semaphore {
        rwsem_count_t           count;
        spinlock_t              wait_lock;
        struct list_head        wait_list;
};
```

- The `down()` function checks to see if someone else has already entered the critical code section; if the value of the semaphore is greater than zero, it decrements it and returns. If it is already zero, it will sleep and try again later.

- The `down_interruptible()` function differs in that it can be interrupted by a signal; the other form blocks any signals to the process, and should be used only with great caution. However, you will now have to check to see if a signal arrived if you use this form, so you'll have code like:

```
if (down_interruptible(&sem)) return -ERESTARTSYS
```

which tells the system to either retry the system call or return `-EINTR` to the application; which it does depends on how the system is set up.

- The `down_trylock()` form checks if the semaphore is available, and if not returns, and is thus a non-blocking `down` function (which is why it doesn't need an interruptible form.) It returns 0 if the lock is obtained. For instance, a typical read entry from a driver might contain:

```
....
if (file->f_flags & O_NONBLOCK) {
        if (down_trylock(&iosem))
            return -EAGAIN;
} else
        if (down_interruptible(&iosem))
            return -ERESTARTSYS;
}
```

- The `up()` function increments the semaphore value, waking up any processes waiting on the semaphore. It doesn't require any `_interruptible` form.

- The `_read`, `write` forms give finer control, permitting more than one reader to access the protected resource, but only one writer.

- You have to be careful with semaphores; you can't lower them anywhere where sleeping would be very bad (such as in an interrupt routine) and you have to think things through carefully to avoid race conditions.

- Semaphores may be declared and initialized with the following macros:

```
DECLARE_MUTEX(name);
DECLARE_RWSEM(name);
```

where `name` is an object of type `struct semaphore`.

 Kernel Version Note **Kernel Version Note**

- From kernel version 2.6.37 on you must use

```
DEFINE_SEMAPHORE(name);
```

in place of `DECLARE_MUTEX()`, which is much clearer in intent.

- The value of the semaphore can be directly manipulated with the inline function:

```
void sema_init (struct semaphore *sem, int val);
```

and is often initialized with the following inline convenience functions:

```
static inline void init_MUTEX (struct semaphore *sem){
        sema_init(sem, 1);
}
static inline void init_MUTEX_LOCKED (struct semaphore *sem){
        sema_init(sem, 0);
}
```

- Historically, semaphores have more often been used as binary **mutexes** rather than as counters.

- A semaphore may be more difficult to debug than a mutex in that it can have more than one owner at a time.

- Any new code should use mutexes unless the counting capability of semaphores is really needed. The migration of most existing semaphores to mutexes is gradually and carefully being done.

- An example, culled from **/usr/src/linux/kernel/sys.c**:

```
....
3.0:1116 DECLARE_RWSEM(uts_sem);
....
3.0:1220 SYSCALL_DEFINE2(gethostname, char __user *, name, int, len)
3.0:1221 {
3.0:1222         int i, errno;
3.0:1223         struct new_utsname *u;
3.0:1224
3.0:1225         if (len < 0)
3.0:1226                 return -EINVAL;
3.0:1227         down_read(&uts_sem);
3.0:1228         u = utsname();
3.0:1229         i = 1 + strlen(u->nodename);
3.0:1230         if (i > len)
3.0:1231                 i = len;
3.0:1232         errno = 0;
3.0:1233         if (copy_to_user(name, u->nodename, i))
3.0:1234                 errno = -EFAULT;
3.0:1235         up_read(&uts_sem);
3.0:1236         return errno;
3.0:1237 }
....
3.0:1195 SYSCALL_DEFINE2(sethostname, char __user *, name, int, len)
3.0:1196 {
3.0:1197         int errno;
3.0:1198         char tmp[__NEW_UTS_LEN];
3.0:1199
3.0:1200         if (!ns_capable(current->nsproxy->uts_ns->user_ns, CAP_SYS_ADMIN))
3.0:1201                 return -EPERM;
3.0:1202
3.0:1203         if (len < 0 || len > __NEW_UTS_LEN)
3.0:1204                 return -EINVAL;
3.0:1205         down_write(&uts_sem);
3.0:1206         errno = -EFAULT;
3.0:1207         if (!copy_from_user(tmp, name, len)) {
3.0:1208                 struct new_utsname *u = utsname();
3.0:1209
3.0:1210                 memcpy(u->nodename, tmp, len);
3.0:1211                 memset(u->nodename + len, 0, sizeof(u->nodename) - len);
3.0:1212                 errno = 0;
3.0:1213         }
3.0:1214         up_write(&uts_sem);
```

```
3.0:1215          return errno;
3.0:1216 }
```

Kernel Version Note   **Kernel Version Note**

- With kernel 2.6.26 the effort to remove as many semaphores as possible accelerated. In fact, it is possible they will be removed altogether at some point, with the last remaining cases converted to the **completion** API.

- As part of this effort, the architecture-dependent code was replaced with generic C code, which simplified and reduced the code base.

- At the same time, the type of the `count` field in the `semaphore` structure was changed to `unsigned int` from `atomic_t`.

13.8 Completion Functions

- The completion functions give an alternative method of waiting for events to take place, and are optimized to work in the case where contention is expected, unlike semaphores which are optimized to work in the case of low contention expectation.

```
#include <linux/completion.h>

struct completion {
    unsigned int done;
    wait_queue_head_t wait;
};

void init_completion (struct completion *c);
void wait_for_completion (struct completion *c);
int  wait_for_completion_interruptible (struct completion *c);
void complete (struct completion *c);
void complete_and_exit (struct completion *c, long code);

unsigned long wait_for_completion_timeout (struct completion *c, unsigned long timeout);
unsigned long wait_for_completion_interruptible_timeout (struct completion *c,
                                                unsigned long timeout);
```

- The functional variations with **timeout** in their name will return without a wake up call if the expiration period is reached without one. Both these and the non-interruptible forms have non-void return values and need to be checked.

- The completion structure can be declared and initialized in either of two ways:

```
DECLARE_COMPLETION(x);

struct completion x;
init_completion(&x);
```

- The `complete_and_exit()` function doesn't return if successful, takes an additional argument, `code`, which is the exit code for the kernel thread which is terminating. Obviously, this function should only be used in cases such as terminating a background thread, as it will kill whatever it is doing.

- The correspondence with semaphores is very simple; there is a one to one mapping between the methods:

```
struct semaphore   <--->    struct completion
sema_init()        <--->    init_completion
down()             <--->    wait_for_completion()
up()               <--->    complete()
```

13.9   Reference Counts

- One often needs to maintain a reference counter for an object, such as a data structure. If a resource is used in more than one place and passed to various subsystems, such a reference count is probably required.

- The **kref API** should be used for maintaining such reference counts, rather than having them constructed by hand. The relevant functions are defined in **/usr/src/linux/include/linux/kref.h**:

```
struct kref {
        atomic_t refcount;
};

void kref_init (struct kref *kref);
void kref_set  (struct kref *kref, int num);
void kref_get  (struct kref *kref);
int kref_put (struct kref *kref, void (*release) (struct kref *kref));
```

- It is presumed that the `kref` structure is embedded in a data structure you are using, which can be the object you are reference counting, as in:

```
struct my_dev_data {
   ...
   struct kref my_refcount;
   ...
};
```

- One must initialize with `kref_init()`, and can increment the reference count with `kref_get()`.

- Decrementing the reference count is done with `kref_put()` and if the reference count goes to zero the function referred to in the second argument to `kref_put()` is called. This may not be `NULL` or just `kfree()` (which is explicitly checked for.) This is likely to be something like this:

```
struct my_dev_data *md;

kref_put(md->my_refcount, my_release);

static void my_release (struct kref *kr){
   struct my_dev_data *md = container_of (kr, struct my_dev_data, my_refcount);
   my_dev_free(md);
}
```

where one does whatever is necessary in `my_dev_free()` to free up any memory and other resources.

- Note the use of the `container_of()` macro, which does pointer arithmetic; its first argument is the pointer we are given, the second the type of structure it is embedded in, and the third is its name in that structure. The result returned is a pointer to that structure.

- A good guide to using kernel reference counts can be found in **/usr/src/linux/Documentation/ kref.txt**.

13.10 Labs

Lab 1: Mutex Contention

- Write three simple modules where the second and third one use a variable exported from the first one. The second and third one can be identical; just give them different names.

  Hint: You can use the macro `__stringify(KBUILD_MODNAME)` to print out the module name.

- You can implement this by making small modifications to your results from the modules exercise.

- The exported variable should be a mutex. Have the first module initialize it in the unlocked state.

- The second (third) module should attempt to lock the mutex and if it is locked, fail to load; make sure you return the appropriate value from your initialization function.

- Make sure you release the mutex in your cleanup function.

- Test by trying to load both modules simultaneously, and see if it is possible. Make sure you can load one of the modules after the other has been unloaded, to make sure you released the mutex properly.

Lab 2: Semaphore Contention

- Now do the same thing using **semaphores** instead of mutexes.

Lab 3: Mutex Unlocking from an Interrupt.

- Modify the simple interrupt sharing lab to have a mutex taken out and then released in the interrupt handler.

- This is supposed to be illegal. Is this ignored, enforced, or warned against? Why?

Chapter 14

Bootloaders U-Boot

We'll look at some of the issues of the CPU **reset**, from initializing hardware through **POST** to loading and starting the **Linux** kernel. After a brief survey of candidate systems, we'll summarize **Das U-Boot**.

14.1 ROM Code Stages

- Projects designing embedded products own responsibility for every facet of firmware or software. In this session we concentrate on code that must reside in *non-volatile ROM*, and several other layers that **usually** reside there.

- The **goals** of the code executed early after *reset* or *power-on* typically include:

  - **POST** (Power-On-Self-Test), usually ROM-resident, is code that **initializes** hardware and performs tests to verify that it is functioning properly. In the **PC architecture**, this job is normally done by the **BIOS**. Often POST code *takes the reset vector*, which is jargon meaning that the instruction first fetched by the CPU when it comes out of **reset** is often the first instruction of the POST stage.

  - POST code must have *intimate and detailed* knowledge of all system hardware components, from their **addresses** in memory or I/O space to the specific steps needed to put them into a functioning state.

* *Special initialization sequences* are sometimes needed for components such as **cache** memory systems and **RAM**. Once initialized, normal **use** operation methods apply. (Often it is the case that **memory cannot** be used until RAM is initialized. This programming challenge has led to development of tools such as **ROMCC**, a subset of C that uses only CPU registers. See next section.)

* In some cases, especially with hardware components in the same package as the CPU, the initialization sequences are kept **proprietary** by the vendor, which can in some cases limit the project's choices for acquiring and implementing POST firmware.

* A project should *inventory* all the system hardware components, even (or *especially*) those in the CPU package, to ensure that the design plan includes provisions for acquiring either code or *knowledge* necessary to initialize them.

— **Boot Loader**. Usually started after POST, many boot loaders use **two stages**, sometimes more. For example, a **PC BIOS** usually knows how to load a very small block of code from one of a number of *boot devices*, which are usually tried in a configurable sequence (the *boot order*). If a device is absent, or if a *checksum* on the small block fails, the next device is tried. (Network-boot is fairly standard, in addition to older disk or *disk-like* devices.)

— In some systems, the small block of code loaded by the end of the POST code will load a *second stage* boot loader, which often can be configured to boot any of several operating system images from several physical devices that might be present.

• In general, a project will likely formulate its plans for the system *boot loader* to meet a **set of goals** for the project over its life cycle. Some of these might include:

— **Engineering Design** phase. This first one is obvious, so obvious that occasionally little attention is given to product phases after deployment.

— **Crash Recovery Boot**. This is usually part of the engineering phase, and is often as simple as ensuring that a **stable** version of the operating system can be booted in the event that the version under development fails.

— **Field Upgrade Boot**. Some products have requirements that include upgrading firmware and/or software in the field. Often the requirement is implemented as an application running under the operating system, but in other cases a separate boot image is selected for this purpose. (Frequently an upgrade will write to some type of non-volatile memory.)

— **Extended Diagnostic Boot**. Many products have extended diagnostic packages meant to be run by technicians in the field, or sometimes, remotely via a Internet or other connection. It is rarely the case that such diagnostic code can run as an application under the runtime operating system, as it will need access to the full hardware resources.

14.2   Some GPL Boot Loaders

Das U-Boot

- **Das U-Boot** (**http://www.denx.de/wiki/U-Boot/**) is fast becoming the most popular boot loader for embedded systems. We will take a more extended tour of **U-Boot** in the next section.

ADAM/ADAM2

- **ADAM2**, the **A**valanche **D**evice **A**pplication **M**anager (**http://www.seattlewireless.net/index.cgi/ADAM2**) is a simple bootloader in use, especially in routers. It provides **uart**, **Ethernet**, **tftp** and a minimal shell.

- Many customized versions exist. Some add additional support for facilities such as **wifi** and **dhcp-client**.

Redboot

- **Redboot** (**http://ecos.sourceware.org/ecos/hardware.html**) is a portable bootstrap environment based on the **eCos** real-time operating system.

- It supports **dhcp-client** and **tftp** and can be used with **gdb**.

CFE

- **CFE**, **C**ustom **F**irmware **E**nvironment (**http://www.linux-mips.org/wiki/CFE**) is a firmware developed by **Broadcom** for 64-bit **SBI** (**Swarm**) and 32-bit **BCM37xx SoC**'s. (**http://ecos.sourceware.org/ecos/hardware.html**). It is a portable bootstrap environment based on the **eCos** real-time operating system.

- It supports **dhcp-client** and **tftp** and can be used with **gdb**.

14.3   Das U-Boot

- **Das U-Boot** (**http://www.denx.de/wiki/U-Boot/**) is probably the most actively developed system-initialization project today. Though used mainly in embedded systems, it is not restricted to them.

- **U-Boot** is, and declares an intent to remain, **patent-free**, and completely open under the **GPL**.

- In many supported boards **U-Boot** can *take the reset vector* and perform the *POST* initialization and test steps at system start-up, which is convenient, in that it saves the steps of **chaining** from POST code to the (first) stage of a separate boot loader. In these systems a modular *board* block of initialization code is linked into the same object file as all other **U-Boot** components, simplifying the management of project firmware.

  (Note: on some boards, e.g. the T.I. *Beagle* the full **U-Boot** program doesn't take the reset vector. Instead, a portion of **U-Boot** called *X-Loader* takes the reset vector, then (normally) chains to **U-Boot** when it is done. This is done so that the permanent non-volatile memory may be quite small, and is an example of **U-Boot**'s flexibility.)

- **U-Boot default configurations** are categorized by **board**, each drawing from available **CPU subtype** support source files. The documentation for making a *custom board-support package* is fairly easy to follow, particularly if the custom board is based on the hardware and architecture of a previous board (which is quite commonly done).

  At present, over 460 boards have full or partial support. CPU families include **ARM**, **x86**, **PowerPC**, **SH**, **MIPS**, **m68k** and several others. Most CPU families have support for several sub-types. For example, supported types of **ARM** include about 25 family members from the *720* through the *StrongArm* to *OMAP* and the *Xscale*.

- **U-Boot** has an **interactive command language** which offers a dialog with the user once the (very fast) POST code has run. This language can be **scripted**, with scripts *stored in variables*, which may, in turn, be preserved in *Flash* memory.

  The command language is *consistent* across platforms, but is also easily extended so that *custom commands* may be added.

  The command language is patterned after a simple **Unix** *shell*, and permits (for example) fairly sophisticated boot sequences, involving load addresses and other variables, to be simply scripted, and automatically invoked upon completion of POST.

- **U-Boot** contains a large set of (configurable and selectable) device drivers and **file system** support. Kernel images can be located in `NAND` memory, as well as in supported file systems **ext2**, **FAT**, **ext3**, **jffs2**, and **cramfs**.

  Files may be implemented on a variety of devices, including **MMC** cards and disks.

- In addition to booting from a local device, **U-Boot** can boot from the **network** using the **tftp** protocol, which is the most common network-boot protocol. This is often convenient during development, as it saves, at every kernel iteration, the step of physically installing the new kernel on a local physical device.

  (Of course, methods other than **tftp** boot can use the network to speed kernel iterations. For example, one could use **NFS** or **ftp** with a running kernel to copy a new kernel image to a local device.) Also, for *some* embedded products, it might be feasible to **deploy** several instances of the product where they can all be loaded from a single **boot server**. In these cases, upgrades are simplified by having to upgrade only the image on the server.

- **uImage format**. The default format for kernels loaded by **U-Boot** is the *uImage* format, which is a "wrapper" around the compressed kernel image (**zImage**),which can be directly loaded by other boot loaders, such as GRUB.

  The uImage wrapper is installed by a **U-Boot** *tool* program named **mkimage**. Use of this tool is usually integrated into the **Linux** kernel **Kbuild** system in the `arch/<CPU-type>` kernel tree by adding a *Makefile* target **make uImage**.

  (For example, if the kernel source tree has been configured for `ARCH = arm`, then the uImage target will be in the configured Makefile: **/usr/src/linux/arch/arm/boot/Makefile**.)

14.4 Labs

Lab 1: Configure and build the U-Boot loader for the *Beagle*.

- **Acquiring U-Boot source.** Your instructor has a source code tree that will be provided. Extract with:

```
$ cd ${HOME}/beagle
$ tar xfvj /misc/instr/s_THIS_S_NO/u-boot-2011.03.tar.bz2
```

- The home **git** repository for **U-Boot** is at `git.denx.de/u-boot.git`. However, from time to time work is done *out of tree* for a particular board or system, and only posted back to the main repository at a later time. As with the *Linux kernel*, source trees found in the main repository may, or may not, operate properly on the target system, with no clearly posted indications of which versions are appropriate. In the case of the source code provided for this class, the author checked out the **v2011.03** tag, verified that it operates for the purposes needed for this class, and also checked with some contacts to verify that code needed to properly initialized the **C4** version of the board are in place.

```
$ # NOTE:  THE INSTRUCTOR DID THIS COMMANDS.  You do NOT need to do them!
$ git clone git://git.denx.de/u-boot.git u-boot
$ # NOTE:  THE INSTRUCTOR CREATED THE TARBALL FROM THE RESULTING
$ #   DIRECTORY u-boot
```

- Configure and compile **U-Boot** using the cross-toolchain we previously built with the **Buildroot** tool:

```
$ cd ${HOME}/beagle/u-boot
$ git tag
    . . .
v2010.12
v2010.12-rc1
v2010.12-rc2
v2010.12.rc3
v2011.03
v2011.03-rc1
v2011.03-rc2
$ git branch top-o-tree v2011.03
$ git checkout top-o-tree
$ make CROSS_COMPILE=arm-linux- mrproper
$ make CROSS_COMPILE=arm-linux- omap3_beagle_config
$ make CROSS_COMPILE=arm-linux-
```

- As noted in the previous section, on some systems **U-Boot** can *take the reset vector*, that is, provide the first instruction fetched by the CPU after reset, or power-on. Use **nm** to examine the first few symbols in the (statically linked) **U-Boot** object file:

```
$ arm-linux-nm -n u-boot | head -8
80e80000 T _start
80e80020 t _undefined_instruction
80e80024 t _software_interrupt
80e80028 t _prefetch_abort
```

```
80e8002c t _data_abort
80e80030 t _not_used
80e80034 t _irq
80e80038 t _fiq
```

- A little searching reveals that the code at `_start` is in an assembly-language file specific to the CPU type on the Beagle: `cpu/arm_cortexa8/start.S`

- Since we just encountered an *assembly-language* file, it's worth mentioning that the standard utility program for inspecting object files, `objdump` includes a **disassembler**. For example, we can disassemble any or all of the object file. For example, the first instruction *u-boot* can be obtained with:

  ```
  $ arm-linux-objdump -d u-boot | head

  u-boot:     file format elf32-littlearm


  Disassembly of section .text:

  80e80000 <_start>:
  80e80000:       ea000012        b       80e80050 <reset>
  ```

- This tool can be handy at times, for example, if there is confusion as to *which* file was compiled and linked into the object: you can directly query the object to see what us there.

- The **U-Boot** command language is implemented in directory `common`. The `Makefile` there permits conditional compilation of *configured commands*, using semantics similar to that used in the **Linux** kernel **Kbuild** system. A fragment of this file shows several *mandatory* components and also two instances of *configurable* components:

```
include $(TOPDIR)/config.mk

LIB     = $(obj)libcommon.a

AOBJS   =

# core
COBJS-y += main.o
COBJS-y += console.o
COBJS-y += command.o
COBJS-y += dlmalloc.o
COBJS-y += exports.o
COBJS-$(CONFIG_SYS_HUSH_PARSER) += hush.o
COBJS-y += image.o
COBJS-y += memsize.o
COBJS-y += s_record.o
COBJS-$(CONFIG_SERIAL_MULTI) += serial.o
COBJS-y += stdio.o
COBJS-y += xyzModem.o
```

Chapter 15

SMP and Threads

We'll review how **Linux** implements Symmetric Multi Processing (**SMP**). We'll see how to compile the kernel and modules appropriately, We will show how processor **affinity** can be set for processes as well as interrupt handling in a number of ways including the use of **CPUSETS**. We'll review how **SMP** affects kernel algorithms.

15.1 SMP Kernels and Modules

- **SMP** stands for **S**ymmetric **M**ulti **P**rocessing. In such a system both memory and I/O processing are shared among all the CPU nodes, rather than tied to particular ones.

- **SMP** support is turned on with

  ```
  #define CONFIG_SMP
  ```

- Most of the `#ifdef`'s involving **SMP** are confined to kernel headers; there should be no (or at least very few) explicit references. Coding for **SMP** should be very transparent.

- The `CONFIG_SMP` macro must be turned on during kernel compilation as well as for any modules that will be linked to it if one wants to use more than one CPU. Non-**SMP** modules cannot be mixed with an **SMP** kernel, and vice-versa.

- An **SMP** kernel will run on machines with only one CPU with very little or no performance penalty.

- It is possible under **Linux** to specify bit masks for what CPUs a given process may be allowed to run on. Additionally one can force the handling of any particular interrupt to be confined to certain CPUs.

- The 2.6 kernel contains an optional feature known as **kernel-preemption**.

- In some ways this makes even a single processor system behave much like an **SMP** system in that all kernel code has to be re-entrant, and bugs that might appear only on **SMP** systems may be induced even on a single CPU.

- Some processors include **hyper-threading** or **multi-core** technology. When either of these are present the machine behaves (in most ways) as if it had more than one CPU.

- While these CPUs behave like an **SMP** system in many ways (and an **SMP**-enabled kernel should be run) they do have some differences.

- In particular they share the same physical memory cache and as a result one does not incur the penalty that usually occurs from having a process migrate from one CPU to another and thereby trashing the cache. To take this into account the scheduler and other kernel algorithms are smart enough to treat these virtual CPUs somewhat differently than physical ones.

- An unusual and fun way to develop properly working **SMP** kernel code is to take advantage of **User Mode Linux (UML)**, whose development has been led by Jeff Dike. Complete documentation can be found at **http://user-mode-linux.sourceforge.net**.

- With **UML** multiple **Linux** instances can be run as virtual machines. Each runs as a non-privileged application. By configuring the kernel running as a virtual machine to pretend it has multiple processors, it is straightforward to mimic true **SMP** functionality.

- Instructions for how to set this up can be found in an article by Jerry Cooperstein at: **http://linux.oreillynet.com/pub/a/linux/2003/03/03/uml_smp.html**

15.2   Processor Affinity

- The default behaviour on an **SMP** system is to permit any process to run on any processor.

- To prevent *ping-ponging*, which causes cache thrashing, **Linux** strives to keep a process on the same CPU it has already been on.

- Forcing a process, or class of processes to be on a certain CPU is termed setting the processor **affinity**; it is also called **binding**, or **pinning** a process to a CPU.

- This is done through use of the `cpus_allowed` field of the `task_struct`, the data structure that describes everything about a task. This is inherited across forks.

- The affinity can be set with two system calls:

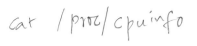

```
int sched_getaffinity (pid_t pid, unsigned int len, unsigned long *old_mask);
int sched_setaffinity (pid_t pid, unsigned int len, unsigned long *new_mask);
```

where `pid` is the process ID for which we are getting or setting the mask pointed to by the third argument, which is of bit-length `len`.

- From the command line one can use **taskset** to get and set affinity masks, as well as launch new processes with a specified mask:

```
$ taskset 0x3 foobar      # Use cpus 0,1 for foobar and start it
$ taskset -c 0,1 foobar   # Use cpus 0,1 for foobar and start it
$ taskset -pc 0,1 7790    # Use cpus 0,1 for running pid=7790
$ taskset -p 0x3 7790     # Use cpus 0,1 for running pid=7790
$ taskset -p 7790         # Show cpus for running pid=7790
```

- It is sometimes advantageous to set **IRQ**-affinity; to force particular interrupts to be dealt with only some subset of all the CPUs, rather than being distributed roughly equally.

- This is done by accessing `/proc/irq/IRQ#/smp_affinity`. One can not turn off all CPUs in the mask, and won't work if the physical **IRQ** controller doesn't have the capability to support an affinity selection.

- The **irqbalance** daemon dynamically adjusts the **IRQ** affinity in response to system conditions. It takes into account performance (latency and cache coherence) and power consumption (keeping **CPUs** no more active than necessary when system load is light.)

- There was also an in-kernel **IRQ**-balancing option, but this was deprecated and finally removed in kernel version 2.6.29 in favor of the user-space solution. Full documentation about the daemon method can be found at **http://www.irqbalance.org**.

- You can examine the current set of cpus online by looking at **/sys/devices/system/cpu/ online**, and you can turn particular cpu's off and on by echoing values to **/sys/devices/system/ cpu/cpu#/online**.

15.3 CPUSETS

- **Cpusets** offer a far more robust way of handling processor affinity. Instead of just assigning a mask of allowable CPU's to a particular process, one can form a whole group of processes that share the same properties in this regard.

- One should note that affinity is inherited from parent to child process, and so the simple affinity setting calls can be used to set up some of the cpuset infrastructure, although control is not as robust.

- There are a number of reasons to take advantage of cpusets, and of setting affinity in particular.

- Consider a server running different applications, for example a database and a web server. It may be advantageous to not have the two loads interfere with each other. It may be permissible to have one application to get relatively saturated while the other must proceed unimpeded.

- NUMA systems running high performance computing applications are likely to want to have **soft partitions** of the work.

- In any case, one also needs dynamical adjustment to be possible as the mix of work changes, without impacting other running jobs.

- A cpuset is a set of allowed CPUS and memory nodes (on NUMA systems.) Every task on the system belongs to a particular cpuset. Once a task is confined to a cpuset affinity changes are confined to subsets of the cpuset.

- Child cpusets can be created that are a subset of the parent cpuset. Furthermore **exclusive cpusets** can be created that do not overlap with any other cpuset.

- Controlling and interfacing with the cpuset is done through the **cgroup** pseudo-filesystem; creating a new cpuset is as simple as making a new subdirectory. First the pseudo-filesystem must be mounted:

```
$ mkdir /dev/cpuset
$ mount -t cgroup -o cpuset cpuset /dev/cpuset
$ ls -l /dev/cpuset

total 0
drwxr-xr-x  2 root root    0 Mar 30 14:52 ./
drwxr-xr-x 16 root root 5100 Mar 30 14:52 ../
-r--r--r--  1 root root    0 Mar 30 14:52 cgroup.procs
-rw-r--r--  1 root root    0 Mar 30 14:52 cpuset.cpu_exclusive
-rw-r--r--  1 root root    0 Mar 30 14:52 cpuset.cpus
-rw-r--r--  1 root root    0 Mar 30 14:52 cpuset.mem_exclusive
-rw-r--r--  1 root root    0 Mar 30 14:52 cpuset.mem_hardwall
-rw-r--r--  1 root root    0 Mar 30 14:52 cpuset.memory_migrate
-r--r--r--  1 root root    0 Mar 30 14:52 cpuset.memory_pressure
-rw-r--r--  1 root root    0 Mar 30 14:52 cpuset.memory_pressure_enabled
-rw-r--r--  1 root root    0 Mar 30 14:52 cpuset.memory_spread_page
-rw-r--r--  1 root root    0 Mar 30 14:52 cpuset.memory_spread_slab
-rw-r--r--  1 root root    0 Mar 30 14:52 cpuset.mems
-rw-r--r--  1 root root    0 Mar 30 14:52 cpuset.sched_load_balance
-rw-r--r--  1 root root    0 Mar 30 14:52 cpuset.sched_relax_domain_level
-rw-r--r--  1 root root    0 Mar 30 14:52 notify_on_release
-rw-r--r--  1 root root    0 Mar 30 14:52 release_agent
-rw-r--r--  1 root root    0 Mar 30 14:52 tasks
```

  The entries in this directory show and control the properties of the root cpuset, which contains all CPU's and memory nodes on the system.

- To create a new cpuset:

```
$ cd /dev/cpuset
$ mkdir newcpuset
```

  The new directory will contain the same entries, but uninitialized . To modify the set of allowed cpus and memory nodes:

```
$ cat cpuset.cpus
0-3
$ cat cpuset.mems
0
$ cat newcpuset/cpuset.cpus newcpuset/cpuset.mems


$ echo 2-3 > newcpuset/cpuset.cpus
$ echo 0   > newcpuset/cpuset.mems
$ cat newcpuset/cpuset.cpus newcpuset/cpusets.mems
```

```
2-3
0
```

Note that while this is being done on a non-NUMA system, one still has to set the memory node. Now assign the current shell to this cpuset::

```
$ echo $$ > newcpuset/tasks
$ cat  newcpuset/tasks
20069
20174
```

where `$$` = 20069 is the current shell pid, and the second number is the **cat** process.

15.4 SMP Algorithms - Scheduling, Locking, etc.

- The **Linux** kernel implements multi-threading through use of the `__clone()` system call, which creates a new process like `fork()` does. However, the child process shares the memory space, table of file descriptors, and table of signal handlers with the parent process,

- Multi-threading can be done on a single CPU, but on **SMP** systems it can become particularly useful. The **pthreads** library (**P**osix **threads**) is the portable way of doing so.

- When compiling applications using the **pthreads** library, one has to make sure to use the compiler flag `-D__REENTRANT` and link to the library with `-lpthread`, or use the compiler flag `-pthread`, which automatically takes care of both.

- All processors share the same main memory and use the same physical addresses. All processors use the same I/O subsystem.

- Sanity requires that certain operations and blocks of code be **atomic** with respect to other processes, and this is especially true in **SMP** mode.

- Within the kernel (and modules) one uses the various synchronization methods including **spinlocks** and semaphore operations; the `up()`, `down()` functions and their variants are all **SMP**-aware and safe.

- **Linux** has been evolving from *coarse-grained* to *fine-grained* locks; i.e., from the entire kernel being locked by only a small number of locks, to one with more locks used for shorter times. This reduces latencies, but increases overhead.

- Signal handling, interrupts, and scheduling is now all fine-grained and **SMP**-safe.

- As the **Linux SMP** implementation progressed, performance went from a situation in which CPU-bound work parallelized well but I/O-bound work did badly, to one in which true parallelization occurs.

- Each processor executes the scheduler function and selects its from its own queue of eligible processes, none of which are already on another CPU. The kernel strives to keep processes on the same CPU if possible, which is especially worthwhile if each processor has its own second level cache. Load balancing software migrates processes between CPUs periodically.

- The `current` macro expands to the task structure of the currently running process on the particular CPU on which the kernel is running; i.e., there is a `current` for each CPU.

- There are some miscellaneous functions of use, which do things like return the current CPU ID, the total number of processors, and send messages from one CPU to another.

- Message passing (on **x86**) is done using interrupts 13 and 16. The first is the unused FPU interrupt from 386 days. Since **SMP** requires at least a 486 this is not a problem. IRQ 13 is used as a fast handler which does not need a kernel lock and thus can always be processed. It can't be used to trigger the scheduler, but only to distribute messages. IRQ 16 is a slower handler which waits for the kernel lock and can trigger scheduling, and is used to start schedulers on other processors.

15.5   Labs

Lab 1: Using CPUSETS

- Mount the **cpuset** filesystem as discussed previously and create a new CPUSET. Do not forget to initialize the allowed mask for allowed processors and memory nodes.

- Assign one or more already running tasks on your system to the cpuset by echoing their **pid**'s into the `tasks` pseudofile.

- Verify that it took hold by doing all of these methods:

```
$ taskset -p <pid>
$ cat /proc/<pid>/status
$ cat /proc/<pid>/cpuset
$ cat /proc/<pid>/cgroup
```

Chapter 16

Memory Management and Allocation

We'll see how **Linux** distinguishes between virtual and physical memory and has them work together. We'll discuss the memory zone allocator scheme. We'll consider how memory is organized into pages and the various algorithms used to control and access them. We'll consider the various methods **Linux** uses to allocate memory within the kernel and device drivers, distinguishing between the kmalloc() and vmalloc() methods, and how to allocate whole pages or ranges of pages at once. We'll also consider how to grab larger amounts of memory at boot.

16.1 Virtual and Physical Memory

- **Linux** uses a **virtual memory** system (**VM**), as do all modern operating systems: the virtual memory is **larger** than the physical memory.

- Each process has its own, **protected** address space. Addresses are virtual and must be translated to and from physical addresses by the kernel whenever a process needs to access memory.

- The kernel itself also uses virtual addresses; however the translation can be as simple as an offset depending on the architecture and the type of memory being used.

- In the following diagram (for 32-bit platforms) the first 3 GB of virtual addresses are used for user-space memory and the upper GB is used for kernel-space memory (Other architectures have the same setup, but differing values for PAGE_OFFSET; for 64-bit platforms the value is in the stratosphere.)

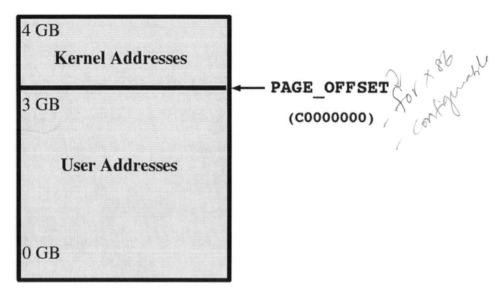

Figure 16.1: **User and Kernel Address Regions**

- The kernel allows fair shares of memory to be allocated to every running process, and coordinates when memory is shared among processes. In addition, **mapping** can be used to link a file directly to a process's virtual address space. Furthermore, certain areas of memory can be be protected against writing and/or code execution.

- For a comprehensive review of **What Every Programmer Should Know About Memory**, see Ulrich Drepper's long article at **http://people.redhat.com/drepper/cpumemory.pdf**. This covers many issues in depth such as proper use of cache, alignment, **NUMA**, virtualization, etc.

16.2   Memory Zones

- **Linux** uses a **zone allocator** memory algorithm, which is implemented in **/usr/src/linux/mm / page_alloc.c**. In this scheme, which has an object-oriented flavor, each zone has its own methods for basic memory operations such as allocating and freeing pages of memory.

- There are three memory **zones**:

  - **DMA**-capable memory must be used for **DMA** data transfers. Exactly what this means depends on the platform; for example, on **x86 ISA** devices it means the memory must lie below 16 MB.
  - **High** memory requires special handling and has meaning only certain platforms. It allows access for up to 64 GB of physical memory. On the 32-bit **x86** it means memory at and above 896 MB.
  - **Normal** memory is everything else.

- By looking at **/proc/zoneinfo** one can ascertain usage statistics for each operative zone.

(Task struct holds context switch information)

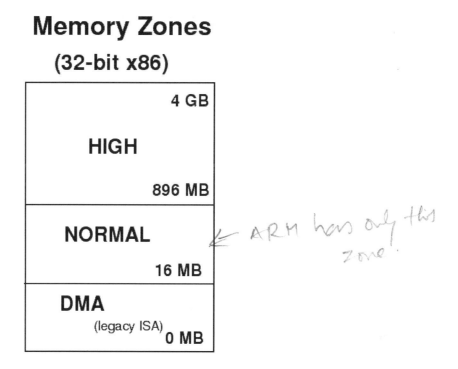

ARM has only this zone!

Figure 16.2: **DMA, Normal and High Memory**

- When memory is allocated the kernel examines what flags were associated with the request and on that basis constructs a list of memory zones that can be used. When the flag GFP_DMA is requested, only pages in the **DMA** zone are considered. If GFP_HIGHMEM is specified, all three zones can be used to get a free page. If neither of these flags are given, both the **normal** and **DMA** zones are considered. On platforms where high memory is not a concept, GFP_HIGHMEM has no effect; i.e., all memory is low memory, and memory is **flat**.

- While **Linux** permits up to 64 GB of memory to be used on 32-bit systems, the limit **per process** is a little less than 3 GB. This is because there is only 4 GB of address space (i.e., it is 32-bit limited) and the topmost GB is reserved for kernel addresses. The little is somewhat less than 3 GB because of some address space being reserved for memory-mapped devices.

16.3 Page Tables

- Memory is broken up into **pages** of fixed size (4 KB on **x86**). Portable code should never depend on a particular page size. To obtain the actual value kernel code can use the PAGE_SIZE macro and user-space programs can call the function getpagesize().

- For 4K pages, the lower 12 bits of the virtual address contain the **offset**; the remaining bits contain the **virtual page frame number** (PFN).

- Pages of virtual memory may be in any order in physical memory. The processor converts the virtual PFN into a physical one, using **page tables**. Each entry in the page table contains a **valid** flag, the PFN, and access control information.

- If the requested virtual page is not **valid**, the kernel gets a **page fault** and then tries to get the proper page into physical memory. **Demand Paging** will try and bring the page in. The page may have been swapped out to disk.

- If a page has been modified and there are insufficient free physical pages, a page is marked as **dirty** and will either be written to disk if the page corresponds to file-based data, or written to the **swap** file. Pages to be discarded are chosen with a **LRU** (Least Recently Used) algorithm.

- **Linux** uses a **four-level Page Table**, even though the 32-bit **x86** processors have only two levels of page tables. (Before version 2.6.10, **Linux** used a three-level scheme.) This permits using the same functional methods for all architectures; traversing the superfluous levels involves fall-through functions.

- If you use the 64 GB option on **x86**, **Linux** uses the **PAE** (Physical Address Extension) facility which gives an extra 4 bits of address space. In this it uses a true three-level scheme, rather than one in which one dimension is collapsed.

16.4 kmalloc()

- The most common functions for allocating and freeing memory in the **Linux** kernel are:

```
#include <linux/slab.h>

void *kmalloc (unsigned int len, gfp_t gfp_mask);
void kfree (void *ptr);
```

- Possible values for the `gfp_mask` argument are detailed in **/usr/src/linux/include/linux/gfp.h** and can be:

Table 16.1: **GFP Memory Allocation Flags**

Value	Meaning
GFP_KERNEL	Block and cause going to sleep if the memory is not immediately available, allowing preemption to occur. This is the normal way of calling `kmalloc()`.
GFP_ATOMIC	Return immediately if no pages are available. For instance, this might be done when `kmalloc()` is being called from an interrupt, where sleep would prevent receipt of other interrupts.
GFP_DMA	For buffers to be used with **ISA DMA** devices; is OR'ed with `GFP_KERNEL` or `GFP_ATOMIC`. Ensures the memory will be contiguous and falls under `MAX_DMA_ADDRESS=16 MB` on **x86** for **ISA** devices; for **PCI** this is unnecessary. The exact meaning of this flag is platform dependent.
GFP_USER	Used to allocate memory for a user . May sleep, and is a low priority request.
GFP_HIGHUSER	Like `GFP_USER`, but allocates from high memory
GFP_NOIO	Not to be used for filesystem calls, disallows I/O initiation.
GFP_NFS	For internal use.

- Drivers normally use only the values GFP_KERNEL, GFP_ATOMIC, and GFP_DMA.

- The `in_interrupt()` macro can be used to check if you are in interrupt or process context. For instance:

```
char *buffer = kmalloc (nbytes, in_interrupt() ? GFP_ATOMIC : GFP_KERNEL);
```

A similar macro, `in_atomic()`, also checks to see if you are in a preemptible context.

- **Note:** `GFP_ATOMIC` allocations are allowed to draw down memory resources more than those with `GFP_KERNEL` to lessen chances of failure; thus they should not be used when they are not necessary.

- To allocate cleared memory, use

  ```
  void *kzalloc (size_t size, gfp_t flags);
  ```

  which calls `kmalloc(size, flags)` and then clears the allocated memory region.

- One can also resize a dynamically allocated region with:

  ```
  void *krealloc (const void *p, size_t new_size, gfp_t flags);
  ```

- `kmalloc()` will return memory chunks in whatever power of 2 that matches or exceeds `len`. It doesn't clear memory, and will return `NULL` on failure, or a pointer to the allocated memory on success. The largest allocation that can be obtained is 1024 pages (4 MB on **x86**). For somewhat larger requests (more than a few KB) it is better to use the `__get_free_page()` functions.

- Furthermore `kmalloc()` always returns physically contiguous memory such as that need for **DMA** transfers.

16.5 __get_free_pages()

- To allocate (and free) entire pages (or multiple pages) of memory in one fell swoop one can use:

  ```
  #include <linux/mm.h>

  unsigned long get_zeroed_page  (gfp_t gfp_mask);
  unsigned long __get_free_page  (gfp_t gfp_mask);
  unsigned long __get_free_pages (gfp_t gfp_mask, unsigned long order);

  void free_page  (unsigned long addr);
  void free_pages (unsigned long addr, unsigned long order);
  ```

  [handwritten: → 2^order will be returned]

- The `gfp_mask` argument is used in the same fashion as in `kmalloc()`.

- `order` gives the number of pages (as a power of 2). The limit is 1024 pages, or `order` = 10 (4 MB on **x86**). There is a function called `get_order()` defined in **/usr/src/linux/include/asm-generic/page.h** which can be used to determine the order given a number of bytes.

- The `__get_free_pages()` function returns a pointer to the first byte of a memory area that is several pages long, and doesn't zero the area. Note that these pages will always be physically contiguous.

- The `__get_free_page()` function doesn't clear the page; it is preferred over `get_zeroed_page()` because clearing the page might take longer than simply getting it.

- It is important to free pages when they are no longer needed to avoid kernel memory leaks.

Example:

```
tty->read_buf = (unsigned char *) __get_free_page(
                             (in_interrupt()) ? GFP_ATOMIC : GFP_KERNEL);
if (!tty->read_buf)
            return -ENOMEM;
```

16.6   vmalloc()

- vmalloc() allocates a contiguous memory region in the **virtual** address space:

  ```
  #include <linux/vmalloc.h>

  void *vmalloc (unsigned long size);
  void vfree (void *ptr);
  ```

- vmalloc() can't be used when the real physical address is needed (such as for DMA), and can't be used at interrupt time; internally it uses kmalloc() with GFP_KERNEL.

- While the allocated pages may not be physically adjacent the kernel sees them as a contiguous range of addresses. The resulting virtual addresses are higher than the top of physical memory.

- More overhead is required than for __get_free_pages(), so this method shouldn't be used for small requests. In principle, vmalloc() can return up to the amount of physical RAM, but in reality one may obtain far less, depending on the platform and the amount of physical memory.

Example:

```
in_buf[dev]=(struct mbuf *)vmalloc(sizeof(struct mbuf));

if (in_buf[dev] == NULL)
 {
   printk(KERN_WARNING "Can't allocate buffer in_buf\n");
   my_devs[dev]->close(dev);
   return -EIO;
  }
```

- Current vmalloc() allocations are exposed through **/proc/vmallocinfo**.

16.7 Early Allocations and bootmem()

- The maximum amount of contiguous memory you can obtain through the various `__get_free_page()` functions is 1024 pages (4 MB on **x86**.) If you want more you can not do it from a module, but the kernel does offer some functions for doing this during boot:

```
#include <linux/bootmem.h>
```

```
void *alloc_bootmem          (unsigned long size);
void *alloc_bootmem_low      (unsigned long size);
void *alloc_bootmem_pages    (unsigned long size);
void *alloc_bootmem_low_pages (unsigned long size);
```

not flexible

- The functions with **_pages** in their name allocate whole pages; the others are not page-aligned. The functions with **_low** make sure the memory locations obtained lie below `MAX_DMA_ADDRESS`. Otherwise, the memory allocation will be above that value.

- It is impossible to free any memory allocated using these functions. However, once you have grabbed this large memory chunk you are free to run your own kind of memory allocator to reuse the memory as needed.

- These functions are primarily intended for critical data structures that are allocated early in the boot process and are required throughout the life of the system. However, they can be used for other purposes.

16.8 Slabs and Cache Allocations   *(Slab cache)*

- Suppose you need to allocate memory for an object that is less than a page in size, or is not a multiple of a page size and you don't want to waste space by requesting whole pages. Or suppose you need to create and destroy objects of the same size repeatedly, perhaps data structures or data buffers. These may be page size multiples or not.

- In either case it would be very wasteful for the kernel to continually create and destroy these objects if they are going to be reused, and it is additionally wasteful to induce the kind of fragmentation that results from continually requesting partial pages.

- You could allocate your own pool of memory and set up your own caching system, but **Linux** already has a well defined interface for doing this, and it should be used. **Linux** uses an algorithm based on the well-known **slab allocator** scheme. As part of this scheme you can create a special memory pool, or **cache** and add and remove objects from it (all of the same size) as needs require.

- The kernel can dynamically shrink the cache if it has memory needs elsewhere, but it will not have to re-allocate a new object every time you need one if there are still wholly or partially unused **slabs** in the cache. Note that more than one **object** can be in a **slab**, whose size is going to be an integral number of pages.

- The following functions create, set up, and destroy your own memory cache:

```
#include <linux/slab.h>
```

```
struct kmem_cache *kmem_cache_create (
    const char *name, size_t size,
    size_t offset, unsigned long flags,
    void (*ctor)(void *, struct kmem_cache *, unsigned long flags),
}
int kmem_cache_shrink  (struct kmem_cache *cache);
void kmem_cache_destroy (struct kmem_cache *cache);
```

- These create a new memory cache of type `struct kmem_cache`, with the `name` argument serving to identify it. All objects in the cache (there can be any number) are `size` bytes in length, which cannot be more than 1024 pages (4 MB on **x86**).

- The `offset` argument indicates alignment, or offset into the page for the objects you are allocating; normally you'll just give 0.

- The last argument to `kmem_cache_create()` points to an optional **constructor** function used to initialize any objects before they are used; the header file contains more detailed information about the arguments and flags that can be passed to this rarely used function.

- The `flags` argument is a bitmask of choices given in **/usr/src/linux/include/linux/slab.h**; the main ones are:

Table 16.3: **Memory Cache Flags**

Flag	Meaning
SLAB_HWCACHE_ALIGN	Force alignment of data objects on cache lines. This improves performance but may waste memory. Should be set for critical performance code.
SLAB_POISON	Fill the slab layer with the known value, a5a5a5a5. Good for catching access to uninitialized memory.
SLAB_RED_ZONE	Surround allocated memory with **red zones** that scream when touched, to detect buffer overruns.
SLAB_PANIC	Cause system panic upon allocation failure.
SLAB_DEBUG_FREE	Perform expensive checks on freeing objects
SLAB_CACHE_DMA	Make sure the allocation is in the **DMA** zone.

- When your cache has been deployed, `name` will show up under **/proc/slabinfo**, and will show something like:

```
slabinfo - version: 1.1
kmem_cache          59      78     100     2     2     1
mycache              0       1    4096     0     1     1
ip_conntrack         0      11     352     0     1     1
tcp_tw_bucket        0       0      96     0     0     1
tcp_bind_bucket     12     113      32     1     1     1
.....
size-8192(DMA)       0       0    8192     0     0     2
size-8192            0       1    8192     0     1     2
....
size-32(DMA)         0       0      32     0     0     1
size-32            888    8814      32    69    78     1
```

where the meanings of the fields are:

  - Cache name
  - Number of active objects
  - Total objects
  - Object size

- Number of active slabs

- Total slabs

- Number of pages per slab

- A dynamic and interactive view of the various caches on the system can be obtained by using the **slabtop** utility, where the elements can be sorted in many ways. One can see the same information by using the command `vmstat -m`.

- Now that you have created your memory cache, you can make any number of objects associated with it, and free them, with the functions:

```
void *kmem_cache_alloc( struct kmem_cache *cache, gfp_t gfp_mask);
void kmem_cache_free  ( struct kmem_cache *cache, void *);
```

pointing to the cache you have created as the first argument. The `gfp_mask` argument is the same as for `__get_free_pages()`. (If the memory doesn't already exist in the cache, it will be created using these flags.) The second argument to `kmem_cache_free()` simply points to what you got from `kmem_cache_alloc()`.

- You can use the function `kmem_cache_shrink()` to release unused objects. When you no longer need your memory cache you must free it up with `kmem_cache_destroy()` (which shrinks the cache first); otherwise resources will not be freed. This function will fail if any object allocated to the cache has not been released.

- Note it is also possible to set up a memory cache that never drops below a certain size using a **memory pool**, for which the **API** can be found in **/usr/src/linux/include/linux/mempool.h**. Such memory is taken outside of the normal memory management system and should be used only for critical purposes.

- The 2.6.22 kernel introduced the **SLUB** allocator as a drop-in replacement for the older **SLAB** implementation. Which one to use is a compile time option; in the 2.6.23 kernel **SLUB** was made the default.

- The new allocator has less of the complexity that evolved in the old one, has a smaller memory footprint, some performance enhancements, is better adapted for **NUMA** systems and has easier debugging capabilities.

- Eventually **SLAB** may disappear, but due to the importance of having a stable cache allocator, this will only happen after **SLUB** has withstood the test of large scale deployment. Indeed there has also been development of other alternatives such as the **SLOB** and **SLQB** slab allocators.

16.9   Labs

Lab 1: Memory Caches

- Extend your character driver to allocate the driver's internal buffer by using your own memory cache. Make sure you free any slabs you create.

- For extra credit create more than one object (perhaps every time you do a read or write) and make sure you release them all before destroying the cache.

Lab 2: Testing Maximum Memory Allocation

- See how much memory you can obtain dynamically, using both `kmalloc()` and `__get_free_pages()`.

- Start with requesting 1 page of memory, and then keep doubling until your request fails for each type fails.

- Make sure you free any memory you receive.

- You'll probably want to use `GFP_ATOMIC` rather than `GFP_KERNEL`. (Why?)

- If you have trouble getting enough memory due to memory fragmentation trying writing a poor-man's de-fragmenter, and then running again. The de-fragmenter can just be an application that grabs all available memory, uses it, and then releases it when done, thereby clearing the caches. You can also try the command `sync; echo 3 > /proc/sys/vm/drop_caches` .

- Try the same thing with `vmalloc()`. Rather than doubling allocations, start at 4 MB and increase in 4 MB increments until failure results. Note this may hang while loading. (Why?)

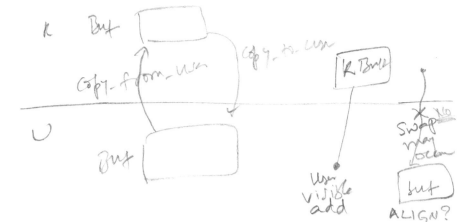

Chapter 17

Transferring Between User and Kernel Space

We'll see how **Linux** handles the transfer of data between user and kernel spaces We'll discuss the various functions such as put_user() and get_user(), and copy_to_user() and copy_from_user(), that are used to accomplish this. We'll consider direct **kernel I/O**, and the get_user_pages() set of functions which can be used to pin memory and enhance I/O throughput. Then we will discuss **memory mapping** and explain the user-space system calls that applications can use to take advantage of it. We will also examine the memory mapping entry point into a character driver. We'll also consider the use of **Relay Channels**. Finally, we'll also show how to access files from within the kernel, while pointing out why. this is generally not a good method to use.

17.1   Transferring Between Spaces

- User-space applications work in a different (virtual) memory space than does the kernel.

- When an address is passed to the kernel, it is the virtual address in user-space. An example would be the pointer to `buf` in the `read()` and `write()` driver entry points.

- Any attempt from within the kernel to directly access these virtual pointers is a good recipe for disaster. As a matter of principle, these addresses may not be meaningful in kernel-space.

- One might indeed get away with dereferencing a pointer passed from user-space - *for a while*. If a page gets swapped out, disaster will occur. The moral of the story is that one should **never** directly dereference a user-space pointer in kernel-space.

- The functions which accomplish the transfers do two distinct things:

  – Verify the user-space address, and handle any page faults that may occur if the page is currently not resident in memory.

  – Perform a copy between the user and kernel addresses.

- Using **raw** I/O or **memory mapping** can avoid copying.

17.2   put(get)_user() and copy_to(from)_user()

- All the following functions can be used only in the context of a process, since they must refer to the current process's `task_struct` data structure in order to do the address translation. Calling them from an interrupt routine is another good recipe for disaster.

- One should never surround the following transfer functions with a spinlock, as they may go to sleep, in which case your driver (or even the system) could get hung, as the spinlock might never be released.

```
#include <linux/uaccess.h>

access_ok (int type, unsigned long addr, unsigned long size);

int get_user (lvalue, ptr);
int __get_user (lvalue, ptr);

int put_user (expr, ptr);
int __put_user (expr, ptr);

unsigned long [__]copy_from_user (
        void __user *to,
        const void *from;
        unsigned long n) ;

unsigned long [__]copy_to_user (
        void *to,
        const void *from,
        unsigned long n) ;

long [__]strncpy_from_user (char *dst, const char *src, long count);
```

```
long  strlen_user (const char *str);
long strnlen_user (const char *str, long n);
unsigned long [__]clear_user (void *mem, unsigned long len);
```

- These functions are the **only** place in the kernel where page faults are resolved as they are in user-space, by demand paging or segmentation faults according to whether or not they are legal.

- This occurs only on pages for the user-space pointer; the kernel never swaps out pages for its own use and always allocates them with urgency and thus never has demand faulting for kernel memory.

access_ok()

- type is VERIFY_READ or VERIFY_WRITE depending on what you want to do in *user-space*. For both use VERIFY_WRITE

- addr is the address to be checked.

- size is a byte count.

- Is called by the most of the following functions; thus rarely needs to be called directly.

- Returns 1 (true) if current process is allowed access; 0 on failure.

get_user()

- Transfers data from **user** space to **kernel** space.

- Assigns to lvalue data retrieved from the pointer ptr.

- Is implemented as a macro, which depends on the type of ptr.

- Calls access_ok() internally.

- Retrieves a single value.

- Returns 0 for success, -EFAULT otherwise.

__get_user()

- Same as get_user() but doesn't call access_ok(). Use when safety is already assured.

put_user(), __put_user()

- Transfers data from **kernel** space to **user** space.

- Same as the get_user() functions, except the direction is reversed; Writes expr data to user space at ptr.

copy_from_user()

- Transfers `len` bytes from **user** space to **kernel** space.

- Calls `access_ok()` internally.

- Also `__copy_from_user(to, from, len)`.

- Returns the number of bytes ***not*** transferred. In error, the driver should return `-EFAULT`

copy_to_user()

- Transfers `len` bytes from **kernel** space to **user** space.

- Calls `access_ok()` internally.

- Also `__copy_to_user(to, from, len)`.

- Returns the number of bytes ***not*** transferred. In error, the driver should return `-EFAULT`

strncpy_from_user(), strlen_user(), clear_user()

- The string functions work just as their names suggest, except the pointer of the string is in user-space.

- The `clear_user()` function clears the contents of the memory location pointed to.

17.3   Direct transfer - Kernel I/O and Memory Mapping

- There are two complementary methods **Linux** can use to avoid using the heretofore described transfer functions.

- In the **kio** method, the kernel is given direct access to user-space memory pointers. The memory is locked down while the transfer goes on, making sure no pages swap out and the pointers remain valid. When the transfer is over the pinning is released. This is the basis of the **raw I/O** implementation. Note that if a file is opened with the non-standard `O_DIRECT` flag, **kio** will be used on that file.

- In the **memory mapping** method, user-space is given direct access to kernel memory buffers, which may be memory regions residing directly on the device. The `mmap()` call is a standard POSIX system call.

- Both methods avoid any buffering or caching for the data being transferred. They require longer to set up and shut down than the copying methods previously discussed. What is the best method depends on a number of factors, such as the size of the transfers, their frequency, the likelihood the data will be reused, etc.

17.4 Kernel I/O

- Sometimes it is desirable to bypass the buffer and page caches entirely, and have I/O operations pass directly through to the device in raw form. This eliminates at least one copy operation. Large data base applications are often users of so-called **raw** I/O operations.

- This facility can be used to lock down user-space buffers and use them directly in the kernel, without use of the `copy_to_user()`, `copy_from_user()` and related functions.

- From user-space, one can force the kernel to use this kind of direct I/O, by opening a file with the `O_DIRECT` flag. This is a GNU extension, so you will also define the macro `_GNU_SOURCE`; i.e, you'll need something like:

```
#define _GNU_SOURCE
...
fd = open (filename, O_DIRECT | O_RDWR | O_CREAT | O_TRUNC, 0666);
```

Whenever this file descriptor is used, kernel I/O will be used.

- Here's an example of a short program which copies a file, using direct I/O on the output file. We use `posix_memalign()` (or the older `memalign()`) instead of ordinary `malloc()` to ensure sector alignment. (All transfers must be sector aligned and an integral number of sectors long.)

```
/*
 args: 1 = input file, 2 = output file, [3 = chunk size]

 usage: %s infile ofile
        %s infile ofile 512
 */

#define _GNU_SOURCE
#define SECTOR_SIZE 512

#include <unistd.h>
#include <fcntl.h>
#include <stdlib.h>
#include <stdio.h>
#include <malloc.h>
#include <string.h>

int main(int argc, char *argv[])
{
        char *buf;
        int fdin, fdout, rcr, rcw;
/* default chunk = 1 page */
        int size = getpagesize();
        if (argc > 3)
                size = atoi(argv[3]);

        /* open input file, must exist */
        fdin = open(argv[1], O_RDONLY);

        /* open output file, create or truncate */
        fdout = open(argv[2], O_DIRECT | O_RDWR | O_CREAT | O_TRUNC, 0666);

        /* use sector aligned memory region */
        /* buf = (char *)memalign (SECTOR_SIZE, size); */
```

```
    posix_memalign(&buf, SECTOR_SIZE, size);

    while ((rcr = read(fdin, buf, size)) > 0) {
            rcw = write(fdout, buf, rcr);
            printf("in = %d, out = %d\n", rcr, rcw);
            if (rcr != rcw)
                    printf
                        ("Oops, BAD values -- not sector aligned perhaps\n");
    }
    close(fdin);
    close(fdout);
    exit(0);
}
```

17.5   Mapping User Pages

- The get_user_pages() function provides a method of exposing user-space memory directly to the kernel, which can help avoid an extra copy; in some sense it is the inverse operation to **memory mapping** which makes kernel memory directly visible to the user side.

- The essential function is:

```
#include <linux/mm.h>

int get_user_pages(struct task_struct *tsk,
                    struct mm_struct *mm,
                    unsigned long start,
                    int len,
                    int write,
                    int force,
                    struct page **pages,
                    struct vm_area_struct **vmas);
```

- The first two arguments are the process and user address space involved; usually they are just current and current->mm.

- The start argument gives the starting address of the user-space buffer of length len pages (not bytes). The write flag should be set if one desires to alter the buffer, and the force flag can be set to force access no matter what current permissions are.

- The return value of this function is the number of pages mapped, and the pages argument receives an array to pointers for page structures. The final argument will be filled with an array of pointers to the vm_area structure containing each page, unless it is passed as NULL.

- A typical use of this function might look like:

```
down_read (&current->mm->mmap_sem);
rc = get_user_pages (current, current->mm, (unsigned long) buf, npages, 1, 0, pages, NULL);
up_read (&current->mm->mmap_sem);
```

where a read lock is placed around the user-space memory region while the access is obtained.

- One important thing to keep in mind is that one obtains only the pointer to the struct page that contains the user address. To get a useful kernel address for the page one has to use macros and functions such as:

```
#include <linux/pagemap.h>
....
char *kbuf = page_address (pages[i]);
```

or do

```
char *kbuf = kmap (pages[i]);
....
kunmap(pages[i]);
```

The second form also handles the case of high memory, but one has to be sure to do the unmapping when done. (In interrupt handlers, one needs to use the functions `kmap_atomic()`,`kunmap_atomic()`, but that can't happen when using `get_user_pages()` since you must be in process context anyway.)

- Note that unless the buffer happens to be **page-aligned**, one only knows that the user address lies **somewhere** in the page; the offset is not furnished. One can produce page-aligned user memory with functions such as `posix_memalign()`, or use utilities which are alignment aware, such as **dd**. Programs such as **cat** are not.

- It is also necessary to cleanup after any modification of the user pages; otherwise corruption may ensue as the virtual memory system has been bypassed. This means marking modified pages as **dirty** and releasing them from the page cache:

```
set_page_dirty_lock(pages[i]);
page_cache_release (pages[i]);
```

17.6 Memory Mapping

- When a file is **memory mapped** the file (or part of it) can be associated with a range of linear addresses. Input and output operations on the file can be accomplished with simple memory references, rather than explicit I/O operations.

- This can also be done on device nodes for direct access to hardware devices; in this case the driver must register and implement a proper `mmap()` entry point.

- This method is not useful for stream-oriented devices. The mapped area must be a multiple of `PAGE_SIZE` in extent, and start on a page boundary.

- Two basic kinds of memory mapping exist:

  - In a **shared** memory map any operation on the memory region is completely equivalent to changing the file it represents. Changes are committed to disk (with the usual delays) and any process accessing the file or mapping it will see the changes.

  - In a **private** memory map any changes are not committed to disk and are not seen by any other process. This is more efficient, but by design is used for a read only situation, or when the final saving of data is to be done by writing to another file.

- Memory mapping can be more efficient than normal disk access, particularly when files are being shared by multiple processes, each one of whom can share access to certain pages, thereby minimizing memory usage and speeding access times.

17.7   User-Space Functions for mmap()

- From the user side, memory mapping is done with:

```
#include <unistd.h>
#include <sys/mman.h>

void *mmap (void  *start,  size_t length, int prot, int flags, int fd, off_t offset);
int munmap (void *start, size_t length);
```

- This requests the mapping into memory of `length` bytes, starting at offset `offset`, from the file specified by `fd`. The offset must be an integral number of pages.

- The address `start` is a preferred address to map to; if 0 is given (the usual case), `mmap()` will choose the address and put it in the return value.

- `prot` is the desired memory protection. It has bits:

Table 17.2: **mmap() Memory Protection Bits**

Value	Meaning
PROT_EXEC	Pages may be executed.
PROT_READ	Pages may be read.
PROT_WRITE	Pages may be written.
PROT_NONE	Pages may not be accessed.

- `flags` specifies the type of mapped object. It has bits:

Table 17.3: **mmap() flags**

Value	Meaning
MAP_FIXED	If `start` can't be used, fail.
MAP_SHARED	Share the mapping with all other processes.
MAP_PRIVATE	Create a private copy-on-write mapping.

  Either `MAP_SHARED` or `MAP_PRIVATE` must be specified. Remember, a **private** mapping does not change the file on disk. Whatever changes are made will be lost when the process terminates.

- Other non-POSIX flags can be specified (see **man mmap**.) In particular, the `MAP_ANONYMOUS` flag permits a mapping only in memory, without a file association.

- Here's a simple example of using anonymous memory mapping to share memory between a parent and child:

```
#include <stdlib.h>
#include <stdio.h>
#include <unistd.h>
#include <string.h>
#include <sys/mman.h>
```

```
#include <sys/types.h>
#include <sys/wait.h>

int main(int argc, char **argv)
{
        int fd = -1, size = 4096, status;
        char *area;
        pid_t pid;

        area =
            mmap(NULL, size, PROT_READ | PROT_WRITE,
                MAP_SHARED | MAP_ANONYMOUS, fd, 0);

        pid = fork();
        if (pid == 0) {                    /* child */
                strcpy(area, "This is a message from the child");
                printf("Child has written: %s\n", area);
                exit(EXIT_SUCCESS);
        }
        if (pid > 0) {                     /* parent */
                wait(&status);
                printf("Parent has read:   %s\n", area);
                exit(EXIT_SUCCESS);
        }
        exit(EXIT_FAILURE);
}
```

- munmap() deletes the mappings and causes further references to addresses within the range to generate invalid memory references.

- See man mmap for further information on error codes.

17.8 Driver Entry Point for mmap()

- From the kernel side, the driver entry point looks like:

```
#include <linux/mm.h>

int (*mmap) (struct file *filp, struct vm_area_struct *vma);
```

- The vma_area_struct data structure is defined in **/usr/src/linux/include/linux/mm.h** and contains the important information. The basic elements are:

```
struct vm_area_struct {
...
   unsigned long vm_start;   /* Our start address within vm_mm. */
   unsigned long vm_end;     /* The first byte after our end address within vm_mm. */
....
   pgprot_t vm_page_prot;    /* Access permissions of this VMA. */
   unsigned long vm_flags;   /* Flags, see mm.h */
....
   /* Function pointers to deal with this struct. */
   const struct vm_operations_struct * vm_ops;

   /* Information about our backing store: */
   unsigned long vm_pgoff;   /* Offset (within vm_file) in PAGE_SIZE
```

```
                        units, *not* PAGE_CACHE_SIZE */
    ....
    };
```

- The `vm_ops` structure can be used to override default operations. Pointers can be given for functions to: `open()`, `close()`, `unmap()`, `protect()`, `sync()`, `advice()`, `swapout()`, `swapin()` ....

- A simple example serves to show how the fields are used:

```
#include <linux/mm.h>

int my_mmap (struct file *file, struct vm_area_struct *vma)
{
  if( remap_pfn_range (vma, vma->vm_start, vma->vm_pgoff,
      vma->vm_end-vma->vm_start, vma->vm_page_prot ))
        return -EAGAIN;
  return 0;
}
```

- Most of the work is done by the function `remap_pfn_range()`:

```
int remap_pfn_range(struct vm_area_struct *vma, /* user vma to map to */
                    unsigned long addr,         /* target user address to start at */
                    unsigned long pfn,          /* physical address of kernel memory */
                    unsigned long size,         /* size of map area */
                    pgprot_t prot);             /* page protection flags for this mapping */
```

Note the `pfn` is the page frame number, so to get it from a particular virtual address you will have to do something like:

```
pfn = __pa(vaddr) >> PAGE_SHIFT;
```

Also note that this function does allow mapping memory above 4 GB on 32-bit systems.

- If you are mapping device I/O memory you should do:

```
vma->vm_page_prot = pgprot_noncached(vma->vm_page_prot);
```

to prevent caching which will slow things down.

- Here is a simple example of a program to test the `mmap()` entry:

```
#include <stdlib.h>
#include <stdio.h>
#include <unistd.h>
#include <string.h>
#include <fcntl.h>
#include <errno.h>
#include <sys/mman.h>

#define DEATH(mess) { perror(mess); exit(errno); }

int main(int argc, char **argv)
{
        int fd, size, rc, j;
        char *area, *tmp, *nodename = "/dev/mycdrv";
        char c[2] = "CX";
```

```
            if (argc > 1)
                    nodename = argv[1];

            size = getpagesize();        /* use one page by default */
            if (argc > 2)
                    size = atoi(argv[2]);

            printf(" Memory Mapping Node: %s, of size %d bytes\n", nodename, size);

            if ((fd = open(nodename, O_RDWR)) < 0)
                    DEATH("problems opening the node ");

            area = mmap(NULL, size, PROT_READ | PROT_WRITE, MAP_SHARED, fd, 0);

            if (area == MAP_FAILED)
                    DEATH("error mmaping");

            /* can close the file now */

            close(fd);

            /* put the string repeatedly in the file */

            tmp = area;
            for (j = 0; j < size - 1; j += 2, tmp += 2)
                    memcpy(tmp, &c, 2);

            /* just cat out the file to see if it worked */

            rc = write(STDOUT_FILENO, area, size);

            if (rc != size)
                    DEATH("problems writing");

            exit(EXIT_SUCCESS);
    }
```

- Here is a simple driver with a mmap() entry point:

```
/* Sample Character Driver with mmap'ing */

#include <linux/module.h>
#include <linux/mm.h>

/* either of these (but not both) will work */
//#include "lab_char.h"
#include "lab_miscdev.h"

static int mycdrv_mmap(struct file *file, struct vm_area_struct *vma)
{
        printk(KERN_INFO "I entered the mmap function\n");
        if (remap_pfn_range(vma, vma->vm_start,
                            vma->vm_pgoff,
                            vma->vm_end - vma->vm_start, vma->vm_page_prot)) {
                return -EAGAIN;
        }

        return 0;
```

```
}

/* don't bother with open, release, read and write */

static const struct file_operations mycdrv_fops = {
        .owner = THIS_MODULE,
        .mmap = mycdrv_mmap,
};

module_init(my_generic_init);
module_exit(my_generic_exit);

MODULE_AUTHOR("Jerry Cooperstein");
MODULE_DESCRIPTION("Sample Memory Map Driver Entry");
MODULE_LICENSE("GPL v2");
```

17.9   Relay Channels

- One often comes up with the need to transfer information between kernel-space and user-space, but not all needs are the same. One may or may not need bi-directionality, efficiency, or promptness. Or one may be working with or without a device driver, and have large or small amounts of data.

- The **Relay Channel** interface (formerly known as **relayfs**) provides a simple to use mechanism that works beautifully when the direction is one way: from kernel to user.

- Kernel clients fill up **channel buffers** with no special constraints on the data form. Users get access to the data with normal system calls, generally **read()** and/or **mmap()**, exercised on data files (by default one for each CPU) that are treated much like normal pipes.

- For each relay channel, there is one buffer per CPU. In turn, each buffer has one or more sub-buffers.

- When a sub-buffer is too full to fit a new chunk of data, or message, the next buffer (if available) is used; messages are never split between sub-buffers (so a message should not be bigger than a sub-buffer.) User-space can be notified that a sub-buffer is full.

- The buffer can be set up in either overwrite or no-overwrite mode (the default); in the second mode, kernel clients will block until readers empty the buffer.

- When the user-space application accesses the data with `read()` calls, any padding at the end of sub-buffers is removed and the buffers are drained.

- When user-space application accesses the data with `mmap()` calls, the entire buffer (including all sub-buffers) must be mapped and no draining occurs. This is more efficient than just using reads, but is also more complex.

- Here's a complete list of the system calls that can be used on a relay channel:

    - `open()`, `close()`: open and close an existing channel buffer. If no other process, or kernel client, is still using the buffer, the channel is freed upon closing.

    - `read()`: Consume bytes from the channel. In no-overwrite mode it is fine if kernel clients are writing simultaneously, but in overwrite mode unpredictable outcomes can happen. Sub-buffer padding is not seen by readers.

    - `mmap()`, `munmap()`: The entire buffer must be mapped and there is no draining.

    - `sendfile()`: Drains like a read.

– poll(): User applications are notified when a sub-buffer boundary is reached, and the flags POLLIN, POLLRDNORM, POLLERR are supported.

- While the work of this mechanism could be done using other methods, such as using the /proc filesystem, ioctl() commands on either real or pseudo devices, improper use of printk() statements, or worst, accessing a log file directly from the kernel, the use of relay channels offers a clean method.

- Relay channels have never been widely adopted in the **Linux** kernel, and everything they can do is probably available using the newer **ftrace** facility, for which there is a strong ongoing development effort.

- Thus we present this material more for its pedagogical value rather than as a recommendation for its use.

17.10 Relay API

- Opening and closing a relay channel is done with

```
#include <linux/relay.h>

struct rchan *relay_open(const char *base_filename,
                         struct dentry *parent,
                         size_t subbuf_size,
                         size_t n_subbufs,
                         struct rchan_callbacks *cb
                         void *private_data);
void relay_close(struct rchan *chan);
```

which associates a file with the channel for each CPU; e.g., if base_filename = "my_chan", the files will be named my_chan0, my_chan1, my_chan2. The associated files will appear in the directory pointed to by parent; if this is NULL, they be in the host filesystem's root directory.

- Each of the n_subbufs sub-buffers is of size subbuf_size, so the total size of the buffer is subbuf_size * n_subbufs. Writes by kernel clients should not be bigger than subbuf_size since they can't be split across sub-buffers.

- When one wants to write into a relay channel, it is done with:

```
void relay_write(struct rchan *chan, const void *data, size_t length);
```

and the information will appear in the associated pseudofile. The final argument to relay_open() is to a table of callback functions:

```
struct rchan_callbacks {
    int (*subbuf_start) (struct rchan_buf *buf,
                         void *subbuf,
                         void *prev_subbuf,
                         size_t prev_padding);
    void (*buf_mapped)  (struct rchan_buf *buf,
                         struct file *filp);
```

```
      void (*buf_unmapped)(struct rchan_buf *buf,
                           struct file *filp);
      struct dentry *(*create_buf_file)(const char *filename,
                           struct dentry *parent,
                           int mode,
                           struct rchan_buf *buf,
                           int *is_global);
      int (*remove_buf_file)(struct dentry *dentry);
}
```

- subbuf_start() is called when one switches to a new sub-buffer. buf_mapped(), buf_unmapped() are called when the buffer is memory mapped or unmapped.

- create_buf_file(), remove_buf_file() create (and remove) the files associated with the relay channel. Note that if the parameter is_global is not zero, there will be only one file even on multiple CPUs; in that case you will explicitly have to take care of any race conditions. The mode argument gives the usual permissions and parent is obviously the parent directory. filename has to be **created/removed** by this method.

- There is no apriori requirement for where these files should go. A convenient place is the debugfs filesystem. In that case one could have:

```
static struct dentry
*create_buf_file_handler(const char *filename,
                         struct dentry *parent,
                         int mode,
                         struct rchan_buf *buf,
                         int *is_global)
{
    return debugfs_create_file(filename, mode, parent, buf,
                               &relay_file_operations);
}
static int remove_buf_file_handler(struct dentry *dentry)
{
    debugfs_remove(dentry);
    return 0;
}
static struct rchan_callbacks relay_callbacks =
{
        .create_buf_file = create_buf_file_handler,
        .remove_buf_file = remove_buf_file_handler,
};
```

where relay_file_operations is the file_operations structure defined in **/usr/src/linux/kernel/relay.c**.

- There are additional callback and utility functions that can be used with relay channels, and one can take control at a lower level than we have indicated. Working with memory mapping requires a little more work than just using read() calls. However, we would recommend starting with what we have described before trying to master some of the intricacies, especially when working in overwrite mode.

17.11   Accessing Files from the Kernel

- A perennial question is "How do I do file I/O from within the kernel?" This is a **bad idea**. It is full of problems involving, stability, race conditions, and security. For an excellent explanation of why this operation is really only suitable as a learning exercise, see **http://www.cs.helsinki.fi/linux/linux-kernel/2003-23/1447.html**.

- You can't accomplish file I/O without a process context; the kernel has to borrow one or create one; borrowing is extremely dangerous as you may corrupt the context of the loaner; creating requires a new kernel thread.

- For a similar method to what is given below, see the article by Greg Kroah-Hartman at **http://www.linuxjournal.com/article/8110**.

- One must set the address space to a user one before dealing with files, and then reset it when done. The macros for handling this are:

```
get_ds();
get_fs();
set_fs(x);
```

  The macro `set_fs(x)` sets which **data segment** to use, where x can be `KERNEL_DS` or `USER_DS`. The macro `get_ds()` is just a shorthand for `KERNEL_DS`. The full definitions can be found in **/usr/src/linux/arch/arm/include/asm/uaccess.h** on most architectures.

- While kernel developers have made directly dealing with files deliberately difficult, however, there does exist a `kernel_read()` function that can be used, and we'll define a `kernel_write()` function below to go along with it.

- Note you can not use these functions from an atomic context as they may sleep; therefore no use in interrupt handlers, timers, etc.

- Here's an example of how to do it:

Example:

```
#include <linux/module.h>
#include <linux/init.h>
#include <linux/uaccess.h>
#include <linux/slab.h>
#include <linux/fs.h>

static char *filename = "/tmp/tempfile";
module_param(filename, charp, S_IRUGO);

int kernel_write(struct file *file, unsigned long offset,
                char *addr, unsigned long count)
{
        mm_segment_t old_fs;
        loff_t pos = offset;
        int result;

        old_fs = get_fs();
        set_fs(get_ds());
        /* The cast to a user pointer is valid due to the set_fs() */
        result = vfs_write(file, (void __user *)addr, count, &pos);
```

```
        set_fs(old_fs);
        return result;
}


#define NBYTES_TO_READ 20

/* adapted from kernel_read() in kernel/exec.c */

static int __init my_init(void)
{
        struct file *f;
        int nbytes, j;
        char *buffer;
        char newstring[] = "NEWSTRING";

        buffer = kmalloc(PAGE_SIZE, GFP_KERNEL);
        printk(KERN_INFO "Trying to open file = %s\n", filename);
        f = filp_open(filename, O_RDWR, S_IWUSR | S_IRUSR);

        if (IS_ERR(f)) {
                printk(KERN_INFO "error opening %s\n", filename);
                kfree(buffer);
                return -EIO;
        }

        nbytes = kernel_read(f, f->f_pos, buffer, NBYTES_TO_READ);

        printk(KERN_INFO "I read nbytes = %d, which were: \n\n", nbytes);
        for (j = 0; j < nbytes; j++)
                printk(KERN_INFO "%c", buffer[j]);

        strcpy(buffer, newstring);
        nbytes = kernel_write(f, f->f_pos, buffer, strlen(newstring) + 1);
        printk(KERN_INFO "\n\n I wrote nbytes = %d, which were %s \n", nbytes,
                newstring);

        filp_close(f, NULL);
        kfree(buffer);

        return 0;
}

static void __exit my_exit(void)
{
        printk(KERN_INFO "\nclosing up\n");
}

module_init(my_init);
module_exit(my_exit);
```

- Such a method should never be used in code that is submitted to the kernel tree.

17.12 Labs

Lab 1: Using get_user() and put_user().

- Adapt your character driver to use `get_user()` and `put_user()`.

Lab 2: Mapping User Pages

- Use the character device driver, adapt it to use `get_user_pages()` for the `read()` and `write()` entry points.

- To properly exercise this you'll need to use a page-aligned utility such as **dd**, or write page-aligned reading and writing programs.

Lab 3: Memory Mapping an Allocated Region

- Write a character driver that implements a `mmap()` entry point that memory maps a kernel buffer, allocated dynamically (probably during initialization).

- There should also be `read()` and `write()` entry points.

- Optionally, you may want to use an `ioctl()` command to tell user-space the size of the kernel buffer being memory mapped.

Lab 4: Using Relay Channels.

- Write a kernel module that opens up a relay channel and makes the associated files visible in the **debugfs** filesystem.

- Have the initialization routine write a series of entries into the channel. While the kernel module is loaded, try reading from it using `read()` and `mmap()`.

- If you read more than once on the open file descriptor what do you see?

- For more advanced exercises, you might try making sure your kernel client writes over sub-buffer boundaries, or writes into the channel from other functions such as an interrupt routine, or other entry points.

Chapter 18

ioctls

We'll consider the **ioctl** method (I/O Control) which is a grab bag which can be used in many different ways for applications to communicate with device drivers. We discuss what **ioctl**'s are, how they are called, and how to write driver entry points for them.

18.1 What are ioctls?

- **ioctl**'s (input output control) are special functions which are unique to a device or class of device. ioctl() is both a call from user-space, as well as a driver entry point (i.e., like `write()`, `read()`, etc.)

- Various **commands** can be implemented which either send to or receive information from a device. One can control device driver behaviour; i.e, shutdown, reset and modify. One can send out-of-band messages even while reads and writes are pending.

- Excessive use of **ioctl**'s is not favored by **Linux** kernel developers, as by their very nature they can be used to do almost anything, including adding what are essentially new system calls.

- To use **ioctl**'s, one has to first open a device using the `open()` system call, and then send the appropriate ioctl() command and any necessary arguments.

```
#include <sys/ioctl.h>

int ioctl(int fd, int command, ...);
```

- The third argument is usually written as `char *argp`. The use of the dots usually means a variable number of arguments. Here it indicates that type checking should not be done on the argument, so we are utilizing a trick. You shouldn't pass more than three arguments to the `ioctl()` call.

- On success 0 is returned, and on error -1 is returned with `errno` set. The possible error returns are:

Table 18.1: **ioctl() Return Values**

Value	Meaning
EBADF	Bad file descriptor.
ENOTTY	File descriptor not associated with a character special device, or the request does not apply to the kind of object the file descriptor references.
EINVAL	Invalid command or argp.

Example:

```
int fd = open ("/dev/mydrvr", O_RDWR);

if ( ioctl( fd, MYDRVR_SET, buf) < 0)
        perror( "MYDRVR_SET ioctl failed" );
```

18.2   Driver Entry point for ioctls

- The entry point for `ioctl()` looks like:

```
#include <linux/ioctl.h>

static int mydrvr_unlocked_ioctl (struct file *file, unsigned int cmd, unsigned long arg);
```

  where `arg` can be used directly either as a `long` or a pointer in user-space. In the latter case, the proper way to is though the `put_user()`, `get_user()`, `copy_to_user()`, `copy_from_user()` functions.

Example:

```
static int mydrvr_unlocked_ioctl (struct file *file, unsigned int cmd,  unsigned long arg)
{
        if (_IOC_TYPE(cmd) != MYDRBASE)
            return (-EINVAL);

        switch (cmd) {

        case MYDRVR_RESET :
        /* do something */
                return 0;

        case MYDRVR_OFFLINE :
        /* do something */
                return 0;
```

```
case MYDRVR_GETSTATE :
if (copy_to_user ((void *)arg, &mydrvr_state_struct, sizeof(mydrvr_state_struct)))
        return -EFAULT;
return 0;

default:
        return -EINVAL;
    }
}
```

18.3 Locked and Lockless ioctls

- From the early days of **Linux**, the ioctl() entry point actually had the following prototype:

  ```
  int ioctl(struct inode *inode, struct file *filp, unsigned int cmd, unsigned long arg);
  ```

  Unfortunately these **locked** ioctl() calls took out the **BKL** (Big Kernel Lock); if they took a long time to run they could cause large latencies in potentially unrelated areas.

- Note, however, the BKL is allowed to sleep unlike other locks and thus joining a wait queue was not enough to bottle up the system; you actually had to do some work that tied up some CPU time.

- The **unlocked** entry point we have shown was introduced to avoid the **BKL** and if it were present in the file_operations structure, it was used instead of the locked variation.

- In the 2.6.36 kernel, the locked version of the ioctl() entry point was finally removed. Drivers can no longer use it.

- Removal of the locked ioctl() system call was part of the active project to move the BKL out of the innards of system calls and drivers with the goal of one-by-one elimination.

- It also should be noted that ioctl() is not the only entry point that takes out the BKL in character drivers; in particular so do open() and fsync(). Another project is ongoing to eliminate the BKL from all of these entry points unless there is a true need for them.

18.4 Defining ioctls

- Before using ioctl() one must choose the numbers corresponding to the integer **command** argument. Just picking arbitrary numbers is a bad idea; they should be unique across the system.

- There are at least two ways errors could arise:

  - Two device nodes may have the same major number.
  - An application could make a mistake, opening more than one device and mixing up the file descriptors, thereby sending the right command to the wrong device.

  Results might be catastrophic and even damage hardware.

- Two important files are **/usr/src/linux/include/asm-generic/ioctl.h** and **/usr/src/linux/Documentation/ioctl/ioctl-number.txt**.

- In the present implementation `command` is 32 bits long; the command is in the lower 16 bits (which was the old size.) There are four bit-fields:

Table 18.3: **ioctl() command bit fields**

Bits	Name	Meaning	Description
8	_IOC_TYPEBITS	type	magic number to be used throughout the driver
8	_IOC_NRBITS	number	the sequential number
14	_IOC_SIZEBITS	size	of the data transfer
2	_IOC_DIRBITS	direction	of the data transfer

- The direction can be one of the following:

```
_IOC_NONE
_IOC_READ
_IOC_WRITE
_IOC_READ | _IOC_WRITE
```

and is seen from the point of view of the *application*.

- The size and direction information can be used to simplify sending data back and forth between user-space and kernel-space, using `arg` as a pointer. Note there is no enforcement here; you can send information either way no matter what direction is used to define the command. The largest transfer you can set up this way is 16 KB, since you have only 14 bits available to encode the size.

- You are not required to pay attention to the split up of the bits in the command, but it is a good idea to do so.

Useful macros:

- Encode the `ioctl` number:

```
_IO(  type, number)
_IOR( type, number, size)
_IOW( type, number, size)
_IOWR(type, number, size)
```

One has to be careful about how the parameter `size` is used. Rather than passing an integer, one passes the actual data structure, which then gets a `sizeof()` primitive applied to it; e.g.,

```
MY_IOCTL = _IOWR('k', 1, struct my_data_structure);
```

This won't work if `my_data_structure` has been allocated dynamically, as in that case `sizeof()` will return the size of the pointer.

- Decode the `ioctl` number:

```
_IOC_DIR( cmd)
_IOC_TYPE(cmd)
_IOC_NR(  cmd)
_IOC_SIZE(cmd)
```

Example:

```
#define MYDRBASE 'k'
#define MYDR_RESET _IO( MYDRBASE, 1)
#define MYDR_STOP  _IO( MYDRBASE, 2)
#define MYDR_READ  _IOR( MYDRBASE, 2, my_data_buffer)
```

18.5   Labs

Lab 1: Using ioctl's to pass data

- Write a simple module that uses the **ioctl** directional information to pass a data buffer of fixed size back and forth between the driver and the user-space program.

- The size and direction(s) of the data transfer should be encoded in the command number.

- You'll need to write a user-space application to test this.

Lab 2: Using ioctl's to pass data of variable length.

- Extend the previous exercise to send a buffer whose length is determined at run time. You will probably need to use the _IOC macro directly in the user-space program. (See linux/ioctl.h.)

Lab 3: Using ioctl's to send signals.

- It is sometimes desirable to send a signal to an application from within the kernel. The function for doing this is:

```
int send_sig (int signal, struct task_struct *tsk, int priv);
```

where **signal** is the signal to send, **tsk** points to the task structure corresponding to the process to which the signal should be sent, and **priv** indicates the privilege level (0 for user applications, 1 for the kernel.)

- Write a character driver that has three **ioctl** commands:

  - Set the process ID to which signals should be sent.
  - Set the signal which should be sent.
  - Send the signal.

- Remember you'll have to use `pid_task(find_vpid(pid), PIDTYPE_PID)` to connect the `pid` to the task structure it corresponds with.

- You'll also have to develop the sending program.

  # include < linux /signal.h >

  - If given no arguments it should send **SIGKILL** to the current process.
  - If given one argument it should set the process ID to send signals to.
  - If given two arguments it should also set the signal.

current => 4/linux/sched.h

Chapter 19

Unified Device Model and sysfs

We'll consider the **unified device model**, it's main data structures and how they apply to real devices and examine the **sysfs** pseudo-filesystem.

19.1   Unified Device Model

- A **unified device model** (or **integrated device model**) was introduced in the 2.6 kernel series. Under this scheme all devices are handled in one framework, with similar data structures and functional methods. Additionally, this framework is represented as a device tree rooted on the system buses.

- For the most part, device drivers need not interact directly with this underlying model, but register as devices under the type of bus they are connected to, such as **pci**. Information about the devices is exposed in the **sysfs** filesystem, to which drivers can optionally export data for viewing, as a more modern alternative to the use of the **/proc** filesystem and **ioctl()** commands.

- At the root of the driver model are **kobjects**, which contain simple representations of data related to any object in a system, such as a name, type, parent, reference count, lock, etc. A set of kobjects identical in type is contained in a **kset**.

- The data structures incorporated in the driver model contain information for each device such as what driver is used for them, what bus they are on, what power state they are in and how they suspend and resume. They also map out the structure of the system buses, how they are connected to each other and what devices can be attached and are attached.

19.2   Basic Structures

- For every device there is a generic structure defined in **/usr/src/linux/include/linux/device.h**

```
3.0: 551 struct device {
3.0: 552         struct device          *parent;
3.0: 553
3.0: 554         struct device_private  *p;
3.0: 555
3.0: 556         struct kobject kobj;
3.0: 557         const char             *init_name; /* initial name of the device */
3.0: 558         const struct device_type *type;
3.0: 559
3.0: 560         struct mutex           mutex;  /* mutex to synchronize calls to
3.0: 561                                         * its driver.
3.0: 562                                         */
3.0: 563
3.0: 564         struct bus_type *bus;          /* type of bus device is on */
3.0: 565         struct device_driver *driver;  /* which driver has allocated this
3.0: 566                                         device */
3.0: 567         void               *platform_data; /* Platform specific data, device
3.0: 568                                         core doesn't touch it */
3.0: 569         struct dev_pm_info     power;
3.0: 570         struct dev_power_domain *pwr_domain;
3.0: 571
3.0: 572 #ifdef CONFIG_NUMA
3.0: 573         int                numa_node;   /* NUMA node this device is close to */
3.0: 574 #endif
3.0: 575         u64                *dma_mask;   /* dma mask (if dma'able device) */
3.0: 576         u64                coherent_dma_mask;/* Like dma_mask, but for
3.0: 577                                         alloc_coherent mappings as
3.0: 578                                         not all hardware supports
3.0: 579                                         64 bit addresses for consistent
3.0: 580                                         allocations such descriptors. */
3.0: 581
3.0: 582         struct device_dma_parameters *dma_parms;
3.0: 583
3.0: 584         struct list_head       dma_pools;   /* dma pools (if dma'ble) */
3.0: 585
3.0: 586         struct dma_coherent_mem *dma_mem; /* internal for coherent mem
3.0: 587                                         override */
3.0: 588         /* arch specific additions */
3.0: 589         struct dev_archdata    archdata;
3.0: 590
3.0: 591         struct device_node     *of_node; /* associated device tree node */
3.0: 592
3.0: 593         dev_t                  devt;   /* dev_t, creates the sysfs "dev" */
3.0: 594
3.0: 595         spinlock_t             devres_lock;
3.0: 596         struct list_head       devres_head;
3.0: 597
3.0: 598         struct klist_node      knode_class;
3.0: 599         struct class           *class;
3.0: 600         const struct attribute_group **groups;  /* optional groups */
3.0: 601
3.0: 602         void   (*release)(struct device *dev);
3.0: 603 };
```

- After important fields are initialized, the device is registered with and unregistered from the system core with:

```
int  device_register   (struct device *dev);
void device_unregister (struct device *dev);
```

- Reference counts for the device are atomically incremented and decremented with:

```
struct device *get_device (struct device *dev);
void put_device (struct device *dev);
```

- The pointer to a structure of type `device_driver` describes the **driver** for the **device**:

```
3.0: 185 struct device_driver {
3.0: 186         const char              *name;
3.0: 187         struct bus_type         *bus;
3.0: 188
3.0: 189         struct module           *owner;
3.0: 190         const char              *mod_name;     /* used for built-in modules */
3.0: 191
3.0: 192         bool suppress_bind_attrs;        /* disables bind/unbind via sysfs */
3.0: 193
3.0: 194         const struct of_device_id       *of_match_table;
3.0: 195
3.0: 196         int (*probe) (struct device *dev);
3.0: 197         int (*remove) (struct device *dev);
3.0: 198         void (*shutdown) (struct device *dev);
3.0: 199         int (*suspend) (struct device *dev, pm_message_t state);
3.0: 200         int (*resume) (struct device *dev);
3.0: 201         const struct attribute_group **groups;
3.0: 202
3.0: 203         const struct dev_pm_ops *pm;
3.0: 204
3.0: 205         struct driver_private *p;
3.0: 206 };
```

- Drivers are registered/unregistered with the appropriate bus with:

```
int  driver_register   (struct device_driver *drv);
void driver_unregister (struct device_driver *drv);
```

and reference counts are incremented/decremented with:

```
struct device_driver *get_driver (struct device_driver *drv);
void                  put_driver (struct device_driver *drv);
```

- Next we consider how this generic infrastructure connects to real devices.

19.3 Real Devices

- Actual device drivers rarely work directly with the structures we have so far described; rather they are used by the internal code used for each specific type of bus and/or device.

- For example, **PCI** devices have two important structures:

```
struct pci_dev {
.....
   struct pci_driver *driver;
....
   struct device dev;
.....
}

struct pci_driver {
.....
   struct device_driver driver;
....
}
```

and **drivers** are registered with the system with

```
#include <linux/pci.h>

int  pci_register_driver   (struct pci_driver *);
void pci_unregister_driver (struct pci_driver *);
```

Devices, on the other hand, are registered, or discovered, directly by the probe callback function or by `pci_find_device()`.

- How is this connected with the generic infrastructure? Because the generic `device` structure is embedded in the `pci_dev` structure, and the generic `device_driver` structure is embedded in the `pci_driver` structure, one must do pointer arithmetic.

- This is done through use of the macro `to_pci_dev()` as in:

```
struct device *dev;
.....
struct pci_dev *pdev = to_pci_dev (dev);
```

  which is implemented in terms of the `container_of()` macro:

```
#define to_pci_dev(n) container_of(n, struct pci_dev, dev)
```

  where the first argument is a pointer to the `device` structure, the second the type of structure it is contained in, and the third is the name of the `device` structure in the data structure.

- Likewise, one can gain access to the `pci_driver` structure from its embedded `device_driver` structure with:

```
struct device_driver *drv;
.....
struct pci_driver *pdrv = to_pci_drv (drv);
```

- With a few exceptions (such as when doing **DMA** transfers) device drivers do not involve the generic structures and registration functions. For example, **PCI** devices fill in the `pci_driver` structure, and call `pci_register_driver()` (and some other functions) in order to get plugged into the system. However, these functions are written in terms of the underlying device model.

- We have peeked at how **PCI** devices hook into the unified device model; we could do the same for other kinds of devices, such as **USB** and **network** and we would find the same kind of structural relations and embedded structures. Adding a new kind of device is just a question of following along the same path.

19.4   sysfs

- Support for the **sysfs** virtual filesystem is built into all 2.6 kernels, and it should be mounted under `/sys`. However, the unified device model does not require mounting **sysfs** in order to function.

- Let's take a look at what can be found using the 2.6.36 kernel; we warn you the exact layout of this filesystem has a tendency to mutate. Doing a top level directory command yields:

```
$ ls -F /sys
block/ bus/ class/ devices/ firmware/ fs/ kernel/ module/ power/
```

which displays the basic device hierarchy. The device model **sysfs** implementation also includes information not strictly related to hardware.

- Network devices can be examined with:

```
$ ls -lF /sys/class/net
total 0
drwxr-xr-x 5 root root 0 Oct 13 04:27 eth0/
drwxr-xr-x 5 root root 0 Oct 13 04:27 eth1/
drwxr-xr-x 5 root root 0 Oct 13 04:27 lo/
```

and looking at the first Ethernet card gives:

```
$ ls -l /sys/class/net/eth0/
total 0
-r--r--r-- 1 root root 4096 Oct 13 16:19 addr_assign_type
-r--r--r-- 1 root root 4096 Oct 13 04:27 address
-r--r--r-- 1 root root 4096 Oct 13 16:19 addr_len
-r--r--r-- 1 root root 4096 Oct 13 16:19 broadcast
-r--r--r-- 1 root root 4096 Oct 13 16:19 carrier
lrwxrwxrwx 1 root root    0 Oct 13 04:27 device ->
                    ../../../devices/pci0000:00/0000:00:1e.0/0000:04:02.0
-r--r--r-- 1 root root 4096 Oct 13 16:19 dev_id
-r--r--r-- 1 root root 4096 Oct 13 16:19 dormant
-r--r--r-- 1 root root 4096 Oct 13 16:19 duplex
-r--r--r-- 1 root root 4096 Oct 13 16:19 features
-rw-r--r-- 1 root root 4096 Oct 13 09:27 flags
-rw-r--r-- 1 root root 4096 Oct 13 16:19 ifalias
-r--r--r-- 1 root root 4096 Oct 13 09:27 ifindex
-r--r--r-- 1 root root 4096 Oct 13 16:19 iflink
-r--r--r-- 1 root root 4096 Oct 13 16:19 link_mode
-rw-r--r-- 1 root root 4096 Oct 13 16:19 mtu
-r--r--r-- 1 root root 4096 Oct 13 16:19 operstate
drwxr-xr-x 2 root root    0 Oct 13 16:19 power
drwxr-xr-x 3 root root    0 Oct 13 04:27 queues
-r--r--r-- 1 root root 4096 Oct 13 16:19 speed
drwxr-xr-x 2 root root    0 Oct 13 09:28 statistics
lrwxrwxrwx 1 root root    0 Oct 13 09:27 subsystem -> ../../net
-rw-r--r-- 1 root root 4096 Oct 13 16:19 tx_queue_len
-r--r--r-- 1 root root 4096 Oct 13 04:27 type
-rw-r--r-- 1 root root 4096 Oct 13 16:19 uevent
```

Notice that typing out the simple entries just reads out values:

```
$ cat /sys/class/net/eth0/mtu
1500
```

in the way we are accustomed to getting information from the `/proc` filesystem. The intention with **sysfs** is to have one text value per line, although this is not expected to be rigorously enforced.

- The underlying device and driver for the first network interface can be traced through the `device` and (the to be seen shortly) `driver` symbolic links. The directory for the first **PCI** bus looks like:

```
$ ls -F /sys/devices/pci0000:00
0000:00:00.0/   0000:00:1a.2/   0000:00:1c.5/   0000:00:1d.7/   0000:00:1f.3/      uevent
0000:00:01.0/   0000:00:1a.7/   0000:00:1d.0/   0000:00:1e.0/   firmware_node@
0000:00:1a.0/   0000:00:1b.0/   0000:00:1d.1/   0000:00:1f.0/   pci_bus:0000:00@
0000:00:1a.1/   0000:00:1c.0/   0000:00:1d.2/   0000:00:1f.2/   power/
```

There is a subdirectory for each device, with the name giving the bus, device and function numbers; e.g., `0000:00:0a.0` means the first bus (0), eleventh device (10), and first function (0) on the device. Looking at the directory corresponding to the Ethernet card we see:

```
$ ls -l /sys/class/net/eth0/device/
total 0
drwxr-xr-x 3 root root        0 Oct 13 04:27 ./
drwxr-xr-x 4 root root        0 Oct 13 04:27 ../
-rw-r--r-- 1 root root     4096 Oct 13 09:27 broken_parity_status
lrwxrwxrwx 1 root root        0 Oct 13 04:27 bus -> ../../../../bus/pci/
-r--r--r-- 1 root root     4096 Oct 13 09:27 class
-rw-r--r-- 1 root root      256 Oct 13 09:27 config
-r--r--r-- 1 root root     4096 Oct 13 09:27 consistent_dma_mask_bits
-r--r--r-- 1 root root     4096 Oct 13 09:27 device
-r--r--r-- 1 root root     4096 Oct 13 09:27 dma_mask_bits
lrwxrwxrwx 1 root root        0 Oct 13 04:27 driver -> ../../../../bus/pci/drivers/skge/
-rw------- 1 root root     4096 Oct 13 09:27 enable
-r--r--r-- 1 root root     4096 Oct 13 09:27 irq
-r--r--r-- 1 root root     4096 Oct 13 09:27 local_cpulist
-r--r--r-- 1 root root     4096 Oct 13 09:27 local_cpus
-r--r--r-- 1 root root     4096 Oct 13 09:27 modalias
-rw-r--r-- 1 root root     4096 Oct 13 09:27 msi_bus
lrwxrwxrwx 1 root root        0 Oct 13 09:27 net:eth0 -> ../../../../class/net/eth0/
drwxr-xr-x 2 root root        0 Oct 13 09:27 power/
--w--w---- 1 root root     4096 Oct 13 09:27 remove
--w--w---- 1 root root     4096 Oct 13 09:27 rescan
--w------- 1 root root     4096 Oct 13 09:27 reset
-r--r--r-- 1 root root     4096 Oct 13 09:27 resource
-rw------- 1 root root    16384 Oct 13 09:27 resource0
-rw------- 1 root root      256 Oct 13 09:27 resource1
-r-------- 1 root root   131072 Oct 13 09:27 rom
lrwxrwxrwx 1 root root        0 Oct 13 09:27 subsystem -> ../../../../bus/pci/
-r--r--r-- 1 root root     4096 Oct 13 09:27 subsystem_device
-r--r--r-- 1 root root     4096 Oct 13 09:27 subsystem_vendor
-rw-r--r-- 1 root root     4096 Oct 13 04:27 uevent
-r--r--r-- 1 root root     4096 Oct 13 09:27 vendor
-rw------- 1 root root    32768 Oct 13 09:27 vpd
```

- To see the full spectrum of information that is available with **sysfs** you'll just have to examine it.

19.5 Labs

Lab 1: Using libsysfs and sysfsutils.

- The **systool** multipurpose utility gives an easy interface for examining the `/sys` device tree, and is part of either the **sysfstools** or **sysfsutils** package. Currently it uses **libsysfs**, which is being deprecated in favor of **libhal**.

- Do **man systool** and run the **systool** command without arguments. It should portray all bus types, devices classes, and root devices. Do `systool -h` to see how to use some of the additional arguments and options.

- Explore!

Chapter 20

Sleeping and Wait Queues

We'll discuss **wait queues**. We'll consider how tasks can be put to sleep, and how they can be woken up. We'll also consider the **poll()** entry point.

20.1 What are Wait Queues?

- **Wait queues** are used when a task running in kernel mode has reached a condition where it needs to wait for some condition to be fulfilled. For instance it may need to wait for data to arrive on a peripheral device.

- At such times it is necessary for the task to go to **sleep** until whatever condition or resource it is waiting for is ready. When the resource becomes available, or the condition becomes true, (perhaps signalled by the arrival of an interrupt) it will become necessary to **wake up** the sleeping task.

- There can be many wait queues in the system and they are connected in a linked list. In addition more than one task can be placed on a given wait queue.

- Another way to understand wait queues is to think of **task organization** and queues. There is a linked list of all tasks who have TASK_RUNNING in the state field of their task_struct, called the **runqueue**. A task which is scheduled out but would like to run as soon as a timeslice is available is **not sleeping**; it still has TASK_RUNNING as its state.

- **Sleeping** tasks (those with a state of `TASK_INTERRUPTIBLE`, `TASK_UNINTERRUPTIBLE`, or `TASK_KILLABLE`) go instead into one of many possible wait queues, each of which corresponds to getting woken up by a particular event or class of events, at which point the sleeping task can go back to the runqueue.

- The sleeping and waking up functions come in two forms, **interruptible** and **uninterruptible**. Uninterruptible sleep is not woken up by a signal and as such should be rarely used, especially in device drivers. It is quite difficult to get out of a task hung in this situation; short of a reboot one may be able to cause a wake up function to be called by terminating an ancestor process.

- The `TASK_KILLABLE` state is woken up only a **fatal** signal (while `TASK_INTERRUPTIBLE` wakes up with **any** signal.) It was introduced in the 2.6.25 kernel.

- When a wait queue is woken up, all tasks on the wait queue are roused (unless an **exclusive** sleep is used, as we shall see.)

- It is very easy to hang a system with improper use of wait queues. In particular, kernel threads of execution such as interrupt service routines should **never** go to sleep.

- The data structure used by wait queues is of the type `wait_queue_head_t`, usually just called a **wait queue**. It is explicitly declared and initialized with with the statements

```
#include <linux/sched.h>

wait_queue_head_t wq;
init_waitqueue_head (&wq);
```

- If the wait queue is not allocated at run time it can be declared and initialized with the macro

```
DECLARE_WAIT_QUEUE_HEAD(wq);
```

  Don't forget to initialize a wait queue.

20.2   Going to Sleep and Waking Up

- Now that we have set up a wait queue, we need to use functions for putting a task to sleep and for waking it up. These are

```
#include <linux/wait.h>

wait_event               (wait_queue_head_t wq, int condition);
wait_event_interruptible (wait_queue_head_t wq, int condition);
wait_event_killable      (wait_queue_head_t wq, int condition);

void wake_up                  (wait_queue_head_t *wq);
void wake_up_interruptible    (wait_queue_head_t *wq);
```

- The `wait_event()` calls are actually macros, not functions. They take `wq`, not `*wq`, as their argument.

- The proper wake up call should be paired with the originating sleep call. (However, `wait_event_killable()` should be paired with `wake_up()`, which isn't obvious.)

- In general you will want to use the **interruptible** wait functions which return 0 if they return due to a wake up call and `-ERESTARTSYS` if they return due to a signal arriving. The other forms are not aborted by a signal and are only used by critical sections of the kernel, such as while waiting for a swap page to be read from disk.

- When you use the interruptible forms, you'll always have to check upon awakening whether you woke up because a signal arrived, or there was an explicit wake up call. The `signal_pending(current)` macro can be used for this purpose.

- The `condition` test has two important purposes:

  - It helps avoid the race condition in which a task is designated to sleep but the wake up call arrives before the change in state is complete; the condition is checked before putting the task to sleep.

  - The condition is checked upon waking up and if it is not true the task remains asleep. This helps avoid another class of race conditions where a task is put to sleep again before it has a chance to really wake up.

- You will still have to call one of the **wake_up** functions when using these macros; they do not just set up a spinning `while` loop until the argument given in `condition` evaluates as true (non-zero).

- Sometimes you want to ensure you don't sleep too long. For this purpose one can use:

```
wait_event_timeout              (wait_queue_head_t wq, int condition, long timeout);
wait_event_interruptible_timeout (wait_queue_head_t wq, int condition, long timeout);
```

  where the timeout is specified in `jiffies`. If the task returns upon timeout, these functions return 0. If they return earlier, they return the remaining `jiffies` in the timeout period. If the interruptible form returns due to a signal, it returns -ERSTARTSYS.

- The waking functions will rouse **all** sleepers on the specified wait queue. There is no guarantee about the order in which they will be woken up; they will be scheduled in by priority algorithms rather than **FIFO** or **LIFO**. Furthermore, the tasks can be woken up on any CPU. A little more control can be obtained with the function:

```
void wake_up_interruptible_sync (wait_queue_head_t *wq);
```

  which checks whether the task being woken up has a higher priority than the currently running one, and if so, invokes the scheduler if possible. However, this is rarely done.

- Thus a simple use of wait queues would include a code fragment like:

```
#include <linux/sched.h>
DECLARE_WAIT_QUEUE_HEAD(wq)
static int fun1 ( ... )
{
    ...
    printk(KERN_INFO "task %i (%s) going to sleep\n", current->pid, current->comm);
    wait_event_interruptible(wq, dataready);
    printk(KERN_INFO "awoken %i (%s)\n", current->pid, current->comm);
    if (signal_pending (current))
            return -ERESTARTSYS;
    ...
    dataready = 0;
}
static int fun2 ( ... )
{
    ...
    printk(KERN_INFO "task %i (%s) awakening sleepers...\n", current->pid, current->comm);
    dataready = 1;
    wake_up_interruptible(&wq);
    ...
}
```

(Note the variable `dataready` should probably be an atomic one, or be protected by some kind of lock.)

20.3   Going to Sleep Details

- Let's look in some detail at the code for entering a wait, or going to sleep. The macro `wait_event()` is defined in **/usr/src/linux/include/linux/wait.h**:

```
3.0: 217 #define wait_event(wq, condition)                                \
3.0: 218 do {                                                             \
3.0: 219     if (condition)                                              \
3.0: 220             break;                                               \
3.0: 221     __wait_event(wq, condition);                                \
3.0: 222 } while (0)
....
3.0: 192 #define __wait_event(wq, condition)                              \
3.0: 193 do {                                                             \
3.0: 194     DEFINE_WAIT(__wait);                                         \
3.0: 195                                                                  \
3.0: 196     for (;;) {                                                   \
3.0: 197             prepare_to_wait(&wq, &__wait, TASK_UNINTERRUPTIBLE); \
3.0: 198             if (condition)                                       \
3.0: 199                     break;                                       \
3.0: 200             schedule();                                          \
3.0: 201     }                                                            \
3.0: 202     finish_wait(&wq, &__wait);                                   \
3.0: 203 } while (0)
```

- The first thing to do is to check if `condition` is true, and if so, avoid going to sleep at all. This avoids the race condition in which the condition is reset and a wake up call is issued after the task is requested to go to sleep but before it actually does so.

- Then one enters the macro where the real work is done, `__wait_event()`, where the first thing to do is `DEFINE_WAIT (name)`, which is equivalent to:

```
wait_queue_t name;
init_wait (&name);
```

which creates and initializes the wait queue.

- The next thing to do is to add the wait queue entry to the queue, and reset the state of the task, which is done by:

```
void prepare_to_wait (wait_queue_head_t *queue, wait queue_t *wait, int state);
```

- Once again one checks `condition` to avoid a race condition, e.g., a missed wake up call, in which case the sleep is once again avoided. Assuming this condition is not true, one calls `schedule()` to schedule in another task; the current one can't be scheduled in because its state is `TASK_UNINTERRUPTIBLE`.

- The next lines of code will only be entered after the state has been reset by a wake up call, and the task is again available for scheduling and has been granted a time slice. The `for()` loop makes sure the `condition` is really true, and if not continues sleep until it is.

- When the sleep is truly finished, one calls:

```
void finish_wait (wait_queue_head_t *queue, wait_queue_t *wait);
```

which does whatever cleanup is needed.

- The `wait_event_interruptible()` macro is almost the same except that it sets the state to `TASK_INTERRUPTIBLE` and the `for()` loop is replaced with:

```
3.0: 267     for (;;) {                                                        \
3.0: 268             prepare_to_wait(&wq, &__wait, TASK_INTERRUPTIBLE);        \
3.0: 269             if (condition)                                            \
3.0: 270                     break;                                            \
3.0: 271             if (!signal_pending(current)) {                           \
3.0: 272                     schedule();                                       \
3.0: 273                     continue;                                         \
3.0: 274             }                                                         \
3.0: 275             ret = -ERESTARTSYS;                                       \
3.0: 276             break;                                                    \
3.0: 277     }                                                                 \
```

which checks to see if the sleep ended because of an incoming signal, and if so returns the value
-ERESTARTSYS.

- The **timeout** variations use for the for() loop:

```
3.0: 228     for (;;) {                                                        \
3.0: 229             prepare_to_wait(&wq, &__wait, TASK_UNINTERRUPTIBLE);      \
3.0: 230             if (condition)                                            \
3.0: 231                     break;                                            \
3.0: 232             ret = schedule_timeout(ret);                              \
3.0: 233             if (!ret)                                                 \
3.0: 234                     break;                                            \
3.0: 235     }                                                                 \
```

in which schedule_timeout() causes the scheduler to get called if the timeout period elapses.

20.4   Exclusive Sleeping

- So far we have dealt only with so-called **non-exclusive** sleeping tasks. For instance, a number of tasks
  may be waiting for termination of a disk operation, and once it has completed they will all need to wake
  up and resume.

- If more than one task is waiting for **exclusive** access to a resource (one that only one can use at a time)
  then this kind of wake up is inefficient and leads to the **thundering herd** problem, where all sleepers
  are woken up even though only one of them can use the resource at a time.

- In this case new functions are required. Setting up the wait involves the inline macro function:

```
wait_event_interruptible_exclusive (wait_queue_head_t wq, int condition);
```

(There is no non-interruptible exclusive sleep macro.)

- The usual wake up functions can be used; in this case only one sleeper will be woken up. If more control
  is needed a number of new wake up functions can be used:

```
void wake_up_all                 ( wait_queue_head_t *wq);
void wake_up_interruptible_all   ( wait_queue_head_t *wq);
void wake_up_nr                  ( wait_queue_head_t *wq, int nr)
void wake_up_sync_nr             ( wait_queue_head_t *wq, int nr)
void wake_up_interruptible_nr    ( wait_queue_head_t *wq, int nr)
void wake_up_interruptible_sync_nr ( wait_queue_head_t *wq, int nr)
```

- The ones with all in the name wake up all tasks in the queue, just as in the non-exclusive case, but
  those with _nr awaken only nr tasks (typically nr=1.)

20.5   Waking Up Details

- All the wake up calls are macros that invoke the basic `__wake_up()` call and are defined in **/usr/src/ linux/include/linux/wait.h**:

```
3.0: 170 #define wake_up(x)                  __wake_up(x, TASK_NORMAL, 1, NULL)
3.0: 171 #define wake_up_nr(x, nr)           __wake_up(x, TASK_NORMAL, nr, NULL)
3.0: 172 #define wake_up_all(x)                __wake_up(x, TASK_NORMAL, 0, NULL)
3.0: 173 #define wake_up_locked(x)           __wake_up_locked((x), TASK_NORMAL)
3.0: 174
3.0: 175 #define wake_up_interruptible(x)    __wake_up(x, TASK_INTERRUPTIBLE, 1, NULL)
3.0: 176 #define wake_up_interruptible_nr(x, nr)  __wake_up(x, TASK_INTERRUPTIBLE,
                                                              nr, NULL)
3.0: 177 #define wake_up_interruptible_all(x)      __wake_up(x, TASK_INTERRUPTIBLE, 0,
                                                              NULL)
3.0: 178 #define wake_up_interruptible_sync(x)    __wake_up_sync((x),
                                                              TASK_INTERRUPTIBLE, 1)
```

    where

```
TASK_NORMAL = TASK_INTERRUPTIBLE | TASK_UNINTERRUPTIBLE
```

- The code for the core `__wake_up()` function is in **/usr/src/linux/kernel/sched.c**:

```
3.0:4490 void __wake_up(wait_queue_head_t *q, unsigned int mode,
3.0:4491                      int nr_exclusive, void *key)
3.0:4492 {
3.0:4493         unsigned long flags;
3.0:4494
3.0:4495         spin_lock_irqsave(&q->lock, flags);
3.0:4496         __wake_up_common(q, mode, nr_exclusive, 0, key);
3.0:4497         spin_unlock_irqrestore(&q->lock, flags);
3.0:4498 }
3.0:4499 EXPORT_SYMBOL(__wake_up);
```

    which takes out an interrupt blocking spinlock, and then passes the work off to `__wake_up_common()`:

```
3.0:4466 static void __wake_up_common(wait_queue_head_t *q, unsigned int mode,
3.0:4467                      int nr_exclusive, int wake_flags, void *key)
3.0:4468 {
3.0:4469         wait_queue_t *curr, *next;
3.0:4470
3.0:4471         list_for_each_entry_safe(curr, next, &q->task_list, task_list) {
3.0:4472                 unsigned flags = curr->flags;
3.0:4473
3.0:4474                 if (curr->func(curr, mode, wake_flags, key) &&
3.0:4475                             (flags & WQ_FLAG_EXCLUSIVE) && !--nr_exclusive)
3.0:4476                         break;
3.0:4477         }
3.0:4478 }
```

- The function cycles through the linked list of wait queues, and for each task placed on a wait queue it calls the wake up function (`curr->func()`) which by default is set to be `default_wake_function()`. (The ability to use an alternative wake up function appeared in the 2.6 kernel) After doing so it checks to see whether or not it is an exclusive wait, and if so properly decrements the number of remaining tasks to be woken up.

- The default wake up function in turn just calls `try_to_wake_up()`:

```
3.0:4450 int default_wake_function(wait_queue_t *curr, unsigned mode, int wake_flags,
3.0:4451                                void *key)
3.0:4452 {
3.0:4453         return try_to_wake_up(curr->private, mode, wake_flags);
3.0:4454 }
3.0:4455 EXPORT_SYMBOL(default_wake_function);
```

- Now we actually do the wake up with

  ```
  int try_to_wake_up (task_t * p, unsigned int state, int sync);
  ```

  which is a long and complicated function, mostly because of the necessity of ensuring a task is not already running on another cpu. If not, it will set the state to `TASK_RUNNING`, and enable the task to be rescheduled.

20.6 Polling

- Applications often keep their eye on a number of file descriptors to see whether or not it is possible to do I/O on one or more of them at any given time. The application will either sit and wait for one of the descriptors to go active, or perhaps dedicate one thread for that purpose while other threads do work.

- Such multiplexed and asynchronous I/O is at the basis of the traditional **Posix** system calls `select()` and `poll()`, as well as the **Linux**-only `epoll` system calls which scale the best to large numbers of descriptors.

- In order to make `poll()` work on a file descriptor corresponding to a character device, one needs to add the entry point to the `file_operations` table as usual:

  ```
  static struct file_operations mycdrv_fops = {
      .owner = THIS_MODULE,
      ....
      .poll = mycdrv_poll,
  };

  static unsigned int mycdrv_poll (struct file *file, poll_table * wait);
  ```

  Whenever an application calls `poll()`, `select()` or uses `epoll` this method will be called.

- First one must call the function

  ```
  void poll_wait (struct file *filp, wait_head_queue_t *wq, poll_table *wait);
  ```

  for each wait queue whose change of status is to be noted.

- Secondly one must return a bit-mask which can be checked to see which (if any) I/O operations are available. A number of flags can be combined in this mask:

Table 20.1: **poll() Flags**

Value	Meaning
POLLIN	Normal or priority band data can be read without blocking.
POLLRDNORM	Normal data can be read. Usually a readable device returns POLLIN | POLLRDNORM
POLLRDBAND	Priority band data can be read. (This flag is unused.)
POLLPRI	High priority out of band data can be read, causing select() to report an exception.
POLLHUP	Reaching end of file on device.
POLLERR	An error has occurred.
POLLOUT	The device can be written without blocking.
POLLWRNORM	Normal data can be written. Usually a writable device returns POLLOUT | POLLWRNORM
POLLWRBAND	Priority band data can be written.

- An example of an entry point might look like:

```
static unsigned int mycdrv_poll (struct file *file, poll_table * wait)
{
    unsigned int revents = 0;
    poll_wait (file, &wq_read, wait);
    poll_wait (file, &wq_write, wait);

    if ( atomic_read (&data_ready_to_read))
        revents |= POLLIN | POLLRDNORM;
    if ( atomic_read (&data_ready_to_write))
        revents |= POLLOUT | POLLWRNORM;
    return revents;
}
```

Look for :-
drivers / char / pcm cia
cm 4040-cs.c

20.7 Labs

Lab 1: Using Wait Queues

- Generalize the previous character driver to use wait queues,

- Have the `read()` function go to sleep until woken by a `write()` function. (You could also try reversing read and write.)

- You may want to open up two windows and read in one window and then write in the other window.

- Try putting more than one process to sleep, i.e., run your test read program more than once simultaneously before running the write program to awaken them. If you keep track of the **pid**'s you should be able to detect in what order processes are woken.

- There are several solutions given:

  - Using `wait_event_interruptible()`. You may want to use **atomic** functions for any global variables used in the logical condition.
  - Using `wait_for_completion()`.
  - Using **semaphores**.
  - Using **read/write semaphores**.
  - Using exclusive waiting on the many readers solution.. How many processes wake up?

- If you test with **cat**, **echo**, or **dd**, you may see different results than if you use the supplied simple read/write programs. Why?

Lab 2: Killable Sleep

- Modify the `wait_event()` lab to use `wait_event_killable()`. After a reading process goes to sleep, send it a non-fatal signal, such as

  ```
  $ kill -SIGCONT <pid>
  ```

  followed by a kill signal, such as `SIGKILL`.

Lab 3: Using poll()

- Take the `wait_event()` solution and extend it to have a `poll()` entry point.

- You'll need an application that opens the device node and then calls `poll()` and waits for data to be available.

interrupt ———————→ (disable all IRQ's)

Interrupt Handler

Critical work	Top Halve
	Bottom Halve

enable all interrupts ←———————

Tasklet   work Que

New:
Threaded interrupt
handlers.

Chapter 21

Interrupt Handling: Deferrable Functions and User Drivers

We'll continue our examination of how the **Linux** kernel handles interrupts, focussing on how the labor is split between top and bottom halves, and what some of the methods are for implementation. We'll investigate the use of deferrable functions, including **tasklets**, **work queues**, and spinning off **kernel threads**. We'll consider the use of threaded interrupt handlers. Finally we'll cover methods of interrupt handling from user-space.

21.1 Top and Bottom Halves

- Efficient interrupt handlers often have **top halves** and **bottom halves**.

- In the **top half**, the driver does what must be done as quickly as possible. This may just mean acknowledging the interrupt and getting some data off a device and into a buffer.

- Technically speaking the top half **is** the interrupt handler. A typical top half:

  - Checks to make sure the interrupt was generated by the right hardware; this is necessary for interrupt sharing.

- Clears an **interrupt pending** bit on the interface board.

- Does what needs to be done immediately (usually read or write something to/from the device.) The data is usually written to or read from a device-specific buffer, which has been previously allocated.

- Sets up handling the new information later (in the bottom half.)

- In the optional **bottom half**, the driver does whatever processing has been deferred. While interrupts are enabled when a bottom half runs, they can be disabled if necessary. However, generally this should be avoided as it goes against the basic purpose of having a bottom half.

- The various kinds of bottom halves behave differently:

    - **Tasklets** can be run in parallel on different CPUs, although the same tasklet can only be run one at a time. They are never run in process context. Tasklets will run only on the CPU that scheduled them. This leads to better cache coherency, and serialization, as the tasklet can never be run before the handler is done, which leads to better avoidance of race conditions.

    - **Work queues** run in process context, and thus sleeping is permitted. Because each work queue has its own thread on each CPU, such sleeping will not block other tasks. A bottom half implemented in this fashion can run on a different CPU than the one that scheduled it.

- Depending on the kind of bottom half, they are launched in different ways; work queues are scheduled in like other tasks, while tasklets are invoked whenever the system checks to see if any are pending after any kind of exception is handled, including interrupts and system calls.

- Another way of implementing a bottom half is through maintaining a **kernel thread**. One starts off the kernel thread upon device initialization or open, and then has it sleep until it has work to do. Scheduling a bottom half then becomes waking up the thread to deal with the work, after which it goes back to sleep. Killing such a thread when a driver is unloaded has to be done with care.

- It is not required to have a bottom half; if there is little processing to be done, it may be more efficient to just do it in the top half, rather than incur the overhead of scheduling and launching a bottom half, and having to be careful about synchronization questions.

Example (using tasklets):

```
static struct my_dat { .... } my_fun_data;

static void t_fun (unsigned long t_arg){ .... }

DECLARE_TASKLET (t_name, t_fun, (unsigned long) &my_data);

static void my_interrupt (int irq, void *dev_id)
{
    /* do some stuff */
    .....
    tasklet_schedule (&t_name);
    return IRQ_HANDLED;
}
```

21.2   Deferrable Functions and softirqs

- **Deferrable functions** perform non-critical tasks at a later (deferred) time, usually as soon as possible. When the functions are run they may be interrupted.

- There are two main types: **softirqs** (of which **tasklets** are one kind) which run in interrupt context and are not allowed to go to sleep, and **workqueues**, which run under a pseudo-process context and are allowed to sleep.

- There are a number of different kinds of softirqs defined. In order of decreasing priority they are:

Table 21.1: **Softirq Types**

Name	Priority	Purpose
HI_SOFTIRQ	0	High-priority tasklets.
TIMER_SOFTIRQ	1	Scheduled timers.
NET_TX_SOFTIRQ	2	Network packet transmission.
NET_RX_SOFTIRQ	3	Network packet reception.
BLOCK_SOFTIRQ	4	Block device related work.
TASKLET_SOFTIRQ	5	Normal-priority tasklets.
SCHED_SOFTIRQ	6	Used in the **CFS** scheduler.
HRTIMER_SOFTIRQ	7	Used if high resolution timers are present.

- The various kinds of deferred functions differ mostly in whether or not they operate in process context and their behaviour on multi-processor systems.

Table 21.2: **Deferred Function Types**

Type	Process Context?	SMP Behaviour	SMP Serialization
softirq	No	Same ones can be run on different CPUs simultaneously	Run on the CPU that schedules them and must be fully re-entrant.
tasklet	No	Can be run simultaneously on different CPUs, but not if they use the same `tasklet_struct`.	Run on the CPU that scheduled them and are thus serialized.
workqueue	Yes	Can be run on any CPU.	Can be delayed and serialized.

- Softirqs are called, or consumed in either of two ways:

  - After an interrupt is serviced the kernel checks if any softirqs are pending; if so it executes them in priority order.
  - The kernel thread **ksoftirqd[cpu]** is scheduled in like other processes, and consumes them in like fashion.

- The second mechanism is required to prevent priority inversion due to **softirq storms**, which can happen when a softirq resubmits itself, or when softirqs from other sources build up before they can be run.

- To avoid this the function `__do_softirq()` is allowed to restart processing only `MAX_SOFTIRQ_RESTART=10` times; it all tasks are not consumed by then, further processing is deferred and the a wake up call is issued to the kernel **softirqd** process which can then be scheduled in to consume additional tasks.

21.3   Tasklets

- **Tasklets** are used to queue up work which can be done at a later time. They are frequently used in interrupt service routines; a typical **top half** does whatever needs to be done to get data off or onto a device and resets it and re-enables interrupts. Further data processing may be done in tasklets while the device is ready for new data.

- Tasklets may be run in parallel on multiple CPU systems. However, the same tasklet can not be run at the same time on more than one CPU.

- A tasklet is always run on the CPU that scheduled it; among other things this optimizes cache usage. (This however can cause delays which may not be worth the cache savings; **work queues** can be used instead.) As a result, many kinds of race conditions are naturally avoided; the thread that queued up the tasklet must complete before the tasklet actually gets run.

- The tasklet code is explained in **/usr/src/linux/include/linux/interrupt.h**. The important data structure is:

```
struct tasklet_struct{
    struct tasklet_struct *next;
    unsigned long state;
    atomic_t count;
    void (*func)(unsigned long);
    unsigned long data;
};
```

- The `func` entry is a pointer to the function that will be run, which can have data passed to it through `data`. The `state` entry is used to determine whether or not the tasklet has already been scheduled; if so it can not be done so a second time.

- The main macros and functions involving tasklets are:

```
DECLARE_TASKLET(name, function, data);
DECLARE_TASKLET_DISABLED(name, function, data);

void tasklet_init (struct tasklet_struct *t,
        void (*func)(unsigned long), unsigned long data);

void tasklet_schedule (struct tasklet_struct *t);
void tasklet_enable   (struct tasklet_struct *t);
void tasklet_disable  (struct tasklet_struct *t);
void tasklet_kill     (struct tasklet_struct *t);
```

- A tasklet must be initialized before being used, either by allocating space for the structure and calling `tasklet_init()`, or by using the `DECLARE_...()` macros, which take care of both steps although they must be used in the global space.

- `DECLARE_TASKLET()` sets up a `struct tasklet_struct` `name` in an **enabled** state; the second form `DECLARE_TASKLET_DISABLED()` being used means the tasklet can be scheduled but won't be run until the tasklet is specifically enabled.

- The `tasklet_kill()` function is used to kill tasklets which reschedule themselves.

- When a tasklet is scheduled, the the inline function `tasklet_schedule()` is called as defined in **/usr/src/linux/include/linux/interrupt.h**:

```
3.0: 542 static inline void tasklet_schedule(struct tasklet_struct *t)
3.0: 543 {
3.0: 544     if (!test_and_set_bit(TASKLET_STATE_SCHED, &t->state))
3.0: 545             __tasklet_schedule(t);
3.0: 546 }
```

which makes sure the tasklet is not already scheduled, by checking the `state` field of the `tasklet_struct`. Note that failure brings a **quiet** dropping of the tasklet as the function has no return value.

- A trivial example:

```
#include <linux/module.h>
#include <linux/sched.h>
#include <linux/interrupt.h>
#include <linux/slab.h>
#include <linux/init.h>

static void t_fun(unsigned long t_arg);

static struct simp {
        int i;
        int j;
} t_data;

static DECLARE_TASKLET(t_name, t_fun, (unsigned long)&t_data);

static int __init my_init(void)
{
        t_data.i = 100;
        t_data.j = 200;
        printk(KERN_INFO " scheduling my tasklet, jiffies= %ld \n", jiffies);
        tasklet_schedule(&t_name);
        return 0;
}

static void __exit my_exit(void)
{
        printk(KERN_INFO "\nHello: unloading module\n",
                cleanup_module);
}

static void t_fun(unsigned long t_arg)
{
        struct simp *datum;
        datum = (struct simp *)t_arg;
        printk(KERN_INFO "Entering t_fun, datum->i = %d, jiffies = %ld\n",
                datum->i, jiffies);
        printk(KERN_INFO "Entering t_fun, datum->j = %d, jiffies = %ld\n",
                datum->j, jiffies);
}

module_init(my_init);
module_exit(my_exit);
```

Kernel Version Note   Kernel Version Note

- There is an ongoing discussion about eliminating tasklets from the **Linux** kernel.

- First, because tasklets run in software interrupt mode, you cannot sleep, refer to user-space, etc., so one has to be quite careful.

- Second, since tasklets run as software interrupts they have higher priority than any other task on the system, and thus can produce uncontrolled latencies in other tasks if they are coded poorly.

- The idea is to replace almost all tasklet uses with workqueues, which run in a sleepable pseudo-user context, and get scheduled like other tasks. A proof of concept implementation in which all tasklets were converted to work queues with a wrapper did not cause terrible problems.

- However, there were developers who were very unhappy with the proposed changes, in particular those who work on network device drivers. In this case testing becomes very laborious.

- If history is any guide the most likely outcome is that the use of tasklets will gradually diminish in that they will be deprecated in new code, and some or a lot of old code will be converted one instance at a time rather than globally. If tasklet use becomes rare it may be eliminated at some point in one fell swoop, but don't lose any sleep waiting for it to happen.

21.4 Work Queues

- A **work queue** contains a linked list of tasks which need to be run at a deferred time (usually as soon as possible).

- The tasks are run in process context; a kernel thread is run on each CPU in order to launch them. Thus not only is sleeping legal, it will not interfere with tasks running in any other queue. Note that you still can't transfer data to and from user-space as there isn't a real user context to access.

- Unlike tasklets, a task run on a work queue may be run on a different processor than the process that scheduled it. Thus they are a good choice when such serialization (and hoping to minimize cache thrashing) is not required, and can lead to faster accomplishment of the deferred tasks.

- The code for work queues can be found in **/usr/src/linux/include/linux/workqueue.h** and **/usr/src/linux/kernel/workqueue.c**. The important data structure describing the tasks put on the queue is:

```
typedef void (*work_func_t)(struct work_struct *work);

struct work_struct {
    atomic_long_t data;
    struct list_head entry;
```

```
        work_func_t func;
};
```

- Here func() points to the function that will be run when the work is done. The other arguments are for internal use and are usually not set directly.

- Note that the data entry is used like the state entry for tasklets; if multiple identical work queues are requested, all but the first will be quietly dropped on the floor in the same way.

- The earliest implementation of workqueues had an explicit data pointer that was passed to the function. This was modified so that the function now receives a pointer to a work_struct data structure.

- In order to pass data to a function, one needs to embed the work_struct in a user-defined data structure and then to pointer arithmetic in order to recover it. An example would be:

```
static struct my_dat
{
    int irq;
    struct work_struct work;
};

static void w_fun (struct work_struct *w_arg)
{
    struct my_dat *data = container_of (w_arg, struct my_dat, work);
    atomic_inc (data->irq);
}
```

- A work_struct can be declared and initialized at compile time with:

```
DECLARE_WORK(name, void (*function)(void *));
```

where name is the name of the structure which points to queueing up function() to run. A previously initialized work queue can be initialized and loaded with the two macros:

```
INIT_WORK(   struct work_struct *work, void (*function)(void *));
PREPARE_WORK(struct work_struct *work, void (*function)(void *));
```

where work has already been declared as a work_struct. The INIT_WORK() macro initializes the list_head linked-list pointer, and PREPARE_WORK() sets the function pointer. The INIT_WORK macro needs to be called at least once, and in turn calls PREPARE_WORK(); it should not be called while a task is already in the work queue.

- While it is possible to set up your own work queue for just your own tasks, in most cases a default work queue (named **events**) will suffice, and is easier to use. Tasks are added to and flushed from this queue with the functions:

```
int schedule_work (struct work_struct *work);
void flush_scheduled_work (void);
```

- flush_scheduled_work() is used when one needs to wait until all entries in a work queue have run,

- Note that these are the only work queue functions that are exported to all modules; the others are exported only to **GPL**-compliant modules. Thus creating your own work queue and using it is reserved only for **GPL**-licensed code.

- A work queue can be created and destroyed with:

```
struct workqueue_struct *create_workqueue (const char *name);
void destroy_workqueue (struct workqueue_struct *wq);
```

where `name` is up to 10 characters long and is the command listed for the thread, and the `struct workqueue_struct` describes the work queue itself (which one never needs to look inside), Note that `destroy_workqueue()` flushes the queue before it returns.

- Adding a task to the work queue, and flushing it is done with:

```
int queue_work (struct workqueue_struct *wq, struct work_struct *work);
void flush_workqueue (struct workqueue_struct *wq);
```

- It is possible to postpone workqueue execution for a specified timer interval using:

```
struct delayed_work { struct work_struct_work, struct timer_list timer;}
int schedule_delayed_work (struct delayed_work *work, unsigned long delay);
int cancel_delayed_work (struct delayed_work *work);

DECLARE_WORK(name, void (*function)(void *));
INIT_WORK(   struct delayed_work *work, void (*function)(void *));
PREPARE_WORK(struct delayed_work *work, void (*function)(void *));
```

where `delay` is expressed in `jiffies`. One can use `cancel_delayed_work()` to kill off a pending delayed request.

- One has to be careful when taking advantage of a task's ability to sleep on a workqueue; when it sleeps, no other pending task on the queue can run until it wakes up!

- The workqueue implementation also provides a method of ensuring a function runs in process context:

```
typedef void (*work_func_t)(struct work_struct *work);
struct execute_work {
        struct work_struct work;
};

int execute_in_process_context (work_func_t fn, struct execute_work *ew);
```

- If this function is called from process context it will return a value of 0 and `fn(data)` will be run immediately. If this function is called from interrupt context it will return a value of 1 and the function will be called with

```
schedule_work(&ew_work);
```

21.5   Creating Kernel Threads

- **kernel threads** of execution differ in many important ways from those that operate on behalf of a process. For one thing they always operate in kernel mode.

- The functions and macros for creating and stopping kernel threads are given in **/usr/src/linux/ include/linux/kthread.h**:

```
#include <linux/kthread.h>

struct task_struct *kthread_run (int (*threadfn)(void *data),
                    void *data, const char namefmt[], ...);
struct task_struct *kthread_create (int (*threadfn)(void *data),
                    void *data, const char namefmt[], ...);
void kthread_bind (struct task_struct *k, unsigned int cpu);
int kthread_stop (struct task_struct *k);
int kthread_should_stop (void);
```

- The created thread will run `threadfn(data)`, which will use `namefmt` and any succeeding arguments to create its name as it will appear with the **ps** command.

- The function `kthread_create()` initializes the process in a sleeping state; usually one will want to use the `kthread_run()` macro which follows this with a call to

```
int wake_up_process (struct task_struct *tsk);
```

- However, one may want to call `kthread_bind()` first, which will bind the thread to a particular cpu.

- Terminating the thread is done with `kthread_stop()`. This sets `kthread_should_stop()`, wakes the thread and waits for it to exit.

- For example one might execute a loop such as:

```
do {  .... } while (!kthread_should_stop());
```

where the loop will probably include sleeping, and then issue a call to `kthread_stop()` from an exit routine.

- Kernel threads can only be created from process context as their implementation can block while waiting for resources. Calling from atomic context will lead to a kernel crash.

- An older function

```
int kernel_thread(int (*fn)(void *), void * arg, unsigned long flags);
```

is still used in many places in the kernel. It is more complicated to use and requires more work to accomplish successful termination. It should not be used in new code.

21.6 Threaded Interrupt Handlers

- The 2.6.30 kernel introduced a new method of writing interrupt handlers in which the bottom half is taken care by a scheduled thread. This feature arose in the **realtime** kernel tree and unsurprisingly has as its goal reducing latencies and the amount of time interrupts may need to be disabled.

- The API is only slightly different than that used in the normal interrupt handler; an IRQ is now requested with the function:

```
int request_threaded_irq (unsigned int irq, irq_handler_t handler,
        irq_handler_t thread_fn, unsigned long flags, const char *name, void *dev);
```

the new aspect being the third argument, `thread_fn` which is essentially a bottom half. There is a also a new return value for the top half, `IRQ_WAKE_THREAD`, that should be used when the threaded bottom half is being used.

- Thus the top half is called in a hard interrupt context, and and must first check whether the interrupt originated in its device. If not it returns `IRQ_NONE`; otherwise it returns `IRQ_HANDLED` if no further processing is required, or `IRQ_WAKE_THREAD` if the thread function needs to be invoked.

- This method has been used to replace tasklets and work queues in many device drivers, and adoption is only likely to increase.

- If the kernel is booted with the command line option, `threadirqs` as in:

  `linux kernel /vmlinuz-3.0.0 .... threadirqs`

  all interrupt handlers will be forced into threading, except those which have been explicitly flagged with `IRQF_NO_THREAD`.

21.7   Interrupt Handling in User-Space

- Device drivers written in user-space may offer certain advantages:

  - Potentially better security and stability.
  - Keeping the core kernel code base smaller.
  - Avoiding some licensing constraints.

- Of course not everyone would consider each one of these properties as an advantage.

- It has long been the case that many device drivers are written in user-space using either the `iopl()` or `ioperm()` functions to get application access to I/O ports, or are layered on top of in-kernel lower-level drivers such as those for the parallel, serial or **USB** ports. Such is the case, for example, with drivers for printers and scanners.

- What was long lacking in terms of infrastructure was a general method of having a user-space driver handle interrupts. The kinds of drivers mentioned above often work in **polling** modes; e.g., the **X** driver checks for mouse activity many times per second by reading I/O ports instead of directly responding to interrupts.

- The **UIO** project (Userspace **I/O**) was finally integrated in the 2.6.23 kernel as a method of handling interrupts from user-space.

- For full documentation see **/usr/src/linux/Documentation/DocBook/uio-howto.tmpl**, or to see it in the pdf form produced from kernel sources go to:
  http://training.linuxfoundation.org/course_materials/LF339/uio-howto.pdf.

- The first device created will cause the appearance of the device node **/dev/uio0**, the second **/dev/uio1** etc. An application reading from these device nodes will block until an interrupt appears and can read an unsigned integer from it containing the total number of interrupts. Instead of a blocking read, you can also use `select()`, `poll()` etc and sit on the file descriptors and wait for activity.

- If all you need to do is know when an interrupt appears a user-space driver alone may suffice. It can be written using all available user-space libraries and tools and need not have an open-source license.

- However, much of the time you will need to write a small kernel driver as well, which may be required to do things like set up memory mapped regions on the device (which you can access from user-space), clear interrupt bits on device registers etc. There is also a general API for writing a **PCI** user-space driver, all of which is described in the document previously referred to.

- We should note that there are potential difficulties such as the possibilities of losing interrupts if multiple interrupts arrive, special problems with sharing interrupts, and trying to avoid too much polling which disturbs true asynchronousness in the interrupt system and can lead to unacceptable latencies.

- We will do exercises in which we used the **UIO** infrastructure, on the one hand, and implement one of our own, also using a special device node.

21.8 Labs

Lab 1: Deferred Functions

- Write a driver that schedules a deferred function whenever a `write()` to the device takes place.

- Pass some data to the driver and have it print out.

- Have it print out the `current->pid` field when the tasklet is scheduled, and then again when the queued function is executed.

- Implement this using:

  - **tasklets**
  - **work queues**

- You can use the same testing programs you used in the sleep exercises.

- Try scheduling multiple deferred functions and see if they come out in LIFO or FIFO order. What happens if you try to schedule the deferred function more than once?

Lab 2: Shared Interrupts and Bottom Halves

- Write a module that shares its IRQ with your network card. You can generate some network interrupts either by browsing or pinging.

- Make it use a top half and a bottom half.

- Check `/proc/interrupts` while it is loaded.

- Have the module keep track of the number of times the interrupt's halves are called.

- Implement the bottom half using:

  - **tasklets**.
  - **work queues**
  - **A background thread** which you launch during the module's initialization, which gets woken up anytime data is available. Make sure you kill the thread when you unload the module, or it may stay in a zombie state forever.

- For any method you use does, are the bottom and top halves called an equal number of times? If not why, and what can you do about it?

- Note: the solutions introduce a `delay` parameter which can be set when loading the module; this will introduce a delay of that many milliseconds in the top half, which will provoke dropping even more bottom halves, depending on the method used.

Lab 3: Producer/Consumer

- You may have noticed that you lost some bottom halves. This will happen when more than one interrupt arrives before bottom halves are accomplished. For instance, the same tasklet can only be queued up twice.

- Write a bottom half that can "catch up"; i.e., consume more than one event when it is called, cleaning up the pending queue. Do this for at least one of the previous solutions.

Lab 4: Sharing All Interrupts, Bottom Halves

- Extend the solution to share all possible interrupts, and evaluate the consumer/producer problem.

Lab 5: Sharing All Interrupts, Producer/Consumer Problem

- Find solutions for the producer/consumer problem for the previous lab.

Lab 6: Threaded Interrupt Handlers

- If you are running a kernel version 2.6.30 or later, solve the producer/consumer problem with a threaded interrupt handler.

- There are two types of solutions presented, one for just one shared interrupt, one sharing them all, with the same delay parameter as used in the earlier exercises.

Lab 7: User-Space Interrupt Handling

- Adapt the character driver with polling to handle a shared interrupt.

- The read method should sleep until events are available and then deal with potentially multiple events.

- The information passed back by the read should include the number of events.

- You can reuse the previously written testing program that opens the device node and then sits on it with `poll()` until interrupts arrive.

- You can also test it with just using the simple read program, or doing `cat < /dev/mycdrv` and generating some interrupts.

- You can probably also implement a solution that does not involve `poll()`, but just a blocking read.

Lab 8: The UIO API

- In order to write a user-space driver using the **UIO** API with a small kernel stub driver you'll have to do the following:

- Allocate space for a `uio_info` structure, defined in **/usr/src/linux/include/linux/uio_driver.h**:

```
/**
 * struct uio_info - UIO device capabilities
 * @uio_dev:          the UIO device this info belongs to
 * @name:             device name
 * @version:          device driver version
 * @mem:              list of mappable memory regions, size==0 for end of list
 * @port:             list of port regions, size==0 for end of list
 * @irq:              interrupt number or UIO_IRQ_CUSTOM
 * @irq_flags:        flags for request_irq()
 * @priv:             optional private data
 * @handler:          the device's irq handler
 * @mmap:             mmap operation for this uio device
 * @open:             open operation for this uio device
 * @release:          release operation for this uio device
```

```
 * @irqcontrol:           disable/enable irqs when 0/1 is written to /dev/uioX
 */
struct uio_info {
        struct uio_device       *uio_dev;
        const char              *name;
        const char              *version;
        struct uio_mem          mem[MAX_UIO_MAPS];
        struct uio_port         port[MAX_UIO_PORT_REGIONS];
        long                    irq;
        unsigned long           irq_flags;
        void                    *priv;
        irqreturn_t (*handler)(int irq, struct uio_info *dev_info);
        int (*mmap)(struct uio_info *info, struct vm_area_struct *vma);
        int (*open)(struct uio_info *info, struct inode *inode);
        int (*release)(struct uio_info *info, struct inode *inode);
        int (*irqcontrol)(struct uio_info *info, s32 irq_on);
};
```

You'll need to fill in entries for at least name, irq, irq_flags and handler, which should return IRQ_HANDLED.

- The structure should be register and unregistered with:

```
int uio_register_device(struct device *parent, struct uio_info *info);
void uio_unregister_device(struct uio_info *info);
```

- The parent field should be a device structure where you fill in at least the name field and supply a release() method (see your previous firmware exercise) and you should call device_register() on this structure first.

- To exercise this you will have to write a short test program which sits on /dev/uio0 and waits for interrupts to arrive, reading the value as an unsigned long.

Chapter 22

Hardware I/O

We'll see how **Linux** communicates with data buses and I/O Ports and uses memory barriers. We'll see how to read and write to memory mapped devices.

22.1   Memory Barriers

- Operations on I/O registers differ in some important ways from normal memory access. In particular, there may be so-called **side-effects**. These are generally due to compiler and hardware optimizations.

- These optimizations can cause reordering of instructions. In conventional memory reads and writes there is no problem; a write always stores a value and a read always returns the last value written.

- However, for I/O ports problems can result because the CPU cannot tell when a process depends on the order of memory access. In other words, because of reading or writing an I/O register, devices may initiate or respond to various actions.

- Therefore, a driver must make sure no caching is performed and no reordering occurs. Otherwise problems which are difficult to diagnose, and are rare or intermittent, may result.

- The solution is to use appropriate **memory barrier** functions when necessary. The necessary functions are defined in and indirectly included from **/usr/src/linux/arch/arm/include/asm/system.h** and are:

```
void barrier (void)
```

```
void rmb (void)
void wmb (void)
void mb (void)

void smp_rmb (void)
void smp_wmb (void)
void smp_mb (void)
```

- The `barrier()` macro causes the compiler to store in memory all values currently modified in a CPU register, to read them again later when they are needed. This function does not have any effect on the hardware itself.

- The other macros put hardware memory barriers in the code; how they are implemented depends on the platform. `rmb()` forces any reads before the barrier to complete before any reads done after the barrier; `wmb()` does the same thing for writes, while `mb()` does it for both reads and writes.

- The versions with `smp_` insert hardware barriers only on multi-processor systems; on single CPU systems they expand to a simple call to `barrier()`.

- A simple example of a use of a write barrier would be:

```
io32write (direction, dev->base + OFF_DIR);
io32write (size, dev->base + OFF_SIZE);
wmb();
io32write (value, dev->base + OFF_GO);
```

- Most architectures define convenience macros, which combine setting a value with invoking a memory barrier. In the simplest form they look like:

```
#define set_mb(var, value)  do { var = value; mb();  } while (0)
#define set_wmb(var, value) do { var = value; wmb(); } while (0)
#define set_rmb(var, value) do { var = value; rmb(); } while (0)
```

- Memory barriers may cause a performance hit and should be used with care. One should only use the specific form needed. For instance on **x86** the write memory barrier does nothing as writes are not reordered. However, reads may be reordered, so you should not use `mb()` if `wmb()` would suffice.

22.2   Allocating and Mapping I/O Memory

- Non-trivial peripheral devices are almost always accessed though on-board memory which is remapped and made available to the processor over the bus. These memory locations can be used as buffers, or behave as I/O ports which have side effects associated with I/O operations.

- Exactly how these memory regions are accessed is quite architecture-dependent. However, **Linux** hides the platform dependence by using a universal interface. While some architectures permit direct dereferencing of pointers for these regions, one should never attempt this.

- There are three essential steps in using these regions: allocation, remapping, and use of the appropriate read/write functions.

- Before such a memory region can be used it must be allocated (and eventually freed) with:

```
struct resource *request_mem_region (unsigned long start, unsigned long len, char *name);
void release_mem_region (unsigned long start, unsigned long len);
```

which work on a region of `len` bytes, extending from address `start`, and using `name` to describe the entry created in **/proc/iomem**. The starting address is a characteristic of the device; e.g., for **PCI** devices it may be read from a configuration register, or obtained from the function `pci_resource_start()`.

- One can not directly use the pointer to the `start` address; instead one must remap and eventually unmap it with:

```
#include <linux/io.h>
void *ioremap (unsigned long phys_addr, unsigned long size);
void iounmap (void *addr);
```

- Furthermore, one should refer to this memory only with the functions to be described next, not direct pointer dereferencing.

- Occasionally, one may find it convenient to use the following functions to associate I/O registers, or ports, with I/O memory:

```
#include <asm-generic/iomap.h>

void *ioport_map (unsigned long port, unsigned int count);
void ioport_unmap (void *addr);
```

By using these functions I/O ports appear as memory. These ports will have to be reserved as usual before this is done. After doing this, access is obtained with the read/write functions to be discussed next.

Once again there are bus-specific optional convenience functions, such as

```
void *pci_iomap (struct pci_dev *dev, int bar, unsigned long maxlen);
void pci_iounmap (struct pci_dev *dev, void __iomem * addr);
```

defined in **/usr/src/linux/lib/iomap.c**.

Note these functions do not request the memory regions; that must be done separately.

22.3   Accessing I/O Memory

- Reading and writing from remapped I/O memory is done with the following functions:

```
#include <linux/io.h>

unsigned int ioread8  (void *addr);
unsigned int ioread16 (void *addr);
unsigned int ioread32 (void *addr);

void iowrite8  (u8  val, void *addr);
void iowrite16 (u16 val, void *addr);
void iowrite32 (u32 val, void *addr);
```

- The `addr` argument should point to an address obtained with `ioremap()` (with perhaps an offset), with the read functions returning the value read.

- Reading and writing multiple times can be done with

```
void ioread8_rep  (void *addr, void *buf, unsigned long count);
void ioread16_rep (void *addr, void *buf, unsigned long count);
void ioread32_rep (void *addr, void *buf, unsigned long count);

void iowrite8_rep  (void *addr, void *buf, unsigned long count);
void iowrite16_rep (void *addr, void *buf, unsigned long count);
void iowrite32_rep (void *addr, void *buf, unsigned long count);
```

- These functions do repeated I/O on `addr`, not to a range of addresses, reading from or writing to the kernel address pointed to by `buf`.

- Most 64-bit architectures also have 64-bit reads and writes, with the functions:

```
u64 readq (address);
void writeq (u64 val, address);
```

  used in an obvious way, where the **q** stands for **quad**. Note there are no `ioread64()`, `iowrite64()` functions at this time.

- Working directly with a block of memory can be done with

```
void memset_io (void *addr, u8 val, unsigned int count);
void memcpy_io   (void *dest, void *source, unsigned int count);
void memcpy_toio (void *dest, void *source, unsigned int count);
```

- The above functions do I/O in **little-endian** order, and do any necessary byte-swapping., except for the `mem...()` ones which simply work with byte streams and do no swapping.

- The older I/O functions:

```
unsigned char  readb (address);
unsigned short readw (address);
unsigned long  readl (address);

void writeb (unsigned char val,  address);
void writew (unsigned short val, address);
void writel (unsigned long val,  address);
```

  are deprecated, although they will still work. They are not as safe as the newer functions as they do not do as thorough type checking.

Chapter 23

Platform Drivers

We'll discuss platform drivers.

23.1   What are Platform Drivers?

- Devices on well known buses, such as **PCI** and **USB**, have well defined methods in the **Unified Device Model** for declaring themselves when they are attached or detached through hotplug mechanisms or are discovered during system boot.

- However, may modern **SOC**'s (**S**ystem **O**n **C**hips) have peripherals such as host controllers and other devices already built in and do not inform the kernel in the same way about their presence. Generally such devices have direct addressing from a **CPU** bus, and while they are rarely connected through a segment of some other type of bus, their registers will still be directly addressable.

- To handle such devices **Linux** uses the **platform driver** interface which connects to and resembles the unified device model and permits virtual addition and removal of devices. Each device gets a unique name and is configurable.

- Thus the **platform bus** can be understood as a **pseudo-bus** useful for both integrated peripherals on **SOC**'s, and for **legacy** interconnects, where there is no major maintained specification such as **PCI** or **USB**.

23.2   Main Data Structures

- The main data structures and methods are given in **/usr/src/linux/include/linux/platform_device.h**, with the `platform_device` structure describing the device:

```
3.0:   19 struct platform_device {
3.0:   20     const char      * name;
3.0:   21     int             id;
3.0:   22     struct device   dev;
3.0:   23     u32             num_resources;
3.0:   24     struct resource * resource;
3.0:   25
3.0:   26     const struct platform_device_id *id_entry;
3.0:   27
3.0:   28     /* MFD cell pointer */
3.0:   29     struct mfd_cell *mfd_cell;
3.0:   30
3.0:   31     /* arch specific additions */
3.0:   32     struct pdev_archdata    archdata;
3.0:   33 };
```

  and contains a pointer to the appropriate `device` structure.

- The `platform_driver` structure describes the driver:

```
3.0:  119 struct platform_driver {
3.0:  120     int (*probe)(struct platform_device *);
3.0:  121     int (*remove)(struct platform_device *);
3.0:  122     void (*shutdown)(struct platform_device *);
3.0:  123     int (*suspend)(struct platform_device *, pm_message_t state);
3.0:  124     int (*resume)(struct platform_device *);
3.0:  125     struct device_driver driver;
3.0:  126     const struct platform_device_id *id_table;
3.0:  127 };
```

  and contains a pointer to the appropriate `device_driver`

- Note that as with **PCI** devices there are macros to go back and forth between the connected `device` and `platform_device` structures:

```
3.0:   35 #define platform_get_device_id(pdev)        ((pdev)->id_entry)
3.0:   36  .
3.0:   37 #define to_platform_device(x) container_of((x),
                                        struct platform_device, dev)
```

- As for other devices in the unified driver model framework, while discovery and enumeration of devices is done outside the actual drivers, one must supply `probe()` and `remove()` methods (as well as the usual various power management functions). It is particularly important that the `probe()` method verify the hardware is actually present as platform setup code can not always reliably determine this.

23.3 Registering Platform Devices

- After filling out the `platform_driver` structure register/deregister themselves with:

  ```
  int platform_driver_register(struct platform_driver *);
  void platform_driver_unregister(struct platform_driver *);
  ```

  In cases where the device is known not to be hot-pluggable one can use:

  ```
  int platform_driver_probe(struct platform_driver *driver,
                            int (*probe)(struct platform_device *));
  ```

- Devices are enumerated with:

  ```
  int platform_device_register(struct platform_device *);
  void platform_device_unregister(struct platform_device *);

  platform_add_devices(struct platform_device **, int);
  ```

23.4 An Example

- As a simple example we look at **/usr/src/linux/arch/arm/plat-pxa/pwm.c**, a driver for a pulse width modulator. Starting with the initialization and exit routine we have:

  ```
  3.0: 282 static struct platform_driver pwm_driver = {
  3.0: 283     .driver       = {
  3.0: 284             .name   = "pxa25x-pwm",
  3.0: 285             .owner  = THIS_MODULE,
  3.0: 286     },
  3.0: 287     .probe        = pwm_probe,
  3.0: 288     .remove       = __devexit_p(pwm_remove),
  3.0: 289     .id_table     = pwm_id_table,
  3.0: 290 };
  3.0: 291
  3.0: 292 static int __init pwm_init(void)
  3.0: 293 {
  3.0: 294     return platform_driver_register(&pwm_driver);
  3.0: 295 }
  3.0: 296 arch_initcall(pwm_init);
  3.0: 297
  3.0: 298 static void __exit pwm_exit(void)
  3.0: 299 {
  3.0: 300     platform_driver_unregister(&pwm_driver);
  3.0: 301 }
  3.0: 302 module_exit(pwm_exit);
  ```

  Note the use of `arch_initcall()` rather than `module_init()` as this driver has to be loaded early.

- The `platform_driver` structure is filled out before registration with:

  - A pointer to the underlying **device_driver** structure, which includes a unique name, **"pxa25-pwm"**.
  - A probe function, `pwm_probe()`, we will look at.
  - A remove function, `pwm_remove()`, which has been labeled with `__devexit_p`, which just has the effect of dropping the code if the driver is compiled as builtin.

– A `platform_device_id` table, `pwm_id_table`:

```
3.0: 28 static const struct platform_device_id pwm_id_table[] = {
3.0: 29    /*  PWM     has_secondary_pwm? */
3.0: 30    { "pxa25x-pwm", 0 },
3.0: 31    { "pxa27x-pwm", 0 | HAS_SECONDARY_PWM },
3.0: 32    { "pxa168-pwm", 1 },
3.0: 33    { "pxa910-pwm", 1 },
3.0: 34    { },
3.0: 35 };
3.0: 36 MODULE_DEVICE_TABLE(platform, pwm_id_table);
```

which specifies which devices the driver can handle, as plays the same role as the `pci_id_table` structure, etc.

- Let's take a look at the probe function, which is obviously quite important. First a pointer to the `platform_device_id` table is obtained:

```
3.0: 177 static int __devinit pwm_probe(struct platform_device *pdev)
3.0: 178 {
3.0: 179    const struct platform_device_id *id = platform_get_device_id(pdev);
3.0: 180    struct pwm_device *pwm, *secondary = NULL;
3.0: 181    struct resource *r;
3.0: 182    int ret = 0;
3.0: 183
```

Then it allocates space for a structure of type `pwm_device` (local to this driver):

```
3.0: 46 struct pwm_device {
3.0: 47    struct list_head        node;
3.0: 48    struct pwm_device       *secondary;
3.0: 49    struct platform_device  *pdev;
3.0: 50
3.0: 51    const char      *label;
3.0: 52    struct clk      *clk;
3.0: 53    int             clk_enabled;
3.0: 54    void __iomem    *mmio_base;
3.0: 55
3.0: 56    unsigned int    use_count;
3.0: 57    unsigned int    pwm_id;
3.0: 58 };
```

with:

```
3.0: 184    pwm = kzalloc(sizeof(struct pwm_device), GFP_KERNEL);
3.0: 185    if (pwm == NULL) {
3.0: 186            dev_err(&pdev->dev, "failed to allocate memory\n");
3.0: 187            return -ENOMEM;
3.0: 188    }
```

Then `clk_get()` is called to lookup and obtain a reference to a clock producer, which then has to be enabled.

```
3.0: 189
3.0: 190    pwm->clk = clk_get(&pdev->dev, NULL);
3.0: 191    if (IS_ERR(pwm->clk)) {
3.0: 192            ret = PTR_ERR(pwm->clk);
3.0: 193            goto err_free;
3.0: 194    }
```

```
3.0: 195        pwm->clk_enabled = 0;
3.0: 196
```

Next the usage count is initialized, some structures are filled in, and `platform_get_resource()` and `request_mem_region()` are called to get access to onboard I/O memory:

```
3.0: 197        pwm->use_count = 0;
3.0: 198        pwm->pwm_id = PWM_ID_BASE(id->driver_data) + pdev->id;
3.0: 199        pwm->pdev = pdev;
3.0: 200
3.0: 201        r = platform_get_resource(pdev, IORESOURCE_MEM, 0);
3.0: 202        if (r == NULL) {
3.0: 203                dev_err(&pdev->dev, "no memory resource defined\n");
3.0: 204                ret = -ENODEV;
3.0: 205                goto err_free_clk;
3.0: 206        }
3.0: 207
3.0: 208        r = request_mem_region(r->start, resource_size(r), pdev->name);
3.0: 209        if (r == NULL) {
3.0: 210                dev_err(&pdev->dev, "failed to request memory resource\n");
3.0: 211                ret = -EBUSY;
3.0: 212                goto err_free_clk;
3.0: 213        }
```

This I/O memory is then remapped to give an address that can be used:

```
3.0: 214
3.0: 215        pwm->mmio_base = ioremap(r->start, resource_size(r));
3.0: 216        if (pwm->mmio_base == NULL) {
3.0: 217                dev_err(&pdev->dev, "failed to ioremap() registers\n");
3.0: 218                ret = -ENODEV;
3.0: 219                goto err_free_mem;
3.0: 220        }
3.0: 221
```

This particular device can have a secondary:

```
3.0: 222        if (id->driver_data & HAS_SECONDARY_PWM) {
3.0: 223                secondary = kzalloc(sizeof(struct pwm_device), GFP_KERNEL);
3.0: 224                if (secondary == NULL) {
3.0: 225                        ret = -ENOMEM;
3.0: 226                        goto err_free_mem;
3.0: 227                }
3.0: 228
3.0: 229                *secondary = *pwm;
3.0: 230                pwm->secondary = secondary;
3.0: 231
3.0: 232                /* registers for the second PWM has offset of 0x10 */
3.0: 233                secondary->mmio_base = pwm->mmio_base + 0x10;
3.0: 234                secondary->pwm_id = pdev->id + 2;
3.0: 235        }
3.0: 236
```

Now we are actually ready to add the device:

```
3.0: 237        __add_pwm(pwm);
3.0: 238        if (secondary)
3.0: 239                __add_pwm(secondary);
```

```
3.0: 240
3.0: 241        platform_set_drvdata(pdev, pwm);
3.0: 242        return 0;
3.0: 243
3.0: 244 err_free_mem:
3.0: 245        release_mem_region(r->start, resource_size(r));
3.0: 246 err_free_clk:
3.0: 247        clk_put(pwm->clk);
3.0: 248 err_free:
3.0: 249        kfree(pwm);
3.0: 250        return ret;
3.0: 251 }
```

Note the setting of the private data `driver_data` field embedded in the underlying `device` structure with `platform_set_drvdata()`. The `__add_pwm()` function just adds the device to a linked list of such devices:

```
3.0: 170 static inline void __add_pwm(struct pwm_device *pwm)
3.0: 171 {
3.0: 172        mutex_lock(&pwm_lock);
3.0: 173        list_add_tail(&pwm->node, &pwm_list);
3.0: 174        mutex_unlock(&pwm_lock);
3.0: 175 }
```

- The `remove()` function just reverses these steps and is pretty straightforward:

```
3.0: 253 static int __devexit pwm_remove(struct platform_device *pdev)
3.0: 254 {
3.0: 255        struct pwm_device *pwm;
3.0: 256        struct resource *r;
3.0: 257
3.0: 258        pwm = platform_get_drvdata(pdev);
3.0: 259        if (pwm == NULL)
3.0: 260                return -ENODEV;
3.0: 261
3.0: 262        mutex_lock(&pwm_lock);
3.0: 263
3.0: 264        if (pwm->secondary) {
3.0: 265                list_del(&pwm->secondary->node);
3.0: 266                kfree(pwm->secondary);
3.0: 267        }
3.0: 268
3.0: 269        list_del(&pwm->node);
3.0: 270        mutex_unlock(&pwm_lock);
3.0: 271
3.0: 272        iounmap(pwm->mmio_base);
3.0: 273
3.0: 274        r = platform_get_resource(pdev, IORESOURCE_MEM, 0);
3.0: 275        release_mem_region(r->start, resource_size(r));
3.0: 276
3.0: 277        clk_put(pwm->clk);
3.0: 278        kfree(pwm);
3.0: 279        return 0;
3.0: 280 }
```

- The rest of the driver consists of definitions of various callback functions defined in **/usr/src/linux/ include/linux/pwm.h**:

```
struct pwm_device *pwm_request(int pwm_id, const char *label);
void pwm_free(struct pwm_device *pwm);
int pwm_config(struct pwm_device *pwm, int duty_ns, int period_ns);
int pwm_enable(struct pwm_device *pwm);
void pwm_disable(struct pwm_device *pwm);
```

which are part of the **pwm** class device infrastructure.

23.5   Hardcoded Platform Data

- Hard-coded platform files are in wide use, especially in the world of embedded **ARM** devices. This is because (unlike in the cases of **PCI** or **USB**) a lot of undiscoverable devices are connected directly or indirectly to the **SoC**.

- This has led to a plethora of board- specific files: see **/usr/src/linux/arch/arm/**. One can compare `/usr/src/linux/{x86,sparc,ppc}` with `/usr/src/linux/{arm,mips,sh4}` in order to see this.

- **Pros:**

  - Easy to add new board.

  - Easy to add variants.

  - Simple board configuration through kernel config.

- **Cons:**

  - Lots of duplicated code.

  - Clutters `arch` directory with board data.

  - Hard to maintain as the number of boards grows.

  - Inflexible (e.g. new board ¡-¿ older kernel).

  - Kernel only boots on specific board(!)

  - Configuration done in code(!)

23.6   The New Way: Device Trees

- A **device tree** is a textual representation of a board's hardware configuration. It can be passed to the kernel at boot time.

- Device trees can abstract the board-specific differences into boot-time data and allow generic kernels to run. Boards are thus no longer bound to a single kernel build.

- The basic data format is as follows: The device tree is a simple tree structure of **nodes** and **properties**:

    - **Properties** are key-value pairs.

    - **Nodes** may contain both properties and child nodes.

- For example, the following is a simple tree in the **.dts** format:

```
/ {
    node1 {
        a-string-property = "A string";
        a-string-list-property = "first string", "second string";
        a-byte-data-property = [0x01 0x23 0x34 0x56];
        child-node1 {
            first-child-property;
            second-child-property = <1>;
            a-string-property = "Hello, world";
        };
        child-node2 {
        };
    };
    node2 {
        an-empty-property;
        a-cell-property = <1 2 3 4>; /* each number (cell) is a uint32 */
        child-node1 {
        };
    };
};
```

    Some good references on all this can be found at:
    http://devicetree.org/mediawiki/index.php?title=Device_Tree_Usage, https://lkml.org/lkml/2011/6/13/143 and https://lkml.org/lkml/2011/6/16/14.

- Here is part of the device tree for the **NVIDIA Tegra** board.

```
/{
        compatible = "nvidia,harmony", "nvidia,tegra250";
        #address-cells = <1>;
        #size-cells = <1>;
        interrupt-parent = <&intc>;

        chosen { };
        aliases { };

        memory {
                device_type = "memory";
                reg = <0x00000000 0x40000000>;
        };

        soc {
```

```
                 compatible = "nvidia,tegra250-soc", "simple-bus";
                 #address-cells = <1>;
                 #size-cells = <1>;
                 ranges;

                 intc: interrupt-controller@50041000 {
                         compatible = "nvidia,tegra250-gic";
                         interrupt-controller;
                         #interrupt-cells = <1>;
                         reg = <0x50041000 0x1000>, < 0x50040100 0x0100 >;
                 };

                 serial@70006300 {
                         compatible = "nvidia,tegra250-uart";
                         reg = <0x70006300 0x100>;
                         interrupts = <122>;
                 };

                 i2s-1: i2s@70002800 {
                         compatible = "nvidia,tegra250-i2s";
                         reg = <0x70002800 0x100>;
                         interrupts = <77>;
                         codec = <&wm8903>;
                 };

                 i2c@7000c000 {
                         compatible = "nvidia,tegra250-i2c";
                         #address-cells = <1>;
                         #size-cells = <1>;
                         reg = <0x7000c000 0x100>;
                         interrupts = <70>;

                         wm8903: codec@1a {
                                 compatible = "wlf,wm8903";
                                 reg = <0x1a>;
                                 interrupts = <347>;
                         };
                 };
         };

         sound {
                 compatible = "nvidia,harmony-sound";
                 i2s-controller = <&i2s-1>;
                 i2s-codec = <&wm8903>;
         };
};
```

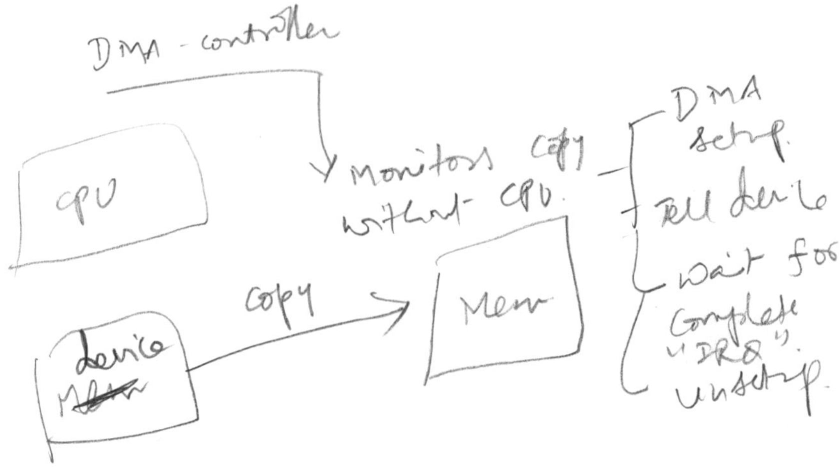
DMA - controller
Monitors copy without CPU.
CPU
copy
Mem
Device
DMA setup.
Tell device
wait for complete "IRQ".
unsetup.

Chapter 24

Direct Memory Access (DMA)

We'll learn about **DMA** under **Linux**. We'll consider how **DMA** uses interrupts for synchronous and asynchronous transfers, how **DMA** buffers must be allocated, and virtual to physical (and bus) address translation. Then we'll look in some detail how **DMA** is deployed for the **PCI** bus, considering both **consistent** and **streaming** transfers, and the use of **DMA Pools**. Finally we'll examine gather/scatter mappings.

24.1 What is DMA?

- Direct Memory Access (**DMA**) permits peripheral devices to transfer data to or from system memory while bypassing CPU control. Proper use of **DMA** can lead to dramatic performance enhancement. Most non-trivial peripherals are likely to have **DMA** capabilities.

- The specifics of **DMA** transfers are very hardware-dependent, both in the sense of the CPU involved (e.g., **x86** or **Alpha**), and the type of data bus (e.g., **PCI**, **ISA**, etc.), and to some degree these degrees of freedom are independent.

- However, since the 2.4 kernel series the goal has been to present a unified, hardware-independent interface. This was achieved in the 2.6 kernel series, permitting one to deal with more abstract methods rather than getting deep into the hardware particularities.

24.2   DMA and Interrupts

- The efficiency of **DMA** transfers is very dependent on proper interrupt handling. Interrupts may be raised when the device acquires data, and are always issued when the data transfer is complete.

- Transfers require a **DMA**-suitable buffer, which must be contiguous and lie within an address range the device can reach, and we will discuss how such buffers can be allocated and released. In the following we will assume that either: such a buffer exists before the transfer and is not released but will be re-used in subsequent transfers; or must be allocated before the transfer begins and released when it is complete.

- Transfers can be triggered **synchronously**, or directly, such as when an application requests or *pulls* data through a `read()`, in which case:

    - The hardware is told to begin sending data.
    - The calling process is put to sleep.
    - The hardware puts data in the **DMA** buffer.
    - The hardware issues an interrupt when it is finished.
    - The interrupt handler deals with the interrupt, acquires the data, and awakens the process, which can now read the data.

- When an application pushes (or writes) data to the hardware one also has a synchronous transfer and the steps are similar.

- Transfers can also be triggered **asynchronously** when the hardware acquires and *pushes* data to the system even when there are no readers at present. In this case:

    - The driver must keep a buffer to warehouse the data until a `read()` call is issued by an application.
    - The hardware announces the arrival of data by raising an interrupt.
    - The interrupt handler tells the hardware where to send the data.
    - The peripheral device puts the data in the **DMA** buffer.
    - The hardware issues an interrupt when it is finished.
    - The interrupt handler deals with the data, and awakens any waiting processes.

- Note that while pushes and pulls have many similar steps, the asynchronous transfer involves two interrupts per transfer, not one.

24.3   DMA Memory Constraints

- **DMA** buffers must occupy *contiguous* memory; Thus you can't use `vmalloc()`, only `kmalloc()` and the `__get_free_pages()` functions. Note you can use also use the abstracted allocation functions we will detail shortly.

- If you specify `GFP_DMA` as the priority the physical memory will not only be contiguous, on **x86** it will also fall under `MAX_DMA_ADDRESS=16 MB`.

- For **PCI** this should be unnecessary and wasteful, but there exist **PCI** devices which still have addressing limitations (sometimes because they were poorly crafted from an **ISA** device.) Thus it is actually necessary to check what addresses are suitable.

- Because the hardware is connected to a peripheral bus which uses **bus addresses** (while both kernel and user code use virtual addresses) conversion functions are needed. These are used when communicating with the Memory Management Unit (MMU) or other hardware connected to the CPU's address lines:

```
#include <asm/io.h>

unsigned long virt_to_bus  (volatile void *address);
void *bus_to_virt  (unsigned long address);

unsigned long virt_to_phys (volatile void *address);
void *phys_to_virt (unsigned long address);
```

You can look at the header file to see how these macros are defined.

- On the **x86** platform bus and physical addresses are the same so these functions do the same thing.

24.4 DMA Directly to User

- High-bandwidth hardware (e.g., a video camera) can obtain lots of speed-up by going straight to the user; i.e., without using **DMA** to first get the data to kernel-space and then transferring to user-space. If one wants to do this by hand it is tricky; the steps are:

    - Lock down the user pages.
    - Set up a **DMA** transfer for each page.
    - When the **DMA** is done, unlock the pages.

- If these steps seem familiar, it is because they are essentially what the `get_user_pages()` **API** does for you; you'll of course still have to do the **DMA** transfers properly.

24.5 DMA API

- The **API** used for **DMA** is platform-independent, and involves a generic structure of type `device`, which may or may not be **PCI** in nature. This structure is embedded in the `pci_dev` structure, so to get at it you'll have to also include **/usr/src/linux/include/linux/pci.h**.

- If one has a device with addressing limitations, the first thing to do is to check whether **DMA** transfers to the desired addresses are possible, with:

```
#include <linux/dma-mapping.h>

int dma_supported (struct device *dev, u64 mask);
```

- For example, if you have a device that can handle only 24-bit addresses, one could do:

```
struct pci_dev *pdev;
if ( dma_supported (pdev->dev, 0xffffff) ){
    pdev->dma_mask = 0xffffff;
} else {
    printk (KERN_WARNING "DMA not supported for the device\n");
    goto device_unsupported;
}
```

- If the device supports normal 32-bit operations, one need not call `dma_supported()` or set the mask.

- In order to set up a **DMA** transfer one has to make a **DMA Mapping**, which involves two steps; allocating a buffer, and generating an address for it that can be used by the device. The details of how this is done are architecture dependent, but the functions for allocating and freeing are the same across platforms:

```
void *dma_alloc_coherent (struct device *dev, size_t size, dma_addr_t *dma_handle, gfp_t flag);
void dma_free_coherent (struct device *dev, size_t size, void *vaddr, dma_addr_t dma_handle);
```

The allocation function returns a kernel virtual address for the buffer, of length `size` bytes. The third argument points to the associated address on the bus (which is meant to be used opaquely.) The `flag` argument controls how the memory is allocated, and is usually `GFP_KERNEL` or `GFP_ATOMIC` if sleeping is not allowed such as when in interrupt context. If the mask requires it, `GFP_DMA` can also be specified. This memory can be freed with `dma_free_coherent()` which requires both addresses as arguments.

- Memory regions supplied with `dma_alloc_coherent()` are used for so-called **Coherent DMA Mappings**, which can also be considered as **synchronous** or **consistent**. These have the following properties:

    - The buffer can be accessed in parallel by both the CPU and the device.

    - A write by either the device or the CPU can immediately be read by either, without worrying about cache problems, or flushing. (However, you may still need to use the various memory barriers functions, as the CPU may reorder I/O instructions to consistent memory just as it does for normal system memory.)

    - The minimum allocation is generally a page. In fact on **x86** one actually always obtains a number of pages that is a power of 2, so it may be expensive.

- Since this method is relatively expensive, it is generally used for **DMA** buffers that persist through the life of the device. A good example of its use would be for network card **DMA** ring descriptors.

- For single operations, one sets up so-called **Streaming DMA mappings**, which can also be considered as **asynchronous**. These are controlled with

```
dma_addr_t dma_map_single (struct device *dev, void *ptr, size_t size,
                           enum dma_data_direction direction);
void dma_unmap_single (struct device *dev, dma_addr_t dma_addr, size_t size,
                           enum dma_data_direction direction);
```

- A pointer to a previously allocated memory region is passed through the `ptr` argument; this must be allocated in **DMA**-suitable fashion; i.e., contiguous and in the right address range. The `direction` argument can have the following values:

Table 24.1: **DMA Transfer Direction Values**

Value	Meaning
PCI_DMA_TODEVICE	Data going to the device, e.g., a write.
PCI_DMA_FROMDEVICE	Data coming from the device, e.g., a read.
PCI_DMA_BIDIRECTIONAL	Data going either way.
PCI_DMA_NONE	Used for debugging; any attempt to use the memory causes failure.

- Streaming **DMA** mappings might be used for network packets, or filesystem buffers. They have the following properties:

    - The direction of a transfer must match the value given during the mapping.

    - After a buffer is mapped, it belongs to the **device**, not the CPU; the driver should not touch the buffer until it has been unmapped.

– Thus for a write the data should be placed in the buffer before the mapping; for a read it should not be touched until after the unmapping (which could be done after the device signals, through an interrupt, that it is through with the transfer.)

- A third kind of mapping is a so-called **Scatter-gather DMA Mapping**. This permits several buffers, which may be non-contiguous, to be transferred to or from the device at one time.

- It is also possible to set up a **DMA pool**, which works pretty much like a memory cache. We'll consider that next.

 Kernel Version Note Kernel Version Note

- Rather than using a generic interface, the 2.4 kernel used a **PCI**-specific interface. The main functions are in one-to-one correspondence with the generic ones and are:

```
#include <linux/pci.h>

int pci_dma_supported (struct pci_dev *dev, u64 mask);
int pci_set_dma_mask (struct pci_dev *dev, u64 mask);
void *pci_alloc_consistent (struct pci_dev *dev, size_t size,
                            dma_addr_t *dma_handle);
void pci_free_consistent (struct pci_dev *dev, size_t size, void *vaddr,
                          dma_addr_t dma_handle);
dma_addr_t pci_map_single (struct pci_dev *dev, void *ptr, size_t size,
                           int direction);
void pci_unmap_single (struct pci_dev *dev, dma_addr_t dma_addr, size_t size,
                       int direction);
```

- While this older **API** has not been removed, it is now just a wrapper around the more general interface, which should be used in any new code.

24.6 DMA Pools

- Suppose you need frequent small **DMA** transfers. For coherent transfers, `dma_alloc_coherent()` has a minimum size of one page. Thus, a good choice would be set up a **DMA Pool**, which is essentially a slab cache intended for use in **DMA** transfers.

- The basic functions are:

```
#include <linux/dmapool.h>

struct dma_pool *dma_pool_create (const char *name, struct device *dev, size_t size,
                                  size_t align, size_t allocation);
void dma_pool_destroy (struct dma_pool *pool);
```

```
void *dma_pool_alloc (struct dma_pool *pool, gfp_t mem_flags, dma_addr_t *handle);
void dma_pool_free (struct dma_pool *pool, void *vaddr, dma_addr_t addr);
```

- No actual memory is allocated by `dma_pool_create()`; it sets up a pool with a name pointed to by `name`, to be associated with the device structure pointed to by `dev`, of `size` bytes.

- The `align` argument (given in bytes) is the hardware alignment for pool allocations. The final argument, `allocation`, if non-zero specifies a memory boundary allocations should not cross. For example, if `allocation=PAGE_SIZE`, buffers in the pool will not cross page boundaries.

- The actual allocation of memory is done with `dma_pool_alloc()`. The `mem_flags` argument gives the usual memory allocation flags (`GFP_KERNEL`, `GFP_ATOMIC`, etc.) The return value is the kernel virtual address of the **DMA** buffer, which is stored in `handle` as a bus address.

- To avoid memory leaks, buffers should be returned to the pool with `dma_pool_free()`, and when all have been released the pool can be wiped out with `dma_pool_destroy()`.

- Note that the memory allocated with the use of the pool will have consistent **DMA** mappings, which means both the device and the driver can use it without using cache flushing primitives.

24.7   Scatter/Gather Mappings

- It is easiest to do a **DMA** transfer if you have only one (large or small) contiguous buffer to work with. Then you can just give a starting address and a length and get the transfer in motion.

- However, one often might have several buffers requiring transfer at the same time, and they might not be physically contiguous. This might occur due to:

    – A `readv()` or `writev()` system call.

    – A disk I/O request.

    – Transfer of a list of pages in a mapped kernel I/O buffer (such as one might have when using `get_user_pages()`.)

- Of course one can chain together a series of individual requests, each one of which represents a contiguous region. But many devices are capable of assisting at the hardware level; a so-called **scatterlist** of pointers and lengths can be given to the device and then it will take care of doing it all as one operation.

- In order to accomplish this you first have to set up an array of structures describing the buffers requiring transfer. For **x86** this structure is described in **/usr/src/linux/arch/arm/include/asm/ scatterlist.h** and looks like:

```
struct scatterlist {
    unsigned long  page_link;
    unsigned int   offset;
    unsigned int   length;
    dma_addr_t     dma_address;
    unsigned int   dma_length;
};
```

Filling in the fields is best done with:

```
void sg_set_page(struct scatterlist *sg, struct page *page, unsigned int len,
                 unsigned int offset);
```

E.g: /drivers/parport/parport.c

defined in **/usr/src/linux/include/linux/scatterlist.h** together with a lot of other useful convenience functions for accessing gather-scatter structures.

- The driver sets the `page`, `offset`, and `length` fields for each buffer in the array; Note `length` is specified in bytes.

- The `dma_address` field will be filled in by the function:

```
int dma_map_sg (struct device *dev, struct scatterlist *sg,
                int nents, enum dma_data_direction direction);
```

where `nents` is the number of buffers in the array. This function returns the number of buffers to transfer. This can be less than `nents` because any physically adjacent buffers will be combined.

- Once this is done it is time to transfer each buffer. Because of architectural differences, one should not refer directly to the elements of the `scatterlist` data structure, but instead use the macros:

```
dma_addr_t sg_dma_address (struct scatterlist *sg);
unsigned int sg_dma_len (struct scatterlist *sg);
```

which return the bus (**DMA**) address and length of the buffer (which may be different than what was passed to `dma_map_sg()` because of buffer coalescence.)

- After the full transfer has been made, one calls

```
int dma_unmap_sg (struct device *dev, struct scatterlist *sg, int nents,
                  enum dma_data_direction direction);
```

where `nents` is the original value passed to the mapping function, not the coalesced value.

24.8 Labs

Lab 1: DMA Memory Allocation

- Write a module that allocates and maps a suitable **DMA** buffer, and obtains the bus address handle.

- Do this in three ways:

  - Using `dma_alloc_coherent()`.
  - Using `dma_map_single()`
  - Using a **DMA Pool**.

  You can use `NULL` for the `device` and/or `pci_dev` structure arguments since we don't actually have a physical device.

- Compare the resulting kernel and bus addresses; how do they differ? Compare with the value of `PAGE_OFFSET`.

- In each case copy a string into the buffer and make sure it can be read back properly.

- In the case of `dma_map_single()`, you may want to compare the use of different `direction` arguments.

- We give two solutions, one with the bus-independent interface, and one with the older **PCI API**.

Chapter 25

USB Drivers

We'll discuss **USB** devices, what they are, the standard that describes them, the topology of the connection of hubs, peripherals and host controllers, and the various descriptors inolved. We'll consider the different kinds of classes and data transfers possible. Then we'll see how **USB** has been implemented under **Linux**. We review registration/deregistration of **USB** devices. We'll describe the entry points to the driver and some of the main functions and data structures in the **USB API**. Finally, we'll do a code walkthrough on a simple **USB** driver.

25.1 What is USB?

- **USB** stands for **U**niversal **S**erial **B**us. It permits easy connection of multiple peripheral devices to one port, and automatic, hotplug, configuration of devices attached (and detached) while the computer is running. Virtually any type of peripheral (with **USB** capability) can be connected to a **USB** port; i.e., scanners, modems, network cards, mice, keyboards, printers, mass storage devices, etc.

- Version 1.0 of the **USB** specification was released in January 1996 by an alliance of Compaq, Intel, Microsoft and NEC. Version 1.1 was released in September 1998, and version 2.0 was released in 1999.

- One thing to be careful about is when considering the **USB** 2.0 standard, is that when the phrase *full speed* or *low speed* is used, it stands in for **USB** 1.1. The newer standard is described as *high speed*.

- Up to 127 devices can be connected simultaneously. The **USB** cable contains four wires; power, ground and two signal wires. In the original standard, the ideal total bandwidth was limited to 12 Mbit/s, but overheads limited this to something like 8.5 Mbit/s and realistic performance was probably as low as 2 Mbit/s. **USB** 2.0 brought a theoretical speed limit of 480 Mbit/s.

- Devices may be either low or high speed, or operate in either mode according to function. A high speed device hooked up to a **USB** 1.1 controller or hub will be limited to lower capabilities.

- Power can be delivered either through the **USB** cable or through a peripheral's own power supply. A total of up to 500 mA can be supplied through each controller. When a device is plugged in it can initially grab up to 100 mA and then request more if limits are not exceeded.

- The kernel contains a lot of **USB**-related documentation in the **/usr/src/linux/Documentation/usb** directory.

- Support for the new **USB** 3.0 standard (also known as **XHCI**) has been included in kernel version 2.6.31, making **Linux** the first operating system to incorporate it.

- **USB** 3.0 is designed for a transfer rate of up to 5 GBit/s, decreases power consumption, and is downwardly compatible with **USB** 2.0.

25.2   USB Topology

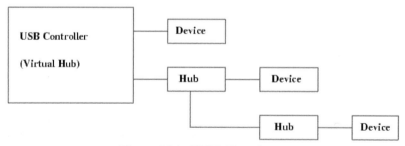

Figure 25.1: **USB Topology**

- **USB** ports are incorporated in all modern motherboards. In most cases there are at least 2 ports. The ports can be connected either directly to devices or to hubs, which themselves can be connected to more hubs or devices. There is a ***virtual root hub*** simulated by the host controller. The total number of ports plus hubs is 127.

- Technically, the physical structure of **USB** is not that of a bus; it is a tree with **upstream** and **downstream** nodes. Each device can have only one upstream connection (with a type *A* connector), but a hub node can have more than one downstream connection (with a type *B* connector.)

- For **USB** 1.x, there are two types of host controllers:

  - **OHCI** (**O**pen **H**ost **C**ontroller **I**nterface) from Compaq.
  - **UHCI** (**U**niversal **H**ost **C**ontroller **I**nterface) from Intel.

  UHCI is simpler and thus requires a somewhat more complex device driver. Peripherals should work equally well with either controller.

- For **USB** 2.0, the standard is **EHCI** (**E**nhanced **H**ost **C**ontroller **I**nterface.)

- Upon being hooked up to the bus, a peripheral identifies itself as belonging to one of several classes. When a particular driver is loaded it will claim the device and handle all communication with it.

25.3 Descriptors

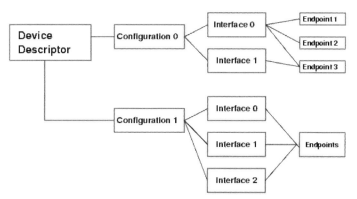

Figure 25.2: **USB Descriptors**

- Each **USB** device has a unique **device descriptor**, assigned to it when the peripheral is connected to the bus. In addition it gets a device number assigned (an integer ranging from 1 to 127). The descriptor has all pertinent information applying to the device and all of its possible configurations.

- A device has one or more **configuration descriptors**. This has specific information about how the device may be used.

- Each configuration points to one or more **interface descriptors**. Each interface might point to various alternate settings about how the device might be used. For instance, a video camera could have three alternate settings, which require different bandwidths: camera activated, microphone activated, and camera and microphone activated.

- Each interface points to one or more **endpoint descriptors**, which give the data source or sink of the device. (All control transfers use an end point of zero.)

25.4 USB Device Classes

- If a device plugged into the **USB** hub belongs to a well-known **device class**, it is expected to conform to certain standards with respect to device and interface descriptors. Thus the same device driver can be used for any device that claims to be a member of that class. The following classes are defined in the standard:

Table 25.2: **USB Device Classes**

Base Class	Descriptor Usage	Description	Examples
00h	Device	Unspecified	Use class information in the interface descriptors
01h	Interface	Audio	speakers, microphones. sound cards
02h	Both	Communications and CDC Control	network adapters, modems, serial port adapters
03h	Interface	HID (Human Interface Device)	mice, joysticks, keyboards
05h	Interface	Physical	force feedback joystick
06h	Interface	Image	digital cameras
07h	Interface	Printer	printers
08h	Interface	Mass Storage	flash drives, MP3 players, memory card readers
09h	Device	Hub	full and high speed hubs
0Ah	Interface	CDC-Data	used together with CDC Control
0Bh	Interface	Smart Card	smart card readers
0Dh	Interface	Content Security	security
0Eh	Interface	Video	webcams
0Fh	Interface	Personal Healthcare	healthcare devices
DCh	Both	Diagnostic Device	USB compliance testing devices
E0h	Interface	wireless controller	bluetooth and wi-fi adapters
EFh	Both	Miscellaneous	ActiveSync devices
FEh	Interface	Application Specific	irda bridge
FFh	Both	Vendor Specific	devices needing vendor specific drivers

- Other devices require a fully customized device driver be written.

25.5 Data Transfer

- There are the following types of data transfer to and from **USB** devices:

- **Control transfers** are short commands that configure and obtain the state of devices. While there may also be device specific commands, most or all devices will support the following standard set defined in **/usr/src/linux/include/linux/usb/ch9.h**:

```
3.0:  79 #define USB_REQ_GET_STATUS        0x00
3.0:  80 #define USB_REQ_CLEAR_FEATURE     0x01
3.0:  81 #define USB_REQ_SET_FEATURE       0x03
```

```
3.0:  82 #define USB_REQ_SET_ADDRESS          0x05
3.0:  83 #define USB_REQ_GET_DESCRIPTOR       0x06
3.0:  84 #define USB_REQ_SET_DESCRIPTOR       0x07
3.0:  85 #define USB_REQ_GET_CONFIGURATION    0x08
3.0:  86 #define USB_REQ_SET_CONFIGURATION    0x09
3.0:  87 #define USB_REQ_GET_INTERFACE        0x0A
3.0:  88 #define USB_REQ_SET_INTERFACE        0x0B
3.0:  89 #define USB_REQ_SYNCH_FRAME          0x0C
3.0:  90
3.0:  91 #define USB_REQ_SET_ENCRYPTION       0x0D       /* Wireless USB */
3.0:  92 #define USB_REQ_GET_ENCRYPTION       0x0E
3.0:  93 #define USB_REQ_RPIPE_ABORT          0x0E
3.0:  94 #define USB_REQ_SET_HANDSHAKE        0x0F
3.0:  95 #define USB_REQ_RPIPE_RESET          0x0F
3.0:  96 #define USB_REQ_GET_HANDSHAKE        0x10
3.0:  97 #define USB_REQ_SET_CONNECTION       0x11
3.0:  98 #define USB_REQ_SET_SECURITY_DATA    0x12
3.0:  99 #define USB_REQ_GET_SECURITY_DATA    0x13
3.0: 100 #define USB_REQ_SET_WUSB_DATA        0x14
3.0: 101 #define USB_REQ_LOOPBACK_DATA_WRITE  0x15
3.0: 102 #define USB_REQ_LOOPBACK_DATA_READ   0x16
3.0: 103 #define USB_REQ_SET_INTERFACE_DS     0x17
```

- **Bulk transfers** send information using up to the full bandwidth. These are *reliable* (i.e., they are checked) and are used by devices like scanners.

- **Interrupt transfers** also can take up to the full bandwidth, but they are sent in response to periodic polling. If the transfer is interrupted, the host controller will repeat the request after a set interval.

- **Isochronous transfers** take up to the full bandwidth as well, but are not guaranteed to be *reliable*. Multimedia devices, audio, video, use these.

25.6   USB under Linux

- There are three layers in the **USB** stack under **Linux**:

  - Host Controller Driver (OHCI, UHCI, EHCI).
  - **USB** Core.
  - Device Drivers.

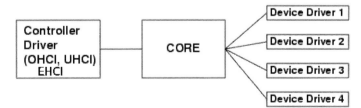

Figure 25.3: **USB: Controller, Core and Device**

- The **USB** core has **API**'s for both the controller drivers and the device drivers. It can be thought of as a library of common routines that both the controller and the peripherals can utilize.

- Device drivers need not concern themselves with the parts of **API** that interact with the host controller. The driver interacts with the **Linux** kernel by going through the **USB** core.

25.7   Registering USB Devices

- **USB** devices are registered and unregistered with the following functions:

```
#include <linux/usb.h>

int  usb_register  (struct usb_driver *drv);
void usb_deregister (struct usb_driver *drv);
```

- usb_register() returns 0 for success, a negative number for failure.

- Before the device is registered the all-important usb_driver structure must be fully initialized. It can be found in **/usr/src/linux/include/linux/usb.h** and looks like:

```
struct usb_driver {
    const char *name;
    int (*probe) (struct usb_interface *intf, const struct usb_device_id *id);
    void (*disconnect) (struct usb_interface *intf);
    int (*ioctl) (struct usb_interface *intf, unsigned int code, void *buf);
    int (*suspend) (struct usb_interface *intf, pm_message_t message);
    int (*resume) (struct usb_interface *intf);
    int (*reset_resume) (struct ubs_interface *intf);
    const struct usb_device_id *id_table;
    struct usb_dynids dynids;
    struct usbdrv_wrap drvwrap;
    unsigned int no_dynamic_id:1;
    unsigned int supports_autsuspend:1;
    unsigned int soft_unbind:1;
};
```

- name is the name of the driver module. It must be unique among all **USB** drivers, and will show up in **/sys/bus/usb/drivers** when the driver is loaded.

- probe() points to the function used to check for the device, and is called when new devices are added to the **USB** bus. If the driver feels it can claim the device (based on the information in the usb_device_id structure passed to it), the routine should initialize the device and return zero. If the driver does not claim the device, it should return a negative error value.

- disconnect() points to the function called when devices are removed from the **USB** bus, while suspend() and resume() point to the functions used for power management.

- ioctl() will get called when a user-space program issues an ioctl() command on the **usbfs** filesystem entry associated with a device attached to this driver. In practice, only the **USB core** uses it for things like hubs and controllers.

- Only the main fields have to be set; others are more optional. Thus one might have:

```
static struct usb_driver my_usb_driver = {
    .name       = "my_usb_device",
    .id_table   = my_usb_id_table,
    .probe      = my_usb_probe,
    .disconnect = my_usb_disconnect,
}
```

- `id_table` points to an identifying structure of type `usb_device_id`, defined in **/usr/src/linux/include/ linux/mod_devicetable.h**:

```
struct usb_device_id {
    /* which fields to match against? */
    __u16           match_flags;

    /* Used for product specific matches; range is inclusive */
    __u16           idVendor;
    __u16           idProduct;
    __u16           bcdDevice_lo;
    __u16           bcdDevice_hi;

    /* Used for device class matches */
    __u8            bDeviceClass;
    __u8            bDeviceSubClass;
    __u8            bDeviceProtocol;

    /* Used for interface class matches */
    __u8            bInterfaceClass;
    __u8            bInterfaceSubClass;
    __u8            bInterfaceProtocol;

    /* not matched against */
    kernel_ulong_t  driver_info;
};
```

- `match_flags` sets which of the other fields in the structure the device should be matched against. Usually this is not set directly; it is initialized by the `USB_DEVICE` macros we'll discuss.

- `idVendor` is the unique **USB** vendor ID for the device, assigned by the **USB** controlling body. `idProduct` is the product ID and is set by the vendor.

- `bcDevice_lo`, `bcDevice_hi` are the low and high ends of the vendor-determined product number

- `bDeviceClass`, `bDeviceSubClass`, `bDeviceProtocol` are assigned by the **USB** controlling body and describe the whole device, including all interfaces.

- `bInterfaceClass`, `bInterfaceSubClass`, `bInterfaceProtocol` describe the individual interface.

- `driver_info` can be used by the driver to distinguish different devices from each other when `probe()` is called.

- The `usb_device_id` table is usually initialized using the following macros:

```
USB_DEVICE(vendor, product)
USB_DEVICE_VER(vendor, product, lo, hi)
USB_DEVICE_INFO(class, subclass, protocol)
USB_INTERFACE_INFO(class, subclass, protocol)
```

in a straightforward way. Thus for a simple driver controlling only one device from one vendor you might have:

```
static struct usb_device_id my_usb_id_table = {
   { USB_DEVICE(USB_MY_VENDOR_ID, MY_VENDOR_PRODUCT_ID) },
   { }  /* Null terminator (required) */
};
MODULE_DEVICE_TABLE (usb, my_usb_id_table);
```

- The `MODULE_DEVICE_TABLE` macro is necessary for user-space hotplug utilities to do their work.

- You may have noticed that the callback functions don't refer directly to the `usb_driver` structure, but instead point to a structure of type `usb_interface`. One can go back and forth between the two structures with:

```
struct usb_device *interface_to_usbdev (struct usb_interface *intf);
void *usb_get_intfdata (struct usb_interface *intf);
void *usb_set_intfdata (struct usb_interface *intf);
```

- The first function retrieves a pointer to the underlying `usb_device`.

- The other two functions get and set a pointer to the `data` element within the `struct device_driver`, pointed to in the `struct usb_driver` pointed to by the `struct usb_interface`. With this private data pointer nested so deep within the structures, these functions are quite useful.

- The `no_dynamic_id` field lets a driver disable addition of dynamic device IDs.

25.8   Example of a USB Driver

- In order to see how it all fits together, let's take a look at **/usr/src/linux/drivers/usb/misc/rio500.c**, a relatively simple driver for a type of **MP3** device that attaches to the **USB** port.

- We will only look at the part of the driver that handles initializing, registering, and probing and disconnecting. The actual data transfer code will of course be quite hardware dependent. It is composed mostly of entry point functions pointed to in the `file_operations` jump table.

- Note that one has reference to a `file_operations` structure as in a character device:

```
3.0: 435 static const struct file_operations usb_rio_fops = {
3.0: 436      .owner =        THIS_MODULE,
3.0: 437      .read =         read_rio,
3.0: 438      .write =        write_rio,
3.0: 439      .unlocked_ioctl = ioctl_rio,
3.0: 440      .open =         open_rio,
3.0: 441      .release =      close_rio,
3.0: 442      .llseek =       noop_llseek,
3.0: 443 };
3.0: 444
3.0: 445 static struct usb_class_driver usb_rio_class = {
3.0: 446      .name =         "rio500%d",
3.0: 447      .fops =         &usb_rio_fops,
3.0: 448      .minor_base =   RIO_MINOR,
3.0: 449 };
```

- The `file_operations` structure is pointed to by an entry in the `struct usb_class_driver`, which will be associated with the device in the `usb_register_dev()` function call, which is made from the `probe()` callback function.

- There is also a structure of type `usb_driver` which points to the callback functions:

```
3.0: 520 static const struct usb_device_id rio_table[] = {
3.0: 521      { USB_DEVICE(0x0841, 1) },              /* Rio 500 */
3.0: 522      { }                                     /* Terminating entry */
3.0: 523 };
3.0: 524
```

```
3.0: 525 MODULE_DEVICE_TABLE (usb, rio_table);
3.0: 526
3.0: 527 static struct usb_driver rio_driver = {
3.0: 528     .name =          "rio500",
3.0: 529     .probe =         probe_rio,
3.0: 530     .disconnect =    disconnect_rio,
3.0: 531     .id_table =      rio_table,
3.0: 532 };
```

- Note that the init function simply registers the usb_driver structure:

```
3.0: 534 static int __init usb_rio_init(void)
3.0: 535 {
3.0: 536     int retval;
3.0: 537     retval = usb_register(&rio_driver);
3.0: 538     if (retval)
3.0: 539         goto out;
3.0: 540
3.0: 541     printk(KERN_INFO KBUILD_MODNAME ": " DRIVER_VERSION ":"
3.0: 542         DRIVER_DESC "\n");
3.0: 543
3.0: 544 out:
3.0: 545     return retval;
3.0: 546 }
3.0: 547
```

- Likewise, the cleanup, or exit, function simply unregisters:

```
3.0: 549 static void __exit usb_rio_cleanup(void)
3.0: 550 {
3.0: 551     struct rio_usb_data *rio = &rio_instance;
3.0: 552
3.0: 553     rio->present = 0;
3.0: 554     usb_deregister(&rio_driver);
3.0: 555
3.0: 556
3.0: 557 }
```

- The real work is done by the probe() and disconnect() functions, as far as setting things up and freeing resources. Note these entry points are called by the **USB** core, not user-space programs.

- The probe() and disconnect() functions are:

```
3.0: 451 static int probe_rio(struct usb_interface *intf,
3.0: 452                 const struct usb_device_id *id)
3.0: 453 {
3.0: 454     struct usb_device *dev = interface_to_usbdev(intf);
3.0: 455     struct rio_usb_data *rio = &rio_instance;
3.0: 456     int retval;
3.0: 457
3.0: 458     dev_info(&intf->dev, "USB Rio found at address %d\n", dev->devnum);
3.0: 459
3.0: 460     retval = usb_register_dev(intf, &usb_rio_class);
3.0: 461     if (retval) {
3.0: 462         err("Not able to get a minor for this device.");
3.0: 463         return -ENOMEM;
3.0: 464     }
3.0: 465
```

```
3.0: 466        rio->rio_dev = dev;
3.0: 467
3.0: 468        if (!(rio->obuf = kmalloc(OBUF_SIZE, GFP_KERNEL))) {
3.0: 469                err("probe_rio: Not enough memory for the output buffer");
3.0: 470                usb_deregister_dev(intf, &usb_rio_class);
3.0: 471                return -ENOMEM;
3.0: 472        }
3.0: 473        dbg("probe_rio: obuf address:%p", rio->obuf);
3.0: 474
3.0: 475        if (!(rio->ibuf = kmalloc(IBUF_SIZE, GFP_KERNEL))) {
3.0: 476                err("probe_rio: Not enough memory for the input buffer");
3.0: 477                usb_deregister_dev(intf, &usb_rio_class);
3.0: 478                kfree(rio->obuf);
3.0: 479                return -ENOMEM;
3.0: 480        }
3.0: 481        dbg("probe_rio: ibuf address:%p", rio->ibuf);
3.0: 482
3.0: 483        mutex_init(&(rio->lock));
3.0: 484
3.0: 485        usb_set_intfdata (intf, rio);
3.0: 486        rio->present = 1;
3.0: 487
3.0: 488        return 0;
3.0: 489 }
```

25.9   Labs

Lab 1: Installing a USB device.

- We are going to write a simple **USB** device driver.

- The driver should register itself with the **USB** subsystem upon loading and unregister upon unloading.

- The `probe()` and `disconnect()` functions should issue printout whenever the device is added or removed from the system.

- By proper use of the `usb_device_id` table, you can configure your driver either to sense any device plugged, or only a specific one. You can obtain the vendor and device ID's by noting the output when the **USB** subsystem senses device connection.

- You will have to make sure your kernel has the proper **USB** support compiled in, and that no driver for the device is already loaded, as it may interfere with your driver claiming the device.

- **Hint:** You'll probably want to do a `make modules_install` to get automatic loading to work properly.

Chapter 26

A Second Driver Example: the USB-EHCI driver

We'll take a detailed walk through the **USB EHCI** controller driver.

26.1   The USB-EHCI Driver

- The main files describing the **EHCI** driver are:

    – /usr/src/linux/drivers/usb/host/ehci.h
    – /usr/src/linux/drivers/usb/host/ehci-hcd.c

- Additional functions are described in:

    – /usr/src/linux/drivers/usb/host/ehci-dbg.c
    – /usr/src/linux/drivers/usb/host/ehci-lpm.c
    – /usr/src/linux/drivers/usb/host/ehci-hub.c
    – /usr/src/linux/drivers/usb/host/ehci-mem.c
    – /usr/src/linux/drivers/usb/host/ehci-q.c
    – /usr/src/linux/drivers/usb/host/ehci-sched.c

- For the **PCI** hardware glue:

    – /usr/src/linux/drivers/usb/host/ehci-pci.c

- There are a number of hardware glue files for different **SoC**'s; we'll concentrate on:

    - **/usr/src/linux/drivers/usb/host/ehci-tegra.c**

- Others include:

    - **/usr/src/linux/drivers/usb/host/ehci-msm.c**
    - **/usr/src/linux/drivers/usb/host/ehci-mxc.c**
    - **/usr/src/linux/drivers/usb/host/ehci-omap.c**

=> ls -alh /dev/sda *

⤷ hard disks

Chapter 27

Block Drivers

We'll introduce block device drivers. We'll consider block buffering. We'll talk about what they are and how they are registered and unregistered. We'll discuss the important `gendisk` data structure. We'll discuss the block driver request function and see how reading and writing block devices is quite different than for character devices.

27.1 What are Block Drivers?

- Drivers for **block devices** are similar in some ways to those for character drivers, but differences are many and deep.

- In normal usage, block devices contain formatted and mountable filesystems, which allow random (non-sequential) access. The device driver does not depend on the type of filesystem put on the device.

- While a particular system call may request any number of bytes, the low-level read/write requests must be in multiples of the block size. All access is **cached** (unless explicitly requested otherwise) which means writes to the device may be delayed, and reads may be satisfied from cache.

- The drivers do not have their own read/write functions. Instead they deploy a **request function**, a callback function which is invoked by the higher levels of the kernel in a fluid way that depends on the use of the cache.

- Block devices may have multiple **partitions**. In most instances the partition number corresponds to the device's minor number, while the whole device shares the same major number. The naming convention for the nodes is:

  Major Name — **Unit** — **Partition**

  e.g., `/dev/hdb4` has a Major Name of `hd`, is Unit `b` (the second), and is Partition 4. Details of the partitioning are contained in the `gendisk` data structure.

- Block devices may also employ removable media such as CD-ROMS and floppy disks.

27.2   Buffering

- Files reside on block devices which are organized in fixed size blocks, although I/O requests, made with system calls, may be for any number of bytes. Thus block devices must be controlled by a buffering/caching system, which is shared for all devices.

- The blocks are cached through the page cache, and a given page may contain more than one block device buffer.

- The device itself should only be accessed if:

  - A block not presently in cache must be loaded on a read request.
  - A block needs to be written (eventually) if the cache contents no longer match what is on the device itself. In this case the block must be marked as *dirty*. Note if a file is opened with the `O_SYNC` flag, no delay is allowed.

- At periodic intervals the **pdflush** system process which causes all modified blocks that haven't been used for a certain amount of time, to be flushed back to the device. Other events may also trigger the flushing, with the object being to keep the number of ***dirty*** blocks in the cache at a minimum, and to make sure that the most important blocks, those describing inodes and superblocks, are kept most consistent.

- The **sync** command writes all modified buffer blocks in the cache. The `fsync()` system call writes back all modified buffer blocks for a single file.

27.3   Registering a Block Driver

- Registering a block device is generally done during the initialization routine, and in most ways is pretty similar to doing it for a character device. Unregistering is generally done during the cleanup routine, just as for a character device. The functions for doing this are:

  ```
  #include <linux/fs.h>

  int register_blkdev (unsigned int major, const char *name);
  int unregister_blkdev (unsigned int major, const char *name);
  ```

  (minor number is the partition)

- `register_blkdev()` returns 0 on success and `-EBUSY` or `-EINVAL` on failure. Supplying a major number of 0 generates a dynamical assignment given as the return value. The value of `major` has to be less than or equal to `MAX_BLKDEV=255`.

- `unregister_blkdev()` returns 0 on success and `-EINVAL` on failure. It checks that `major` is valid and that `name` matches with `major`, but doesn't check if you are the owner of the device you are unregistering.

Kernel Version Note   **Kernel Version Note**

- There also exist more modern block device registration and unregistration functions, `blk_register_region()` and `blk_unregister_region()`.

- The use of these is somewhat complicated and can be read about in an article by John Corbet in his driver porting series: **http://lwn.net/Articles/25711/**.

- The `block_device_operations` structure plays the same role the `file_operations` structure plays for character drivers. It gets associated with the device through an entry in the `gendisk` data structure, as we will show shortly.

- The `block_device_operations` structure is defined in **/usr/src/linux/include/linux/blkdev.h** as:

```
3.0:1294 struct block_device_operations {
3.0:1295         int (*open) (struct block_device *, fmode_t);
3.0:1296         int (*release) (struct gendisk *, fmode_t);
3.0:1297         int (*ioctl) (struct block_device *, fmode_t, unsigned, unsigned long);
3.0:1298         int (*compat_ioctl) (struct block_device *, fmode_t, unsigned, unsigned long);
3.0:1299         int (*direct_access) (struct block_device *, sector_t,
3.0:1300                                           void **, unsigned long *);
3.0:1301         unsigned int (*check_events) (struct gendisk *disk,
3.0:1302                                       unsigned int clearing);
3.0:1303         /* ->media_changed() is DEPRECATED, use ->check_events() instead */
3.0:1304         int (*media_changed) (struct gendisk *);
3.0:1305         void (*unlock_native_capacity) (struct gendisk *);
3.0:1306         int (*revalidate_disk) (struct gendisk *);
3.0:1307         int (*getgeo)(struct block_device *, struct hd_geometry *);
3.0:1308         /* this callback is with swap_lock and sometimes page table lock held */
3.0:1309         void (*swap_slot_free_notify) (struct block_device *, unsigned long);
3.0:1310         struct module *owner;
3.0:1311 };
```

- For simple drivers, one need not even define `open()` and `release()` entry points, as generic ones will do the basic work. However, real hardware will probably need to perform certain steps at these times and will still need specific methods to be written.

- **Example:**

```
static struct block_device_operations mybdrv_fops = {
    .owner=   THIS_MODULE,
    .open=    mybdrv_open,
    .release= mybdrv_release,
    .ioctl=   mybdrv_ioctl
};
```

27.4   gendisk Structure

- The gendisk structure is defined in **/usr/src/linux/include/linux/genhd.h** and describes a partionable device. You'll have to set it up, manipulate it, and free it when done.

- The gendisk structure is:

```
struct gendisk {
    int major;                  /* major number of driver */
    int first_minor;
    int minors;                 /* maximum number of minors, =1 for
                                 * disks that can't be partitioned. */
    char disk_name[32];         /* name of major driver */
    struct hd_struct **part; /* [indexed by minor] */
    int part_uevent_suppress;
    struct block_device_operations *fops;
    struct request_queue *queue;
    void *private_data;
    sector_t capacity;

    int flags;
    struct device *driverfs_dev;
    struct kobject kobj;
    struct kobject *holder_dir;
    struct kobject *slave_dir;

    struct timer_rand_state *random;
    int policy;

    atomic_t sync_io;           /* RAID */
    unsigned long stamp;
    int in_flight;
#ifdef   CONFIG_SMP
    struct disk_stats *dkstats;
#else
    struct disk_stats dkstats;
#endif
};
```

- major is the major number associated with the device, and first_minor is the first minor number for the disk.

- disk_name is the disk name without partition number; e.g., hdb.

- fops points to the block_device_operations structure. Putting it in the gendisk structure is how it is associated with the device.

- request_queue points to the queue of pending operations for the disk. Note there is only one request queue for the entire disk, not one for each partition.

- private data points to an object not used by the kernel and thus can be used to hold a data structure for the device that the driver can use for any purpose.

- capacity is the size of the disk in **512 byte** sectors; even if you have a different sector size, the capacity has to be unitized in this way.

- flags control the way the device operates. Possible values include GENHD_FL_REMOVABLE, GENHD_FL_CD etc.

- The following functions are used to allocate, configure, and free `gendisk` data structures:

```
#include <linux/genhd.h>

struct gendisk *alloc_disk (int minors);
void add_disk (struct gendisk *disk);
void put_disk (struct gendisk *disk);
void del_gendisk (struct gendisk *disk);
void set_disk_ro (struct gendisk *disk);
```

- The first step is to create the `gendisk` data structure. This is done with `alloc_disk()`, whose argument is the largest number of minor numbers, and thus partitions, the disk can accommodate.

- One then fills in the various fields, such as the major number, the first minor (generally 0), and the capacity (which can be done with the `void set_capacity (struct *gendisk, int nsectors)` macro) and point to the proper request queue and device operations table.

- Once any needed initializations are done to the device, the function `add_disk()` is called to activate the device. This increases the reference count for the disk; the function `put_disk()` should be called when the structure is released to decrement the reference count.

- Upon removal of the device, one has to call `del_gendisk()`, although the actual removal won't happen until you subsequently call `put_disk()`.

- To put all partitions on the disk in a read-only status, you can use `set_disk_ro()`.

27.5 Request Handling

- Upper levels of the kernel handle the I/O requests associated with the device, and then group them in an efficient manner and place them on the **request queue** for the device, which causes them to get passed to the driver's **request function**.

- The kernel maintains a request queue for each major number (by default). The data structure is of type `struct request_queue` and is defined in **/usr/src/linux/include/linux/blkdev.h**. The other major data structure involved is of type `struct request` and details each request being made to the driver.

- The request queue must be initialized and cleaned up with the functions:

```
#include <linux/blkdev.h>

struct request_queue *blk_init_queue (request_fn_proc *request, spinlock_t *lock);
void blk_cleanup_queue (struct request_queue *q);
```

and the sector size should be set in this structure with

```
void blk_queue_logical_block_size(struct request_queue *q, unsigned short size);
```

- A spinlock has to be passed to the upper layers of the kernel. This will be taken out when the request function is called, with code like:

```
static spinlock_t lock;
....
spin_lock_init (&lock);
...
my_request_queue = blk_init_queue (my_request, &lock));
```

- The simplest way to see how request handling is done is to look at a trivial request function:

```
static void my_request(struct request_queue *q)
{
        struct request *rq;
        int size, res = 0;
        char *ptr;
        unsigned nr_sectors, sector;
        printk(KERN_INFO "entering request routine\n");

        rq = blk_fetch_request(q);
        while (rq) {
                if (!blk_fs_request(rq)) {
                        printk(KERN_WARNING
                                "This was not a normal fs request, skipping\n");
                        goto done;
                }
                nr_sectors = blk_rq_cur_sectors(rq);
                sector = blk_rq_pos(rq);
                ptr = my_dev + sector * sector_size;
                size = nr_sectors * sector_size;

                if ((ptr + size) > (my_dev + disk_size)) {
                        printk(KERN_WARNING
                                " tried to go past end of device\n");
                        goto done;
                }
                if (rq_data_dir(rq)) {
                        printk(KERN_INFO "writing at sector %d, %ud sectors \n",
                                sector, nr_sectors);
                        memcpy(ptr, rq->buffer, size);
                } else {
                        printk(KERN_INFO "reading at sector %d, %ud sectors \n",
                                sector, nr_sectors);
                        memcpy(rq->buffer, ptr, size);
                }
        done:
                if (!__blk_end_request_cur(rq, res))
                        rq = blk_fetch_request(q);
        }
        printk(KERN_INFO "leaving request\n");
}
```

- Peeling off the first request from the queue is done with `blk_fetch_request()` which returns `NULL` when there are no more requests. The function `blk_fs_request()` checks what kind of request is being delivered. This evaluates as true for normal filesystem requests, as opposed to diagnostic and other kinds of operations.

- The actual copying is done with a simple `memcpy()`. Note, however, the use of the function `rq_data_dir()`, which checks the first bit of the `flags` field of the request structure which is set for writes, and cleared for reads.

Kernel Version Note **Kernel Version Note**

- The 2.6.31 kernel introduced changes in the block driver interface, reworking the `request_queue` structure and introducing some new functions. Furthermore the function `blk_queue_hardsect_size()` was replaced with `blk_queue_logical_block_size()`.

- Here is an example of an older request function:

```
static void my_request(struct request_queue *q)
{
        struct request *rq;
        int size;
        char *ptr;
        printk(KERN_INFO "entering request routine\n");

        while ((rq = elv_next_request(q))) {
                if (!blk_fs_request(rq)) {
                        printk(KERN_INFO
                                "This was not a normal fs request, skipping\n");
                        end_request(rq, 0);
                        continue;
                }
                ptr = my_dev + rq->sector * q->hardsect_size;
                size = rq->current_nr_sectors * q->hardsect_size;

                if ((ptr + size) > (my_dev + disk_size)) {
                        printk(KERN_ERR " tried to go past end of device\n");
                        end_request(rq, 0);
                        continue;
                }
                if (rq_data_dir(rq)) {
                        printk(KERN_INFO "a write\n");
                        memcpy(ptr, rq->buffer, size);
                } else {
                        printk(KERN_INFO "a read\n");
                        memcpy(rq->buffer, ptr, size);
                }
                end_request(rq, 1);
        }
        printk("KERN_INFO leaving request\n");
}
```

- Peeling off the first request from the queue was done with `elv_next_request()` which returns `NULL` when there are no more requests. Exiting the request function ends when the `end_request()` function is called with a second argument of 0 for failure, or 1 for success.

27.6   Labs

Lab 1: Building a Block Driver

- Write a basic block device driver.

- You'll need to implement at least the open() and release() entry points, and include a request function.

- You can either use an unallocated value for the major device number and select a minor device number, or try getting a major number dynamically. Assuming you are using **udev**, the node should be made automatically when you load the driver; otherwise you will have to actually add the node with the mknod command.

- Keep track of the number of times the node is opened. Try permitting multiple opens, or exclusive use.

- Write a program to read (and/or write) from the node, using the standard **Unix** I/O functions (open(), read(), write(), close()). After loading the module with insmod use this program to access the node.

- **NOTE**: Make sure you have enough memory to handle the ram disk you create; The solution has 128 MB allocated.

Lab 2: Mountable Read/Write Block Driver

- Extend the previous exercise in order to put an **ext3** file system (or another type) on your device.

- You can place a filesystem on the device with

```
$ mkfs.ext3 /dev/mybdrv
$ mount /dev/mybdrv mnt
```

where you give the appropriate name of the device node and mount point.

- For an additional enhancement, try partitioning the device with **fdisk**. For this you may need an additional ioctl() for HDIO_GETGEO, and you'll have to include: linux/hdreg.h. This **ioctl** returns a pointer to the following structure:

```
struct hd_geometry {
      unsigned char heads;
      unsigned char sectors;
      unsigned short cylinders;
      unsigned long start;
};
```

Remember the total capacity is (sector size) x (sectors/track) x (cylinders) x (heads). You also want to use a value of 4 for the starting sector.

- If you are using a recent kernel and version of **udev**, the partition nodes should be made automatically when you load the driver; otherwise you will have to actually add them manually.

Chapter 28

Memory Technology Devices

We are going to consider the different types of **MTD** devices, how they are implemented, and the various filesystems used with them.

28.1 What are MTD Devices?

- **Memory Technology Devices (MTD)** are **flash** memory devices. They are often used in various embedded devices.

- Such a device may have all of its memory in flash (which functions like a hard disk in that its values are preserved upon power off) but often it will also have normal RAM of some type.

- Flash memory is a high-speed EEPROM where data is programmed (and erased) in **blocks**, rather than byte by byte as in normal EEPROM.

- **MTD** devices are neither character or block in type; in particular they distinguish between write and erase operations, which block devices don't.

- Normal filesystems are generally not appropriate for use with flash devices for a number of reasons, which we'll detail later, so special filesystems have been designed.

- The **Execute in Place**, or **XIP**, method, in which the CPU maps pages of memory from the flash-residing application directly to its virtual address space, with copying of pages to RAM first, can be useful in embedded devices.

- Some useful references:

Table 28.1: **MTD Links**

http://www.linux-mtd.infradead.org	The main web site for **Linux MTD** development.
http://www.linuxfordevices.com/articles/AT7478621147.html	A white paper by Cliff Brake and Jeff Sutherland about using flash in embedded **Linux** systems.

28.2   NAND vs. NOR

- There are two basic kinds of flash memory: **NOR** and **NAND**.

- **NOR** flash devices are the older variety with these features:

  - A linear addressed device, with individual data and address lines; just like **DRAM**.

  - Addressed can be directly mapped in the CPU's address space and accessed like **ROM**.

  - Programming and erase speeds are respectable; erases are slower than programs.

  - Function like **RAM**, access is random.

  - The number of erase cycles is limited, about 100,000 or so.

  - Recent development of **MLC** (multi-level cell) techniques, in which two bits of memory can be stored per cell, have boosted density and reduced manufacturing costs per unit of memory, although it may come at the cost of reduced performance.

  - Traditionally these devices have been associated with **code** storage.

- **NAND** flash devices are newer, and have these features:

  - Addressing is non-linear; data and commands are multiplexed onto 8 I/O lines. Thus, device drivers are more complex.

  - Access is sequential.

  - Densities are much higher than with **NOR** devices, and the speed is an order of magnitude faster.

  - Bad blocks can be a problem; **NAND** devices may ship with them, but at any rate, blocks will fail with time, and thus device drivers have to do bad block management.

  - Traditionally these devices have been associated with **data** storage.

- Since 1999 **NAND** has grown from about one tenth of the total flash market to most of it.

- Regardless of which method the underlying flash device uses, **Linux** can use the same basic methods to access it.

- Here is a table from **http://www.linux-mtd.infradead.org/doc/nand.html** documenting some of the differences between **NAND** and **NOR** devices:

Table 28.2: **NOR and NAND Device Features**

	NOR	**NAND**
Interface	Bus	I/O
Cell Size	Large	Small
Cell Cost	High	Low
Read Time	Fast	Slow
Program Time (single byte)	Fast	Slow
Program Time (multi byte)	Slow	Fast
Erase Time	Slow	Fast
Power consumption	High	Low, but requires additional RAM
Can execute code	Yes	No, but newer chips can execute a small loader out of the first page
Bit twiddling	nearly unrestricted	1-3 times, also known as "partial page program restriction"
Bad blocks at ship time	No	Allowed

28.3 Driver and User Modules

- The **MTD** subsystem in **Linux** uses a layered approach, in which the lower hardware device driver layer is ignorant of filesystems and storage formats, and need only have simple entry points for methods like **read, write,** and **erase**. Likewise, the upper layer is ignorant of the underlying hardware but handles all interaction with user-space.

- Thus, there are two kinds of **modules** comprise the **MTD** subsystem; **user** and **driver**. These may or may not be actual kernel modules; they can be built-in.

- **User** modules provide a high level interface to user-space, while **Driver** modules provide the raw access to the flash devices.

- Currently implemented **User** modules include:

  - **Raw character:** direct byte by byte access, needed to construct a filesystem or raw storage.
  - **Raw block:** used to put normal filesystems on flash. Whole flash blocks are cached in RAM.
  - **FTL, NFTL:** (Flash Translation Layer Filesystem)
  - **Microsoft Flash Filing System:** Read-only for now.
  - **Journalling Flash File System (JFFS2):** Full read/write, compressed journalling filesystem.

28.4 Flash Filesystems

- Filesystems for flash devices pose some important challenges:

  - Block sizes can be relatively large (64 KB to 256 KB). Under present **Linux** implementations, a block device filesystem can not have a block size bigger than a page of memory (4 KB on **x86** and many other platforms.)
  - **NOR** flash has a finite limit to the number of erase cycles per block; typically about 100,000. It is important to use all parts of the device equally.

- – There may be **bad blocks** which must to be locked out.
- – Flash memory is expensive, so compressed filesystems are attractive.
- – Journalling is important enhancement; it shortens the power-down procedure.
- – Execution in place is often needed in embedded systems, but it is orthogonal to compression.

- A number of different filesystems have been used for flash devices, and let's consider each in term.

- **initrd** (**Init**ial **R**am **D**isk) was originally developed for use on floppy based systems, and then later to load a basic operating system which could then load essential drivers, such as in the case of **SCSI** systems.

- When used with flash memory, **initrd** begins by copying a compressed kernel from flash to RAM and then executes the copy, which in turn decompresses the **initrd** image and mounts it using the ramdisk driver.

- The disadvantages are fixed size, which is wasteful, and loss of changes upon reboot. Better approaches are now available.

- **cramfs** is a compressed read only filesystem, where the compression is done at the unit of pages. An image is placed in flash and important system files are placed there. The filesystem is made with the **mkcramfs** program, and can be checked with the **cramfsck** utility.

- **ramfs** is a dynamically-sized ramdisk, used in a flash filesystem to store frequently modified or temporary data.

- **jffs** and its descendant **jffs2** are complete read/write, compressed, journalling filesystems. **jffs** was originally developed by Axis Communications in Sweden (**http://developer.axis.com/software/jffs**), and had no compression. **jffs2** provides compression and is developed by a team led by David Woodhouse (**http://sourceware.org/jffs2**).

- The **jffs2** filesystem consists of a list of nodes (log entries) containing file information. When the filesystem is mounted the entire log is scanned to figure out how to put together files.

- Nodes are written to flash sequentially from the first block on, and when the end is reached, the beginning is looped over. This spreads out access over the device; i.e., it provides **wear-leveling**.

- Note that more than one filesystem can be used on a flash device. For instance read-only material can be put in a **cramfs** filesystem, frequently changing data can be placed on **ramfs**, and anything requiring read/write access and preservation across reboot can be put on **jffs2**.

28.5 Labs

Lab 1: Emulating MTD in memory

- Even if you don't have any **MTD** devices on your system, you can emulate them in memory, using some built-in kernel features.

- First you'll have to make sure you have all the right facilities built into the kernel. Go to the kernel source directory, run `make xconfig` and turn on the appropriate **MTD** options, as well as including the **jffs2** filesystem.

- The important ones here are: under **MTD**, turn on *Memory Technology Device Support*, pick a level of debugging (3 should show all), turn on *Direct char device access...*, etc. Also turn on *Test driver using RAM* and *MTD emulation using block device*. By default you'll get a disk of 4 MB with 128 KB erase block size. Under *Filesystems*, turn on **JFFS(2)** and pick a verbosity level.

- If you have done everything as modules you **may** get away without a reboot, as long as you run depmod. At any rate, recompile, reboot, etc., into the kernel that now includes **MTD** and **JFFS2**.

- First we'll test the character emulation interface. To do this you have to make sure you create the device node:

```
$ sudo mknod -m 666 /dev/mtd0 c 90 0
```

- Before or after this, you'll have to make sure to do

```
$ sudo /sbin/modprobe mtdram total_size=2048 erase_size=8
```

(or leave out the options to get the default values you compiled into the kernel.) You won't have to run modprobe if you haven't done this as modules.

- You can now use this as a raw character ram disk, reading and writing to it. Experiment using **dd, cat, echo**, etc.

Lab 2: jffs2 filesystem and MTD block interface.

- In order to place a **jffs2** filesystem on a **MTD** device it is easiest to first make a filesystem **image** on another filesystem, and then copy it over. To do this you must have the **mkfs.jffs2** utility, which you can download in source or binary form from **http://sourceware.org/jffs2**.

- You'll need to do

```
$ sudo /sbin/modprobe mtdblock
```

if you haven't built this into the kernel.

- You'll also have to make the proper device node:

```
$ sudo mknod -m 666 /dev/mtdblock0 b 31 0
```

(Note that you have to do the previous lab and leave the module loaded for this lab to work.)

- Populate a directory tree (say ./dir_tree) with some files and subdirectories; the total size should be less then or equal to the size of **MTD** ram disk. Then put a filesystem on it **and** copy it over to the **MTD** block device emulator with:

```
$ sudo mkfs.jffs2 -d ./dir_tree -o /dev/mtdblock0
```

(You may want to separate out these steps so you can keep the initial filesystem image; i.e., do something like

```
$ sudo mkfs.jffs2 -d ./dir_tree -o jfs.image
$ sudo dd if=jfs.image of=/dev/mtdblock0
```

- Now you can mount the filesystem and play with it to your heart's content:

```
$ sudo mkdir ./mnt_jffs2
$ sudo mount -t jffs2 /dev/mtdblock0 ./mnt_jffs2
```

- Note that you can change the contents of the filesystem as you would like, but the updates will be lost when you unload the **MTD** modules or reboot. However, you can copy the contents to an image file and save that for a restore.

- Note that if you have turned on some verbosity you will see messages like

```
Feb 20 09:02:48 p3 kernel: ram_read(pos:520192, len:4096)
Feb 20 09:02:48 p3 kernel: ram_write(pos:393216, len:12)
Feb 20 09:02:48 p3 kernel: ram_read(pos:262144, len:4096)
Feb 20 09:02:48 p3 kernel: ram_read(pos:266240, len:4096)
Feb 20 09:02:48 p3 kernel: ram_read(pos:270336, len:4096)
```

  and other such diagnostic information which will help you examine what is going on in the disk.

- Notice that because **jffs2** is a compressed filesystem, you can accommodate much more than nominal size, depending on your actual contents.

Chapter 29

Notifiers

We'll discuss how the **Linux** kernel implements notifier callback chains so that interested parties can monitor various kernel resources and subsystems. We'll show how to create a notifier chain as well as how to register with a preexisiting one. We'll explain how to write callback functions and insert them in the relevant chain.

29.1 What are Notifiers?

- Sometimes a particular piece of kernel code needs either to inform other parts of the kernel about an event of interest, or needs to be alerted to events that may be of interest to itself. While a number of methods of such notification have been employed in the past, the present **kernel notifier** API was introduced in the 2.6.17 kernel.

- Examples of events which utilize notifiers include:

  - Network device changes.

  - CPU frequency changes.

  - Memory hotplug events.

  - **USB** hotplug events.

  - Module loading/unloading.

  - System reboots.

- There are four kinds of notifier **chains** which can be used:

  - **Blocking:** Callbacks are run in process context and are allowed to block.
  - **Atomic:** Callbacks are run in interrupt/atomic context and are not allowed to block.
  - **Raw:** Callbacks are unrestricted (as is registration and unregistration) but locking and protection must be explicitly provided by callers.
  - **SRCU:** A form of blocking notifier that uses **Sleepable Read-Copy Update** instead of read/write semaphores for protection.

- The blocking and atomic types are the ones used most often and for simplicity we'll restrict our discussion to these two types.

29.2   Data Structures

- The important data structures for notifier chains are the `notifier_block` and the various `notifier_head` structures:

```
#include <linux/notifier.h>

struct notifier_block {
   int (*notifier_call) (struct notifier_block *block, unsigned long event, void *data);
   struct notifier_block *next;
   int priority;
};

struct blocking_notifier_head {
        struct rw_semaphore rwsem;
        struct notifier_block *head;
};

struct atomic_notifier_head {
        spinlock_t lock;
        struct notifier_block *head;
};
```

- The `notifier_call()` is the function to be called when something of interest occurs and it will receive `event` and a pointer to `data` when called.

- The `next` element shows there will be a linked list of notifier functions, called in order of priority.

- The `priority` data element works so that the **final** event called is the one with the highest priority (lowest value for the `priority` field); if the bit `NOTIFIER_STOP_MASK` is set in the callback function return value, any notifier can stop any further processing. Other return values are not confined, but the special values `NOTIFY_STOP` (everything is fine, don't call any more modifiers) and `NOTIFY_OK` (everything is fine, continue calling other callback functions) can be used.

29.3 Callbacks and Notifications

- Registering and unregistering callback functions is done with:

```
int atomic_notifier_chain_register (struct atomic_notifier_head *nh,
                                    struct notifier_block *nb);
int blocking_notifier_chain_register (struct blocking_notifier_head *nh,
                                      struct notifier_block *nb);

int atomic_notifier_chain_unregister (struct atomic_notifier_head *nh,
                                      struct notifier_block *nb);
int blocking_notifier_chain_unregister (struct blocking_notifier_head *nh,
                                        struct notifier_block *nb);
```

- These functions tell the system to call the function specified in the `notifier_block` function whenever traversing the linked list in the notifier head, which may be one you created or which previously existed.

- Signalling an event to the appropriate notifier chain is done with:

```
int blocking_notifier_call_chain (struct blocking_notifier_head *nh, unsigned long event, void *data);
int atomic_notifier_call_chain   (struct atomic_notifier_head *nh, unsigned long event, void *data);
```

  where the `event` is specified and a pointer to `data` can be passed.

- Pre-existing notifier chains generally follow the convention of defining registration/unregistration functions as:

```
void XXX_register_notifier  (struct notifier_block *nb);
void XXX_unregister_NOTIFIER(struct notifier_block *nb);
```

  where `XXX` specifies the notifier; examples include `usb`, `reboot`, `cpu_notifier`, `crypto`, `oom`, and `netdevice`. Occasionally the `XXX` and the `register`, `unregister` elements in the names are swapped.

29.4 Creating Notifier Chains

- Creating blocking and atomic notifier chains can be done in the either by doing:

```
#include <linux/notifier.h>

BLOCKING_NOTIFIER_HEAD(notifier_name);
ATOMIC_NOTIFIER_HEAD(notifier_name);
```

  or

```
struct blocking_notifier_head notifier_name;
BLOCKING_INIT_NOTIFIER_HEAD(notifier_name);

struct atomic_notifier_head notifier_name;
ATOMIC_INIT_NOTIFIER_HEAD(notifier_name);
```

  which create the appropriate **notifier_head** structures:

29.5   Labs

Lab 1: Joining the USB Notifier Chain

- To register and unregister with the already existing notifier chain for hot-plugging of **USB** devices, use the exported functions:

  ```
  void usb_register_notify   (struct notifier_block *nb);
  void usb_unregister_notify (struct notifier_block *nb);
  ```

- You should be able to trigger events by plugging and unplugging a **USB** device, such as a mouse, pendrive, or keyboard.

- Print out the event that triggers your callback function. (Note that definitions of events can be found in **/usr/src/linux/include/linux/usb.h**.).

Lab 2: Installing and Using a Notifier Chain

- Write a brief module that implements its own notifier chain.

- The module should register the chain upon insertion and unregister upon removal.

- The callback function should be called at least twice, with different event values, which should be printed out.

- You may want to make use of the data pointer, modifying the contents in the callback function.

Index